DAVIS!

HOPE YOU ENJOY THE BOOK!

THANKS FOR COMING TO NORTHSTAR!

LOOK FORWARD TO SEEING YOU NEXT YEAR

P.S ANYTHING TO WOUNDED WARRIORS WILL BE APPRECIATED

8/20/15

Wanna Shine, Mister?

10 Cents!

The Life Story of Dennis G. Punches

Written by

Dennis Punches & Dean Hansen

To my children: Debbie, Laurie, Skip, and Emma.
You are the joy of my life!

To Katie: for blessing me with children!

To Bev Wortman: for being my dedicated right-hand
and my friend for so many years!

To the Magnificent Seven:
Joe Treleven, Bill Kagel, Pat Carroll,
Neal Sparby, Susan Mathison, and Al Keely!

To all of those who have helped increase my quality of life.
There are too many to number!

To John Pearce: for coaxing me out of retirement
to do it again down under!

To my new family: Stacy & Alice
who help keep me young!

And most importantly, to Angela:
You brighten every day we are together!

Contents

Introduction

Although I will never admit to slowing down, I recognize that my aging process is occurring and there are some things that I used to do that are now more difficult. While my mental faculties are still with me, I wanted to capture some things that might be of value to someone else.

We have gathered many stories in this book that emphasize the opportunities that have been afforded to me in this great country, the God-given talents that have changed my life, and the sharing by people who are smarter than I am who have shown me how to succeed. I invite you to peruse this book and enjoy the stories, many of which include individuals who impacted me in one way or another and have helped me realize that I couldn't be where I am today were it not for them.

Special credit is due to a number of people, some of whom are not even around anymore, to whom I am so grateful, including, among others: a grade school principle who would send me, as a 10 year-old, to downtown Chicago on errands for her; a high-school coach who not only asked my opinion, but also helped instill confidence in my abilities to achieve; and, a former NFL coach who taught me to not get caught in the garbage of life. Each gave me opportunities, expressed trust and confidence in me, and helped engender confidence in myself, my decision making, and ultimately my ability to sell.

To those young budding entrepreneurs out there who are asking, "Can I still accomplish great things in today's environment?" The answer, my friends, is yes! You can still achieve. There is not a magic formula but there are some things that I have learned, and shared here, that I believe will help you.

Please realize that you may have to burn the candle at both ends, as I did. But, as Edna S. Vincent Millay shared, that can illuminate our path.

> *"My candle burns at both ends*
> *It will not last the night;*
> *But ah, my foes, and oh, my friends -*
> *It gives a glorious light."*

I am grateful for my family, my friends, and for my work associates and partners, who have helped me achieve my dreams. Hopefully you will find something in this book that will help you be a better person, achieve greater things, and realize your dreams.

Special thanks go to Dean Hansen who has spent many hours with me over the recent months listening, reflecting, guiding the conversation, and recording the stories. We have enjoyed the time together sharing and discussing how to weave the stories into the book you hold.

Please join us in a look back at my life adventures in, *Wanna Shine, Mister? 10 Cents!*

Dennis - *November 2013*

Chapter 1 – Birth & Heritage

January 18, 1936 was a snowy, bitterly cold day in the north woods just outside of Eagle River, Wisconsin, and it was extremely uncomfortable in the little cabin that Herb and Dorothy Punches called home. The temperature was negative 48 degrees and the combined heat of the wood and coal stoves in the cabin could not keep up with the cold. On any other day, they would have just been uncomfortable, but today, Dorothy, who was nine months pregnant, realized that she was about to give birth.

The weather precluded having the doctor come from town so a local mid-wife was called to help with the delivery. It didn't matter how much water was put on to boil; it was brutally cold. The delivery proceeded without problems and Dennis George Punches began his mortal life. Even though he was born between the two stoves, and was quickly wrapped in blankets, the tender skin on the face of this newborn was frostbitten. Within a few days his face was completely covered with scab from the injury. Dorothy bathed his little face in olive oil, trying to prevent scarring. Showing signs of the resiliency that would become a hallmark of his life, the olive oil treatment worked, and Dennis' face healed well.

With Dennis' birth it brought to four the number of children in the home. These were difficult times, not only because of the cold, but because of the economic challenges nationwide. The Great Depression had settled in the bones of the U.S. residents like the biting Wisconsin cold, and the Punches family felt the impact. Herb had left school when he was in 8th grade and had later married Dorothy when she was only fifteen years old. When there was money in the economy, wealthy individuals from surrounding communities and states would make their way to Eagle River to hunt and fish. As a respected and talented young sportsman, Herb knew the area well and worked as a guide, leading paying clients to the best fishing holes or to find the biggest buck. He was particularly adept at finding the elusive musky (muskellunge), a fish that was a worthy adversary for any fisherman and would eventually be named the Wisconsin state fish. But now, since many of those individuals had lost their own fortunes, no one offered to pay Herb to be a guide.

There were few jobs to be had in the local economy and when President Roosevelt introduced the Civilian Conservation Corps (CCC), intended to put able bodied individuals to work, it gave working men a chance to complete meaningful tasks that would also benefit the country's infrastructure. Herb was one of many local men, and part of the 500,000 nationwide, who would eventually enter the ranks of the CCC. Although standards required that a man be unemployed and unmarried, with a limit of one six-month enlistment, apparently there were ways around those requirements. Not only did Herb, as a married man, participate, he, along with many others, also re-enrolled in the program. These men worked for many months on road construction, tree planting, park development, bridge construction, or other significant and meaningful projects. Herb's role with the CCC was as a carpenter. The $30 per month[i] (see end notes) that he earned didn't go very far towards supporting his family, but it was better than the alternative of having no job at all.

Why would a family choose to live in northern Wisconsin with its harsh and unforgiving climate, even if the hunting and fishing were good? Family records suggest that the Punches family had migrated to Canada from Germany, and then subsequently moved into upstate New York, most likely in the 1700s. The group from upstate New York eventually made their way to the Midwest to homestead and became farmers in northern Wisconsin. It was here that Herbert Martin Punches was born in 1906 and subsequently spent his boyhood and early manhood working on the family farm. He would see his share of challenging times, not the least of which was during the Great Depression.

One of the more prominent members of the family was a man by the name of Joseph Hewes who hailed from North Carolina. Joseph was one of the signers of the Declaration of Independence.[ii] He had built a prosperous mercantile and shipping business and had amassed a fleet of ships by the beginning of the Revolutionary war. He called his first ship *The Providence*, after his mother. In the early months of 1776, because of his shipping experience, he was appointed as head of the Naval Committee, and when he subsequently turned his fleet over to the newly established Continental Navy, he was named as Secretary of the Navy. In that role, Mr. Hewes appointed John Paul Jones, who would distinguish himself and become a naval hero, to captain the Navy's first commissioned ship.[iii]

Any Hewes' fortune that once existed was either dissipated by Joseph's generosity with the fledgling country, headed on a very different path from that of the Punches family of Eagle River, or was otherwise exhausted. Joseph left only his good name and the effects of his, and the other founding fathers', pursuit of freedom and opportunity for the United States.

After he worked for some time for the CCC, Herb received a job opportunity to become a wood carver. The Punches family, including Herb, Dorothy, and their four children, moved to Chicago. Herb's specialty became religious statues which were sold commercially, some of which are still in the possession of the family. This was a significant change of environment for the family moving from the woods of northern Wisconsin to the inner city of Chicago. Forests, streams, and open spaces were replaced with buildings, streets, and lots of people.

Chapter 2 – Moving to Chicago

As they moved to Chicago, the family rented and lived in a three-bedroom walk-up located at 3517 Dickens Avenue in the city of Chicago. Three small bedrooms were barely adequate for 6 people, even less so after they added two more children, but it was what they had to live in. Such situations sometimes result in novel solutions to problems. Since the three older boys needed to share a room and there was but one bed, all three slept in that same bed with Herb Jr. and Bob sleeping lengthwise and Dennis sleeping across the top of the bed where the pillows would normally be. That would be their sleeping arrangement for 2 to 3 years until Dennis grew too big and no longer fit across the top of the bed. It could be said that in some ways they were a very close family; very close, indeed! Shirley had her own room until Patsy was born and Bill would later add to the contingent in the boy's room.

The home was heated by a single potbelly stove; there was no central air conditioning or central heating that might distribute heat or cooling to all areas of the house. The area closest to the stove was warm but the other rooms could be pretty cold in the winter. Not only was that potbelly stove their only heat source, it required a daily trip to the coal yard where they would purchase, and then carry, coal to the house to burn. During the very warm summer days, the only way to cool the apartment was to open the windows and try to coax a little breeze to come through and move the heavy, warm air.

While the rent for the apartment was only $25 a month, it was always difficult to secure those dollars, and as a result, they were often late getting paid. Dorothy was responsible for stretching the family budget dollars to care for the needs of eight people and there was never enough money to go around. The rent collector, an austere looking man who generally dressed in a black coat and dark glasses, was an imposing and intimidating figure for this young mother. The thought of facing Mr. Harper with yet another late rent payment was not pleasant. Dorothy devised a brilliant plan, one that would limit her exposure to Mr. Harper. She figured that he would go easy on a young boy sent to deliver the rent, even if it was 5 or 10 days late, so Dennis was selected to take the $25, either in cash or a money order. Dorothy would give instructions to be careful with the money and would then send the boy on his way. Since he had no preconceived notion of how he would be received, Dennis was not surprised when Mr. Harper welcomed him into his office. The late rent payment was accepted and Mr. Harper even produced a sucker for the boy to eat on his way home. It was hard to tell who enjoyed the interaction more; Mr. Harper, because he didn't have to go looking for the rent, Dennis, because he enjoyed the sucker from his new benefactor, or Dorothy, because she didn't have to face the embarrassment of being late yet again with the rent. This was indeed a brilliant plan and it worked many times.

As was the case with most young boys, Dennis and his brothers were chased out of the house first thing in the morning with appropriate instructions to check in at the right times, where to play, and what not to do. A vivid memory for Dennis, even as a five-year old, was taking his little toys out to the backyard of the house to play in the dirt. There was no lawn because the grass would not grow in the worn-out soil and in those difficult economic times no one was going to spend the money or the time to fix the problem. While playing in the dirt, perhaps displaying uncommon vigilance for a young boy, he watched carefully what was going on around him. As he looked across the street, his eye rested on grass; real, thick, green grass. Mrs. Hartwig, a local teacher, and her husband had grass in their yard. Well, this young five-year-old determined then and there that someday he was going to play in grass instead of in the dirt. That resolution was his earliest recollection of making a decision based on personal motivation to change something in the way he lived. His family would have a place to play in the grass, and not in the dirt.

A novel way for parents to manage the competitive, and sometimes combative, nature of male children is to buy a couple of pairs of boxing gloves. This allowed for some serious entertainment while the padding in the gloves fairly well protected the combatants from injuring one another. One day Dennis was boxing with his older brother, Bob, and when he stepped back, he tripped over something. It wasn't a misplaced blow that injured the arm; as he fell he tried to catch himself with his left arm, breaking the wrist in the fall. For most children a broken left wrist is an inconvenience but for Dennis it was a particular problem because he was left-handed. His teacher threatened to hold him back a year in school unless he figured out how to write with his right hand. Since writing with his dominant left hand was out of the question, as it was in a cast, and since there was no way that Dennis would willingly stay back a grade, he determined to learn to write with his right hand. Often, such an experience will make it such that the handwriting is poor no matter which hand the student wrote with, but with Dennis, not only did he master the art of penmanship with his right hand, after the cast was off he continued to do so throughout his life. He attributes being ambidextrous to that experience. His left hand was still dominant but he learned that he could vary which hand he used based on what he was trying to do. Later in life being ambidextrous meant that he played tennis, shot guns, and ate left-handed, while throwing and writing right-handed were most comfortable. There have been times when he simply made a decision about which hand he was going to use to eat based on where someone had put the utensils at the plate.

Recognized early on as a young man that could be trusted, Dennis was given responsibilities at Funston Grade School in fifth grade. Mrs. McGregor, the principal of the school had chosen him to run errands for her. While some were run-of-the-mill errands, he was given some chores that were out of the ordinary for a young boy. Periodically, the principal would have papers or packages that needed to go to an office in what was referred to as the loop, Chicago's downtown, a distance of 6 miles or so from the school. The principal would call Dennis out of his classroom, entrust him with some documents to be delivered, and give him thirteen cents. It cost four cents each way to ride on the L (the local train) to downtown and back. The remaining five cents was provided for him to enjoy an ice cream after he had made his delivery.   That was a confidence builder to have the trust of a grownup, especially one in authority.

Even though he might periodically be sent on an errand and would enjoy the ice cream treat, he didn't have the money to participate in the daily milk days. Milk was available to the students for a penny but he seldom had a penny for milk, and he knew he wasn't going to get money from home. Determined to address the situation, rather than go without, he joined the safety patrol. Those who worked safety patrol were invited to have free hot chocolate when they came back into the school after being out in the cold. Hot chocolate was much better than cold milk on a winter day.

Chapter 3 – Shoeshine Business

A consistent source of friction in the Punches' home was the limited money. Herb made almost $100 each week but often there was only a fraction of that income that would trickle into the household budget. Herb had a drinking problem and an ego. That combination led him to spend a significant portion of his income in one of the local taverns.

Herb would often take Dennis with him to the bar on Friday evenings. He seldom, if ever, took one of the older boys, and why he took Dennis remains a bit of a mystery. But once at the bar, Herb would seat his son on a stool at the bar, and Dennis would watch him drink. Once in a while the boy would get a soda, but not often. Herb was a proud man and wanted to be recognized as being important. He would be paid on Fridays and the cash would then accompany him to the bar. The drink selection was fairly limited for this poor working class tavern. The choice was generally limited to a mixed drink called a highball, or a beer. The highball was generally cheap whiskey mixed with 7-Up. The other variation was a boilermaker which was a shot of whiskey followed with a chaser of beer. On many evenings, generally after his second drink, Herb would tell the bartender, "Give the boys a drink!" Even though he had the cash at the time, he could no more afford to pay for other people's drinks than could his son who was seated beside him at the bar. Even though Dorothy begged him for food money, he was such a proud guy that he had to show that he was the big shot.

Dennis was an observant boy and it didn't take long for him to realize that there was money in the tavern on Friday nights. People would lay their money on the bar and if they bought a beer they always left their change right there. The longer he observed the more determined he became to get a share of that money. Since he knew where the prey was, he decided that he was going to become the hunter. The neighborhood sported an avenue where there were four bars on one short section of the street. One particular tavern, the Modern Inn, seemed to be the best hunting ground as its patrons seemed to display the most money.

Dennis gathered up some scrap lumber and built a shoeshine box. He somehow rustled up enough money to buy a single can of polish and a shoe brush, figuring that it wouldn't matter what color the polish was because almost all of his potential clients would be wearing work boots. He had a good idea what time the men would show up at the bar because he had sat there with his father often enough to recognize the flow. So, now armed with a shoe shine box, he was ready to invite potential customers to turn from the bar and place a foot on the box. Dennis was ready to pitch his service.

He had originally recruited his older brother to hawk shoe shines in front of the shoeshine boy, but that didn't last long. His brother lost interest, since he didn't like doing it in the first place, and quit. The enterprise was barely underway and Dennis had already lost his first employee and partner. Not to be deterred, he realized that as soon as the men had a drink or two in them they loosened the grip on their money, and now he wouldn't have to share his earnings. "Wanna shine, mister? Ten cents!" was his sales pitch. Doubtless the men recognized the audacity of a young boy trying to make some money and perhaps took their initial shine to humor him but soon he had developed a regular route of sorts and on a good evening would be able to do five shoe shines, netting himself a 50 cent profit for his efforts. It was an especially productive evening when someone would add a tip.

It was the logic of an eight-year-old who realized there was an opportunity to make some money on Friday nights when the men got paid. Dennis generally avoided the bar where his dad was drinking. His mom knew what he was doing and determined that as long as he was home before dark, which made it tough in the wintertime, it was okay. The environment in the city of Chicago was such that it was safe for a child to be out in the late afternoon and early evening. The neighborhood had an extensive ethnic mix, including Jewish, Polish, Norwegian, Italian, and Irish, all of whom lived on the same block. It was a blended group without the polarization that would subsequently exist in the area. And of course, World War II drew everyone together in thought and purpose. It was generally a pretty happy bunch of people; a bunch that didn't have much money, but they were pretty happy. The shoeshine business lasted for about a year and a half, until Dennis was about 10 years old, after which he determined that there were bigger fish to fry.

Christmas was memorable that first year as he did his shopping with the money from the shoeshine business. There was a small store close to where they lived where he could get a handkerchief for the girls for

$.25 each, and the store staff would even wrap them up in small boxes. It was pretty exciting for a young boy to be in a position to give gifts to grandma, mom, and his sisters. It was important to him to use some of that money to buy presents.

Another money-making venture, this one not quite as profitable as the shoeshine business but profitable none-the-less, involved a bit of larceny. In the early 1940s, people bought quart bottles of beer to take home. A two-cent deposit per bottle was charged to the customer, a deposit that would be paid back to any person who possessed the bottle. Empty beer bottles were put on the back porch, especially in the Jewish apartment buildings. Even though this group didn't drink much, there were still enough of them to make a wander through the neighborhood worthwhile for a young boy, and frankly, these particular buildings were the easiest ones from which to get the beer bottles. Dennis and his friends identified the best hunting ground, and were thrilled when they found four or five of those bottles on the back porches. He soon knew where the bottles would likely be and would establish a route, of sorts, to harvest those 2 cent gems. Of course, they had to pick them up quietly. The boys would sneak up the back steps, quickly grab the bottles, being careful not to clink them together, and then dash away. On a good night a boy might gather 20 cents worth of bottles. They found that a local tavern, one where Dennis would sometimes shine shoes, would take the beer bottles and give the deposit money to the boys. People kept putting the bottles out on the porch even though the boys would often carry them off. Nobody ever complained about empty bottles disappearing, or if they did, they didn't make much of a fuss. This was probably the earliest form of recycling and the boys were glad for a little jingle in their pockets. Even though it showed a little bit of larceny, no one seemed to mind.

Dennis grew up listening to radio in the days prior to television. But with the advent of television, this new and exciting entertainment drew the boys like flies to honey. In their Chicago neighborhood one of the tavern owners purchased one of the early televisions and set it up in the bar. Since few of the families could afford a TV for their homes, the tavern was about the only place someone could go to watch a program. With tacit approval from the tavern owner, the neighborhood boys would make a stop at the local candy store and buy a nickel soda pop, if they had a nickel, before going next-door to the bar. The owner of the bar would allow the kids to sit in the back of the room and watch the television set in the early evening. Since some of the first programs on TV were of wrestling matches, the boys were enthralled watching the programs on that tiny screen and drinking their nickel pop. Even though the boys came out smelling like a brewery, their moms, including Dennis' mom, knew where they were. Most were willing to overlook the setting and let the boys watch television.

Chapter 4 – Life Isn't Always Fair

World War II put tremendous demands on the citizens and the resources of the United States. Gathering materials used in the war effort was common in cities across the country, and Chicago was no exception. People would save their newspapers and other materials and then the school boys would go around the neighborhood, gathering whatever had been saved. Dennis and his friends were happy to get involved. The boys would take string or twine along so they could tie the paper into bundles, each bundle standing a couple of feet tall. They would then haul the bundles in their wagons to the school. Each boy would get credit for the paper that he brought in. Even though there was no money involved in the reward system, instead they would get a certificate that stated the amount of paper that they had gathered, it was enough motivation that the boys were eager and willing to participate.

Not only were the citizens asked to gather metal, newspaper and other materials that might assist, they were asked to contribute money to the war effort. A prime fundraising approach in the U.S. was to sell war bonds to the American public.   Although they were available in different denominations, the least expensive bond cost $18.75 which when held to maturity, generally after 10 years, could be redeemed for $25.00. An appeal to personal patriotism often enticed individuals to give up already meager earnings to purchase a promise from the government to pay them back at some point in the future after the war ended. The sales approaches were many and varied.

Children were even recruited to help with the war bond sales effort as they were invited to sell savings books. For many families the prospect of coming up with the money required to buy even a single bond was daunting. A novel way was found to help overcome that problem. For those who found it difficult to purchase an entire bond at one time, ten cent savings stamps could be purchased and collected in Treasury approved stamp albums until the individual had accumulated enough stamps for a bond purchase. Since the stamp album had little value by itself, it was a natural fit to let the children sell the booklets.

During one particular effort, the reward system was dramatically more lucrative than the paper drives as a bicycle was to be the prize for the person that sold the most savings books or bonds. Since the bicycle was the prize for just their school, the chance of getting the bike was pretty good for someone who wanted to expend the effort. This sales competition became a very personal experience for Dennis as Billy Bombshell (probably spelled Baumshell), or better said, Billy's father, took Dennis out of the running of the contest for that bicycle.

Dennis had decided that he had as good a shot at that bike as anyone and was determined to win. As a result he worked very hard through the designated time period. As the contest was drawing to a close, he was ahead of everyone else to get the bike. On that dreadful day, the last day of the contest, Billy Bombshell's dad bought a large bond, eclipsing everyone else's efforts for the contest and making Billy the winner. Billy was fat, lazy, and not particularly well liked, and it was common knowledge that he had made no effort to go out and sell the booklets. But the actions of Billy's dad had wiped Dennis, along with the rest of the kids, out of the contest. The prize for all of his hard work and efforts was taken away in a moment. Looking back, Dennis realizes that this was his first real experience with capitalism, but at the time, he struggled with the thought, "Not fair! I did all the work and this guy's dad buys the bond. He gets the bike, and I get nothing!" Though Billy's dad could have afforded to just buy the bicycle, he wanted his boy to have the notoriety of the little write up in the local paper touting that Billy Bombshell had won the bicycle.

It was a very disappointing experience for Dennis. He was so close to winning the bike he could feel himself pushing the pedals as he rode down the street. It was especially disappointing because he didn't have a bike at the time. Even though sometimes life isn't fair, the experience caused him to determine that he would never get caught again in a situation like that. It may not be a bond or a bicycle at issue, but he would put himself in a position to control his own destiny.

Chapter 5 – Make a Buck

As with most young men, Dennis was always on the lookout for a way to make some money. For those who pay attention and look for them, moneymaking endeavors will generally present themselves. Although not high on the list of preferable things to do, since winters in Chicago were cold, there was often snow to be shoveled from the sidewalks. Snow shoveling required little investment, just a shovel and the willingness to work. As a result there was always competition from the other boys and young men in the area, but Dennis soon realized that it was generally the person that does the best job that is hired a second time. He understood the lesson.

Sometimes a boy has to be creative to come up with an opportunity, such as with a shoeshine box, but other times the opportunity comes looking for them. Mr. Fierstein owned the local movie theater that was nestled among the taverns. When Dennis was about nine years old, Mr. Fierstein offered him a job to run errands from the projection booth down to the usher, or whatever else Mr. Fierstein wanted him to do. There was no cash involved; the pay was to watch all of the free movies that he wanted to see. Dennis would generally work two nights a week, which would coincide with the two changes of movies that happened during the week. This job lasted for a couple of years, during which time he saw a lot of movies.

The delivery of heating fuel, either oil or coal, to one's home was a luxury. Most families purchased their fuel several times a week but it required going to a retailer who furnished coal or pumped the heating oil into a can for the customer. A neighbor lady who lived next door to the Punches family hired Dennis to get heating oil for her, as her husband had some medical problem such that he couldn't go get the oil. She would pay Dennis 25 cents, generally twice each week, to take his wagon to the store and there purchase a 5 gallon can of heating oil. After hauling the wagon load back home, the real work began. Since she lived on the third floor he had to carry that can of oil up three flights of stairs. For a little kid a 30 pound can of oil was really heavy. Dennis would carry the can up the stairs, take the lid off of the tank attached to the hot stove, and pour the oil into the tank.

During that time period no one thought much about having a child carrying a 5 gallon can of oil. Very few parents today would allow a child to get near that kind of heating oil, let alone close to a hot stove. Yet, Dennis is better for having the experience. He learned a lesson that many of today's kids miss. The lesson was that work is our friend. An associated lesson, although Dennis didn't learn to describe it until some years later, was that life will present stumbling blocks to us. When we learn the importance of facing a stumbling block, backing up and figuring out how to deal with the difficulty, life becomes easier; not for lack of challenges, rather from knowing how to deal with the challenges.

If children don't have an opportunity to face adversity while they are young, how are they going to deal with it when they do bump up against it? Adversity comes to everyone in their lives. Unfortunately, it will hit many of them right smack in the face. Even though he didn't recognize it at the time, Dennis was developing traits of resiliency and tenacity as he figured out how to make and save some money and stay focused on his goal. He was learning the lessons of *"Think and Grow Rich"* even before he read the book.

Dennis spent much of his childhood looking at how to deal with the stumbling blocks in his own life and how to be better because of them, such as when Billy Baumshell did him out of his bicycle in the war bonds competition.   Rather than whine about his misfortune, he worked hard and saved his money from his shoe shines, his beer bottle collecting, and his heating oil enterprise. By the time he was about ten years old, he had finally saved enough money, or so he thought, that he could buy a bike. It wasn't a Schwinn bike; those were expensive! Montgomery Ward sold a Monark bike, a bike designed to be sold to the masses. His mother took him to the Montgomery Ward store where the bike was on sale for $29. He had saved up $24 and was short by $5. His disappointment was short-lived as his mom gave him the additional money, and they bought the bike.

Dennis also had a paper route delivering the Chicago Sun-Times in the Jewish section of town. This was an early exposure to being a self-employed businessman as he had to pay the newspaper company for his papers and then collect the money from his customers for the papers delivered.   He was responsible for any loss, damage, or shortages. It didn't matter what the weather was doing, either; the papers had to be delivered in the rain, the snow, or the heat.   There was never a thought that mom or dad would bail him out and drive him around in the car. It was up to him to get on his bicycle with a bag full of newspapers. Sometimes he could throw the paper, but for many deliveries he had to run the paper to the doorstep. He was really glad to have a bike.

The Punches family did not go to church together. The Cooleys, the next door neighbors, belonged to the Holy Rollers. Since they had a son his age, they thought Dennis should go to church with them and off he would go with them to their storefront church on Fullerton Avenue. Services were very animated, with the expectation that the congregation would respond to the minister and, as he recalls, "They would really jump around." During a particularly memorable service, as one of the assistant pastors demonstrated an event from the Bible, depicting someone climbing a mountain, the man fell from his new perch and broke his leg. That left an impression in the mind of a young boy.

During the services they provided wooden chairs for the congregation to sit on but it seemed that they spent much of their time on their knees with heads down. Dennis found much of what went on to be somewhat humorous, such as a daring assistant pastor with a broken leg, but even though he wanted to laugh, he couldn't, or shouldn't. He would sit or kneel trying to control his laughter.

Dennis did become a Christian soldier when Mrs. Cooley bought him a shirt embroidered with "Christian Soldier" on the front. It was hard to turn down a free shirt, any free shirt. That constituted the majority of his religious upbringing, although he would attend and be confirmed at a Methodist church in Chicago, after having been baptized and circumcised in Eagle River, Wisconsin. Again this occurred with a neighbor, rather than with his parents. His folks didn't discourage his participation but neither did they encourage it.

Chapter 6 – Early Sports

Dennis' tenacity showed itself early in his life as he participated in sports. In fact, he forced himself on the bigger kids when it came to sports. Figuring that he would not be able to learn much from kids his own age, he determined that he would play with the older kids where he could grow his skills. His entry with the big guys playing baseball was offering to be the catcher. Since the other guys all wanted to play in the field, even though they would not let him bat, they let him throw the ball back to the pitcher. Soon he was playing with the big guys, including his oldest brother. Even though Dennis was never invited by his brother, Herb, who was not one to give his younger brother an advantage, there was a certain pride with both boys that little brother could hold his own with big brother's friends.

As noted earlier, during the summer in Chicago, mothers were quick to chase children from the house in the mornings. While each wanted some idea of their child's whereabouts, she mostly wanted the children not to be bothering her while she did her housework. That was fine with the boys as they would quickly get the day's ball game underway and thought nothing of playing all day. In fact, the games were generally at their most critical point just as the dinner hour approached. There was nothing worse than being one run down, with a runner on base, and up to bat when mom calls you to come for dinner. That was a moral dilemma. There have been countless boys through the ages who have silently asked the question, "Do I listen to Mom or do I pretend that I don't hear her," all the while urging the

{ 29 }

pitcher to hurry his delivery. When the boys didn't respond quickly enough Dorothy might show up with a broom to chase her boys home. Though he wasn't certain that she would really use it on him, since Dennis was quicker than she was he made great sport out of avoiding the broom.

The boys played a game called 16-inch Ball, a game that was somewhat unique to the Chicago area. By comparison, a 12-inch ball is used today for fast-pitch softball. Although initially a fairly hard ball, a 16-inch ball would soften up as it was batted. For those who were learning to catch and throw, that big ball provided some advantages, even while it challenged the skills of the boys. When batted, even though the ball didn't carry as far as a baseball or a 12-inch softball, they could still hit it a couple of hundred feet, roughly 2/3 of a ballpark. All of the pitching was underhand. The catching was done with two hands and without a glove, a definite advantage since one didn't have to buy a glove to play. When the ball was thrown, it was overhand with one hand. Dennis honed his ball handling skills while playing 16-inch ball since he was only allowed to be the catcher. When the boys finally let him bat, he could soon hit as well as most of the other boys.

By the time he was eleven it was apparent, not only to him but also to the other boys, that he had some pretty good athletic ability. The boys would put together a team from the neighborhood and head for Humboldt Park[iv] in Chicago on Saturday mornings to play 16-inch ball. A boy who got there early enough could claim one of the four diamonds available. This was prized real estate as there were not many parks in the area. The boy that got there first would stand on the pitching mound with a bat, the signal to the latecomers that he had that diamond. The honor and integrity among the boys would never allow anyone to break that unwritten rule. Dennis was often the one that was sent early to get a diamond because he had a bicycle. He would generally arrive by 7 or 730 in the morning, with the rest of the guys getting there around 8 a.m. Upon the arrival of the rest of their team, they would then invite another team, one who had not been fortunate enough to claim their own diamond, to engage in a game. In that way the boys would choose their opponent for the day.

Dennis also learned to play basketball while living in Chicago. Community teams were often sponsored by a local church and several kids from the same block would generally go play together. The boys had to have a uniform, and since their church sponsor didn't provide one, they would buy sleeveless undershirts for a dollar each, dye them, and then paint a number on the shirt. Dennis and his team had maroon shirts with white numbers. It was in those community leagues when he started to develop his basketball skills and soon realized that he had more coordination than most of the other boys.

Sports were a haven that would let the boys get away from a brewing situation at home. The family financial difficulties really came to a head when Dennis was about ten years old, when his parents divorced. The family had watched as Herb struggled with his alcohol consumption. He would often come home drunk and the arguing was inevitable. Many evenings, as the children would try to sleep, they would cower in their rooms as their parents argued. Dorothy would try to get Herb to stop drinking but the grip of the alcohol was too tight. He was an alcoholic.

After the divorce, Dorothy tried to keep the family together but she couldn't do it on the income she made as a telephone operator with the Bell System. The technology of the day required that, to complete a call, the operator had to physically connect a cord on a circuit board, a job that required some dexterity but didn't pay particularly well. With six children, the financial burden was too great; the family had to split up. The oldest son, Herb, went into the military service. Shirley got married when she was just 17. Bob, the second oldest boy, was adopted by an aunt. That left the three youngest children, Dennis, Patsy, and Bill, at home with mom.

Eventually, even with just the three children at home, when Dorothy determined that she could no longer care for them, she gave up custody, and the children went to live with their father. Some years later, after Dorothy remarried, her youngest son, Bill, returned to live with her. The family was literally torn apart. Unable to make ends meet when they had Herb's income, Dorothy now found that she couldn't afford to provide for them on her own, either.

In retrospect, the years in Chicago were tough ones, probably more so for Dorothy and Herb because they were so poor, but the kids adapted and, for the most part, enjoyed their childhood. Dennis recalls that his childhood in Chicago was fun, and, not knowing any different, it appeared to him that they lived normal lives. Herb would state and reiterate through the years, "Born in 06, married in 26, and kicked out in 46." This was a traumatic time for the family. Divorce and the related upheaval were difficult but they were stumbling blocks which had to be surmounted. Dennis was determined to do so.

Chapter 7 – On to Wauconda

Dorothy had made a valiant effort to keep the family together but it just didn't work out. Herb had moved to Wauconda, Illinois, located about 40 miles northwest of Chicago. After Herb agreed to let them come and live with him, Dorothy relinquished custody of the three youngest children. In 1948, Dennis, as a 12 year-old, went to live with his father.

Herb worked as a carpenter for a development company called Dedo Brothers, building low-cost, single-family housing. It was in the course of a conversation that Dennis found out that his father made almost $100 a week. At the time that was a reasonable income, but when Herb would leave a fair amount of that money at the bar each week it left little else to live on. He never paid alimony or child support and since Dorothy never pursued legal recourse, it ultimately caused her to give him the three younger children. Even as he agreed to take responsibility for the children, there wasn't much that had changed. He was never a particularly engaging father before and he made little effort to build a relationship with his children now that they lived with him.

Herb had purchased a shell, which, true to its name, was just the exterior portion of a house, for about $1500. Even though it was enclosed none of the interior work was completed. That process was up to the homeowner, including the studding for the interior walls and finishing. He had completed a bathroom, including a tub, toilet and sink, although it lacked a shower, but that was the extent of the interior work. Even though the house was unfinished when the children went to live with him, it was where they lived while he finished the house. As time passed he purchased additional materials and worked on various part of the house, adding bedrooms and other interior walls. Eventually Herb, Jr. returned home from the service and helped him finish the inside of the house. The entire project cost, including the shell, was approximately $3,000.

The Chicago school system recognized a graduation from grammar school in the winter and another in the spring of each year. If a student had completed the requirements necessary, they might move up one grade at mid-year. With a January birth date, if Dennis still been in Chicago, he would have graduated from grammar school in January. But with a different approach in Wauconda, rather than starting 9th grade in the fall, Dennis found himself starting eighth grade again. Even though he wasn't pleased at the time to start eighth grade over, eventually he would realize that he got a six months head start physically over the other boys at a time when his body was developing. He could tell almost right away when he made sports teams that his skills were advanced beyond those of his teammates. They were still fumbling around while he could dribble right past them. But that was because his body was developed and more mature. He expected that he would be called a dummy because he had been put back half of a year, and while disappointed, eventually he came to feel that it was actually one of the greatest things that ever happened to him. He had always been a good student, but with the added motivation to show he wasn't a dummy, and with focused effort, his scholastic marks were consistently straight A's.

With the eighth grade basketball season approaching, the other kids informed Dennis that he would never make the team because, as they shared, not only was he was from Chicago, they had already picked the guys who were going to play. No matter how adamant they were, there were a couple of things that the boys failed to understand. The first was that all one had to do was tell Dennis he couldn't do something and he turned that into motivation to prove someone wrong. The second was that the boys forgot that the coach had something to do with picking the team. A very motivated Dennis Punches showed his skills to the coach and within a month he was the starting guard on the basketball team.

Generally kids who are going through the developmental stage between 12 and 16 years of age are somewhat clumsy, especially if they are tall. Dennis was only about 5'5" or 5'6". He was slim and quick and could really handle the ball. He literally dribbled his way onto the team and into the starting five. He would later become the starting guard on the basketball team as a freshman in high school and carried that on through his four years of high school.

In fact, he was a good enough athlete that while still in eighth grade the coaches invited him to play on the high school baseball team. Similar to forcing the older boys to let him play with them in Chicago, he was now playing with the high school kids while still in grammar school. He was quick to display his skills and took every opportunity to improve them.

Chapter 8 – Fish, Hunt, Work

Herb was an outdoorsman, an avid fisherman, and an excellent hunter. Although he never took his boys out specifically to teach them to hunt or fish, after the children moved to Wauconda, he would sometimes allow them to accompany him.   Dennis was given the most opportunities to accompany his father and eventually Herb even allowed Dennis to row the boat, primarily because he didn't have a motor, and it is tough to fish while you row the boat. Dennis had to learn to row just right while Herb was fishing, not an easy task with an impatient and demanding master. There was an almost constant verbal barrage from the back of the boat as Herb chided that Dennis was making too much noise with the oars and that he would scare the fish.   There followed a stream of commands, "faster", "slower", "closer", or "stop." When Herb finally let Dennis hold a fishing pole, it quickly became clear that if he were to really participate, then Dennis would have to buy his own equipment.

It was quite apparent that even though Herb let Dennis go with him, Dad was not trying to teach his son anything other than how to row the boat. Dennis simply provided the labor while Herb fished. Yet, while he rowed, he observed carefully and learned how to fish by watching his dad. He paid careful attention to the way Herb would cast, landing the lure within a couple of inches of where he wanted it to go. Dennis realized that if he was going to be a skilled fisherman, those were skills he needed to develop when he finally got a chance.

As soon as he could save enough money, Dennis bought a True Temper rod and reel so he could go fishing, and although they were cheap, they were his own. Even then, when he had a rod and reel, his dad wouldn't invite Dennis to go fishing with him, so Dennis went by himself or with his neighbor. To his delight, even though they were mostly catching bluegills or crappies, Dennis was fishing.

The opportunity to hunt was a similar one. Dennis' oldest brother would go hunting with his dad. Herb Jr. had a soft-spoken, non-demanding personality and worked with his father as a carpenter. When Dad and brother would go hunt, Dennis' brother would invite him to tag along because he knew Dennis wanted to hunt. Dad also knew that Dennis wanted to hunt and although he didn't object to the boy tagging along, he didn't encourage it, either.

Even though Herb would demand safe hunting practices and talked about gun safety, he wasn't really focused on teaching. As with the fishing pole, Dennis knew that he would never get a chance to shoot unless he purchased his own shotgun. After saving enough money for a Mossberg 12-gauge, bolt-action shotgun, Dennis purchased the gun for $29.99. The action for the gun was worked from the right side, a terrible gun for a left-handed shooter because he had to pull the gun away from his left shoulder, and switch hands holding the gun, to cock it with his right hand. But it was the cheapest gun that he could buy and that won out over any other consideration. With practice, Dennis became a pretty good shot with that gun. No one really understood at the time just how important that ability would become for the family.

Not long after the kids moved in with their father, about the time Dennis started high school, Herb became very ill and was unable to work. He soon exhausted any unemployment compensation benefits so Dennis went to work at a bowling alley setting pins. This change required that he develop stringent time management skills as Dennis juggled new family responsibilities, along with athletics, studies, and work.

Of necessity his hunting skills quickly improved. Early mornings would see Dennis head out of the house to the corn fields or the woods that surrounded Wauconda. Each morning he would be up before 6:30 a.m. so he could go out and shoot a couple of rabbits, a squirrel, or even a pheasant if it got in the way; and he wasn't particular if it was a rooster or a hen. Whatever he shot was important because it meant meat on the table. As he gained experience he became a pretty good shot, learned to conserve his shells and not take foolish shots, and figured out the best way to smoothly work the action on that bolt action shotgun, even though it was quite inconvenient. Perhaps as importantly, he found it quite enjoyable to go out each morning and be able to shoot some game.

One of Dennis' neighbors was a good friend who played with him on the football team. This friend also enjoyed hunting and, though the wild game wasn't important to his family, he was always ready to go hunt with Dennis. Because the boys went hunting nearly every day and would deplete the available animals closer to their homes, they would have to go deeper into the cornfields or into the woods. Yet, they found that when hunting and carrying a gun, time and distance didn't mean much. During a normal morning of hunting, the boys would walk somewhere between five and ten miles, unless there was a deep snow. Since they could follow the tracks the animals made in the snow, it made hunting a lot easier, and they found they didn't have to walk as far. Dennis suggests that they sometimes found themselves praying for snow.

The boys would harvest as many animals as they could in any given hunt because the game was always used but it was unthinkable to waste anything that they shot at. While they didn't want to appear unreasonable if they had occasion for a conversation with the game warden, they were primarily limited by the amount of time that they had to hunt. The game wardens were aware that he was hunting year-round but they also knew that the family was desperately in need of that food and didn't have any money. They left Dennis alone to hunt.

After hunting, Dennis would bring whatever they had shot back home and immediately clean it. If they had scored with some rabbits, he would tack their feet to the wall in the garage, remove the skin, cut a couple of slits to remove the guts, and take off the neck and head. He would then turn the meat over to his dad to make dinner. After Herb got sick that meat was very important to the family.

Periodically the boys came home empty-handed from their hunting trips, and those were sad days. The mainstay of their diet was creamed potatoes with peas. With a piece of rabbit to go with them, the potatoes were tolerable. But absent a piece of meat, the potatoes were wearisome. To this day, Dennis won't eat creamed potatoes with peas. He has eaten enough to last a lifetime.

Dennis was very thrifty and careful with how the money was spent since his meager earnings paid the bills. He realized that they could cut the milk bill in half by using powdered milk. During the stretch when Herb was sickest, he couldn't even get out of bed. There wasn't a house payment because Herb had paid cash for the shell and for the interior improvements in the home, but Dennis was responsible to pay, from his earnings the cost of food, property taxes, household expenses, and gas for the car. Gratefully, gas would be as low as 23.9 cents per gallon, but generally under 30 cents a gallon; a far cry from 2013 prices of over four dollars per gallon.

After the morning hunt, Dennis would take care of his two younger siblings, getting them up and ready for school. With a loaf of bread, a can of evaporated milk, and some eggs, he would make French toast. Though they might wish for something else, that's what they got to eat almost every morning. Then it was time to get them ready and out the door so they could catch the bus to school.

After getting his siblings off to school, Dennis would catch the school bus and spend his day in classes. Nearly every day after school he would have practice for football, basketball, baseball, or track until about 5 p.m. He would take a shower at the school after practice and head to the bowling alley, stopping only to grab a quick bite to eat. There was a little place on the way to the bowling alley where he could buy some food for 20 or 30 cents.

The bowling leagues started at 7 p.m., so he needed to be there before then, ready to go to work. The prevailing wage for a pin setter was 10 cents per line. A line was one game per bowler and each bowler bowled three games during the evening. He was responsible for two alleys with five bowlers on each alley so he set the pins for 30 games, or lines, per league. There was a place to step through between the two alleys that he was working. After each bowler would roll his ball, Dennis was responsible to pick the ball up and set it on the return track, clear the pins that had been knocked down, or reset all of the pins for the next bowler. If someone had thrown a strike, that required that he gather all of the pins to reset them. He soon established a pattern such that he would grab four pins to put in the rack, then the next four, and finally the last two. He would then set them all on the lane ready for the bowler. As he was working both lanes he had to stay right on top of it. He learned by experience that he had to be quick or he might get hit by the flying pins. By working the two leagues from 7 p.m. until about 11 p.m., he could make $6.20 for the evening. He would stay very busy for the entire evening and, because it required so much physical movement, even if in a fairly confined space, he stayed in very good shape. After work he would usually catch a ride home with someone because it was five miles back to where they lived. He was always glad when he got home and there was some of the rabbit that he had shot that morning waiting for him to eat.

The bowling job generally occupied four nights a week, and sometimes a fifth. Those evening work weeks would allow him to make almost $30 per week, a very important sum as that was the family's sole income for an extended period of time.

Because he was a good student, Dennis was given an opportunity to make a very unique deal with the principal of the school as Mr. Warfield was aware of the plight of their family. Mr. Warfield knew that Dennis was a good athlete and that he was working pretty hard in school. He also knew that Dennis was busting his tail to get to school on time because he had to deal with his two younger siblings and his dad before school. Mr. Warfield suggested, "I'll make you a deal. If you keep straight A's on your report card, I will change your study hall to the first hour so that you can come to school an hour later than anybody else. But if you don't keep straight A's, I'll have to take it away." Instead of having to be to school at eight o'clock with the rest of the kids, here was an offer for a chance to delay his arrival until nine o'clock. It didn't take long for Dennis to figure out that this would give him time to ride his bike the five miles to school and be there on time at 9 a.m. That would allow him to get his hunting done, clean the game, feed breakfast to his brother and sister, and get them off to school. That was a very generous gesture on the part of the principal, especially since it was he who suggested such a solution. Both were true to their commitment and they were able to retain that agreement through Dennis' four years of high school.

In spite of that busy schedule, or perhaps partly because of it, Dennis stayed focused on his academics and did well enough that he graduated number two in his class from high school. He had some great teachers and great individuals who influenced him during that time.

Chapter 9 – High School Athlete

Dennis states that it was Coach Hailey that gave him his first opportunity to really think and act like an adult and to realize that he could make important decisions for his life. Perhaps that is a modest statement considering his home responsibilities, but it was a lofty thought, none-the-less. The first football game that Dennis played in, he was the starting quarterback. The school had lost 22 games in a row and had not won a single game the previous two seasons. Here he was, the kid from Chicago, as the starting quarterback. In many eyes, Dennis was the one that would lead the team to their 23rd loss in a row. Coach Hailey assured him that that was not going to happen. Dennis shares that he can still recall what Coach Hailey said. "Look, we're a small team and if you don't throw that ball, we are not going to last three quarters because our guys aren't built as big as this other team. You've got to throw that football!"

Well, long story short, Dennis did throw the football. Wauconda won the game 20 – 0 during which Dennis threw three touchdown passes. Especially thrilling was that, in the process, they broke the losing string of 22 games. They went on to win the Northwest Conference title in Illinois that year. With a strong start for the beginning of his high school football career, Dennis' playing ability ultimately led to a football scholarship for college. That scholarship was the only way that he would have gotten there because he could not have afforded college otherwise.

The success in that football game set the tone for the rest of Dennis' high school athletic career. The conference was very competitive and Wauconda High was at somewhat of a disadvantage because they were such a small school. The Northwest Chicago Suburban Conference included Palatine, Bensenville, Northbrook (which became Glenbrook as it combined with Glenview), Antioch, and Lake Zürich; all of which were bedroom communities on the Northwest side of Chicago. But playing in a small school also had advantages for the athletes. Because the players from which the coach could choose were limited, he had to play those on the team; and if an athlete was good, as Dennis was, he played a lot. Dennis' skills were such that he was on each varsity team in four different sports for all four years of high school.

Winning is important to every high school team and although winning was a hallmark of Dennis' career, they also faced their share of defeats. Through his early high school experience Dennis had never played against a black man in any of his sports. That changed with the experience of playing in the basketball sectional tournament in Waukegan, Illinois, prior to the state tournament. Not only was it novel, and perhaps a little intimidating, Dennis describes, "They beat the hell out of us. We had won 13 games in a row before we ran into this team of black guys, and they killed us! That was an education for us by itself."

Because Dennis was a four-sport athlete and the track and baseball seasons overlapped, there were times during high school when he would have a track meet and a baseball game on the same day, and often at the same time. Dennis would take two pairs of shoes with him that day; his track shoes, and his baseball spikes. He would usually be pitching or catching with the baseball team and would compete in the long jump with the track team. Between innings of the baseball game, he would run over to the track, which, luckily, was just across the field, put on his track shoes, and make his first jump. He would then tell the coaches to call him if anyone beat his distance. Since his first jump would often win the event, generally he only had to jump once. He regularly jumped close to 20 feet and most of the other kids could only muster jumps of 16 to 18 feet. After completing his jump, he would remove his track shoes, quickly put his baseball spikes back on, and return to the baseball game. Since it was a small school there was an expectation that there would be some flexibility to allow that to happen. It was also that flexibility that allowed Dennis to finish with 16 athletic letters in high school. For Dennis, his athletic season never stopped during the school year with football in the fall, basketball right after the football season, and with baseball and track starting about the same time. It was only during the summer when he was not playing a sport.

The coaches, who were generally teachers, were paid almost nothing for their coaching responsibilities, but students don't spend much time thinking about what a coach or a teacher makes. They just look up to a coach or a good teacher, sometimes in a bit of awe, and try to replicate the type of person that they are.

Wauconda High School only had about 400 students. The coaches really had no choice but to use whatever athletes were available if they wanted to have a team. That being said, Dennis didn't get to play on four teams every year just because he was there. As an excellent athlete he contributed to the success of each Wauconda team on which he played. Dennis made the all-conference teams in basketball as a guard, and in football as quarterback. His school and conference long jump records stood for a number of years. In baseball he threw a complete game one-hitter.

Every baseball game was a complete game for the pitchers because they only had two pitchers on the team. Each of those two players, when not pitching, was the catcher for the game. As Dennis recalls, getting behind the plate as the catcher was the toughest thing for him to do in athletics. The coach forced him to do it because the other pitcher had only one pitch, a fastball, and that one was often wild. There was no one other than Dennis who could catch him. When someone else tried to catch for him, invariably the other team would steal a lot of bases on passed balls. When the coach told him he had to get behind the plate Dennis protested, telling him "that bat comes within 6 inches of my head every time the batter swings." He went on to say, "When I first started playing the catcher position I will admit that for the first little while I would close my eyes when the bat would start around but eventually I did get pretty good at it. I played that position for most of high school." Generally speaking, behind the plate is the last place where you want your pitcher to be, as most teams want to protect them, but the coach felt he had no choice.

Dennis had a good curveball, a pitch that would now be called a slider, and a pretty good fastball. When he threw a slider, he held the ball with three fingers to give the ball a backwards spin so that it would break left to right, while his curveball was thrown with a forward spin so it would break right to left.

The competition was good enough that a couple of the guys from the conference made it to the major leagues, even though they were never stars. Dennis was a good enough baseball player that he had an opportunity to try out for the Chicago White Sox at 17 years of age.

The White Sox held a baseball school, called the Rogers Hornsby School, where they brought in up to 100 select high school athletes from the Chicago area for a tryout. Dennis had just pitched his complete game one-hitter. No doubt his coach had something to do with getting a tryout for him, but that was how they selected the kids. Dennis shares, "It was a big thrill to be out there on the diamond where the professionals played every day. During the day I pitched some and I played some shortstop. They liked me at shortstop because I could move fairly well and I had a good arm. I had to have a good arm to pitch every day. They liked that I could make the throw from deep shortstop to first base. The competition was tough, as one can imagine, with 100 kids. While I really didn't put very much into it, knowing that I would not be selected to move forward, it was a great experience. I thought I should give it a shot. It was a thrill to know that they at least looked at you, but it's obvious that I didn't become the next Joe DiMaggio."

In spite of his extensive participation in high school sports and the heavy demands on his schedule, Dennis' father seemed completely oblivious to Dennis' athletic participation. Of course that wasn't unexpected because Herb showed little interest in developing much of any kind of relationship with him. Added to that, Herb never paid a lot of attention to any athletics, let alone his, until one day he read Dennis' name in the paper. Dennis had made the headlines in the newspaper in Waukegan, Illinois after he had thrown a number of touchdown passes and they clinched the league championship. When Herb mentioned that he had read about his football playing, Dennis responded that he had been playing football for a couple of years and maybe Herb should come see him play. Herb came to their homecoming game while Dennis was still playing in high school and then followed his college football career.

High school athletics were heady stuff and Dennis enjoyed the chance to participate. He had good coaches who encouraged excellence. In fact, it was those high school coaches who threatened expulsion from the team for smoking or drinking, no matter who the athlete was, and whether or not the season was underway. They had his attention! Neither smoking nor drinking was an issue for him. Four different sports and seasons allowed him to stay in excellent physical shape. The demand of athletics, academics, and family responsibilities left little time to get in trouble. And frankly, if there was time available, hunting or fishing were always a draw.

Dennis finished his high school athletic experience earning letters each of four years in four separate sports: football, basketball, baseball, and track. It was a stellar career.

Chapter 10 – The Dream

Dennis had an experience early in life that stuck with him, upon which he periodically reflects, and which has regularly made a difference in his life. When he was 16 or 17 years old, he had to have some surgery. All went as planned as he went under the anesthesia and the doctors got underway. However, the anesthesia started wearing off before the surgery was complete. Since he was still asleep, there was nothing that Dennis could do but endure the pain that was intensifying. In the dream that followed, the intense pain was an important element. Men in white coats approached Dennis with clipboards and they were questioning him. If he gave them the right answers, he moved up a rung on a ladder. Even as the pain became greater, he kept moving up the ladder. He knew that if it got to where he couldn't stand the pain that was where he had to stop his climb. Eventually, he looked down and realized that he had come a long way up the ladder. Then the dream ended.

Dennis has contemplated that dream often. Why was it meaningful? He took it as a sign or an omen of where he had to take his life, and that was up that ladder. He recognized that he possessed God-given talents to move up the ladder and failure to use them would not be right. Consequently, whenever he came to an impasse in either business or in his personal life, he would refer back to that ladder and say, "Wait a minute. You were put there for a reason. Now use it!"

That dream has also helped Dennis to take a philosophical approach to life, and to cause moments of introspection. He has shared, "As I look back over my life I see several pivotal events which involve God-given talents, and which were significant in the direction of my life. I realized early on that I had to do something with those talents. It is one thing to have them but another to recognize that you have them. It is also very important that you don't take them for granted. Even at an early age you need to recognize that they are an important asset."

Dennis had developed a significantly competitive approach to life which he combined with those God-given talents, recognizing that he had them, and then moved forward because of them. He was stirred to action when someone suggested that he couldn't do something and he would immediately go to work to prove that they were wrong. But as he did so he also found that he had great abilities to achieve. This not only manifested itself on the athletic field, but also in academics. Dennis was able to maintain a straight A average through high school with what he recalls was a minimum of exertion. It was a good thing that he could listen to and could absorb the instruction. There wasn't a lot of extra time for studying.

He continued, "It is amazing that I was able to be as successful as I was without having extensive study time. I did gain an incredible appreciation for time, something that has stuck with me throughout my life. I understand that I am bound by time and space, which we all are, but the thought came to me early in my life that I had to be organized to get everything done that I wanted to do. It helped that I didn't fall in love until I was 16 although when it did happen, it did screw up the timetable a little bit."

Chapter 11 – Working & Character Building

High school didn't mean just hunting, fishing, athletics or academics. Dennis also found time to work and earn some money. The bowling alley job was critical to the family financial well-being while Herb was sick. Dennis also took other jobs during the summer to make money. He spent one summer as a water meter reader going from house to house. That job would play a pivotal role later in life as he sought a critical business relationship.

Dennis purchased a distraction when he was 16. He bought his first car, a 1941 Plymouth, which ate more oil than it did gas. After paying about $200 for the car, it took about four months to pay it off. Of course, he had to get his own insurance and pay for that himself. Since it was an old car he chose not to purchase collision insurance, just property damage coverage. He would drive the car to school and when the other guys wanted to ride with him in the car, in a true entrepreneurial spirit, Dennis would charge them for the privilege. Everybody needed to put in a dollar for gas, and if they didn't, he let the car sit until he had money for gas from them.

With a car to take care of, it seemed to make sense to take a part-time job one summer working at a gas station in Wauconda. He was responsible to greet customers on the pump island, to fill their cars with gas, do oil changes and grease jobs, and change and repair flat tires. One of the advantages of working at the gas station was that he could keep the used motor oil that was drained out of the other cars and would use it in his own car that burned and leaked a lot of oil. It didn't matter that it was used oil because his car was burning it up anyway, whether it was good or bad. And even though it smelled awful, he carried the can of oil in the backseat of the car since he needed to add oil regularly. It was much more convenient there than in the trunk.

Dennis focused on providing excellent customer service at the station. In fact, one particular customer was so pleased with Dennis' work that he insisted that Dennis was the only one that should work on his car. As he shares the story, "There was an Italian guy, a union official, Mr. Baldino, who had a big Chrysler that was wired for security because he was part of the mafia. His son went to school with me. Mr. Baldino always wanted me to take care of his car because I knew not to set off the alarms. That was a big car. One day when they came to the gas station he gave me a watch. No one had ever given me such a gift, and he said 'Here, Denny, I want you to have this watch.' As I remember, it was an Elgin watch which was made in Elgin, Illinois. A week later they found him under a viaduct in Chicago in the trunk of his car with about 30 bullet holes in his body. It was hard to look at that watch and not associate it with a dead man."

As a carpenter, Herb thought that might be a good trade for Dennis. While Dennis didn't necessarily agree, he did think that it might be a good idea for him to learn the trade. There was an immediate problem as Dennis is left-handed and all of the power tools at the time were made for right-handed people. After unsuccessfully trying to make straight cuts using his left hand and a right-handed tool, Herb strongly criticized him for not being able to cut a straight line. Dennis was bright enough to agree with his dad and even suggested that Herb should probably do the cutting while Dennis did the grunt work. He quickly found himself doing the heavy lifting, carrying things around, but doing nothing technical.

One day they were pouring a cement slab for a garage that Herb had contracted to build, using a technique called puddling. As the concrete mix would come off of the truck they had to quickly run a board back and forth across the concrete in a sawing motion to level the concrete and allow the rocks to settle to the bottom. Herb was a very strong man, not heavy, but very strong and sinewy. Dennis was strong too, but not as adept as his dad. Dennis would be on one end of the board and Herb would be on the other while they sawed back and forth across the concrete. A challenging task anyway, it becomes very difficult if the two workers are not fairly well matched in strength and ability. Invariably one will get ahead of the other, which causes problems. In this case Dennis didn't have gloves and the 2 x 4's were inflicting lots of slivers into his hands. Herb was faster than Dennis and unwilling to slow down at all to let him catch up. So, as Dennis shares, "He would get ahead of me and I was dragging behind. By the time we got done he was telling me what a terrible job I was doing and that I would probably never amount to anything, at least in the construction or carpentry business. I was 17 years old at the time and I thought to myself that he was probably right. So I stopped puddling and said, 'Dad, you're probably right. I am not smart enough to do this kind of work.' I set my end of the board down, walked through the work that we had just done (right through the concrete) and out the other side, and said, 'Dad, I can't do this anymore.' I thought he was gonna beat me to a pulp but we had an understanding from that day on that I was meant to do something else."

Another experience strengthened the feelings for Dennis that he didn't want to work for his dad. One of the many odd jobs that Dennis came up with during high school was that he and a friend hired out to dig basements with shovels. Old houses that were built without a basement would be jacked up such that someone could get under the house and shovel out the dirt. This was grunt work in its purest form, digging a basement by hand. When Herb contracted to build a basement under a house he hired the boys to dig it. They agreed to work for Dennis' dad, expecting to be paid at the end of the job. However, when the boys finished digging the basement, while Herb paid the other guy in cash, he bought Dennis a coat. When Dennis realized that he was not to receive any money, he was bitterly disappointed! He needed the coat to stay warm but he sure was looking forward to the cash. Maybe Herb was getting even with Dennis for walking through the concrete.

Though their relationship had its rocky spots, Dennis would later develop a pretty good relationship with his father. Herb claims he was part Indian, probably Ojibwa, although they have never been able to trace it back. But looking at his profile, one could see that he might be part Indian. His is the side of the family where one would find the stoic, quiet, hard, the Duke (John Wayne) type of personality. Dennis developed little of that type of demeanor.

On the other hand, Dennis' mother was just the opposite as the soft, forgiving, loving person who worked very hard and really cherished her children. Dennis recalls her telling him that he was the special one. He knew that she told that to every other one of his five siblings, but he believed her when she said that he was special. She was a big motivator in his continuing on in school. In fact, during his last summer working construction before going to college, she wouldn't let him cash any of his paychecks. He was making $1.25 per hour, so the paychecks were not huge. But she took each check and saved them all until the end of the summer. Just before he left for school in Wisconsin, she had him take all of his paychecks to cash them. That was what he had to live on to start his college life. As he reflected, he didn't need very many dollars that summer before he went to school because all he did was work and sleep.

As Dennis was growing up, he never put his money in an account at a bank. The lesson that was taught by mom's example was that money was kept in a drawer at home. She would tuck money away in a drawer, or under the mattress, with a firm statement, "You can't touch this. You have to find some other way to make some money but you can't touch the savings." Even with the money accessible, family members knew to leave one other's savings alone.

Dorothy had some wonderful sayings, such as: "If you can't say something good about someone, don't say anything." Dennis will share, "I would say that she was a big influence on my life, the softer side. As you look through the generations and have an opportunity to look at your children, grandchildren, and great-grandchildren, you will be able to recognize the softer side as well as the harder side. Most people will have some mix of both ingredients, which is probably necessary to build character."

Dennis soon gathered up a second distraction when, as if the car wasn't distracting enough, a young lady caught his attention. He was in love. Though she probably felt slighted because of the amount of time that he spent hunting, practicing for athletics, and working, she must have thought she had it made as the girlfriend of the high school quarterback. However, she did manage to break his heart before he left for college as she decided that she preferred one of his football teammates over him. Though it hurt at the time, it is hard not to wonder what changes in direction she might have caused for Dennis if she had not made that decision. He has decided that it was for the best.

Dennis' upbringing was a bit out of the ordinary, causing him to look at life much differently than many of his peers. He had learned the value of time and the importance of focusing on the right things. Yet, here he was, 17 years old, and to his way of thinking, he had the world by the tail. He didn't think that it could get any better. He was the star quarterback and a straight A student. He had $35 in his pocket, a car of his own, and a pretty cheerleader as a girlfriend. Wasn't this hog heaven? But then he realized that he was never going to be 17 again. He had to pay attention to his use of time, and use it well. He would never get the time back. He didn't want to wake up one day at 40 years of age and realize that he had missed the boat. He had to focus and use his time wisely if he wanted to achieve his life's goals.

Dennis graduated 2nd in his class, academically. Though many of his classmates would remain in Wauconda, he had an opportunity to attend college on a football/athletic scholarship at Carroll College in Waukesha, Wisconsin. As a small liberal arts college sponsored by the Presbyterian Church, it was close to family and offered a chance to continue to play sports. Although other colleges made their play for his talents, including another one that offered a scholarship, Dennis determined to go to Wisconsin. This would be a pivotal decision that would impact the rest of his life.

His mentor, Coach Hailey, was a terrific coach and teacher. He had inspired Dennis to be better academically and athletically than he likely would have been otherwise. It is normal to want to pattern your life after someone that you revere and trust, so Dennis determined he would study in college to become a teacher and a coach. Just as teaching and coaching had become Coach Hailey's purpose in life, Dennis determined that would be the case with him, as well.

Chapter 12 – Starting College

As he approached the end of high school, Dennis received two offers to play college football; one from Bradley University in Peoria, Illinois, and the other from Carroll College in Waukesha, Wisconsin. He accepted the scholarship offer from Carroll as it was a much smaller school, he liked the campus and the layout, and he thought he had a much better chance of doing well there. His comfort level came easily as the school was what he had pictured college should be. Dennis moved to Waukesha, Wisconsin in 1954 to start school and begin a new life adventure.

Football practice began that fall and Dennis made the traveling squad his freshman year. Unlike his experience in high school, where he was a four-year starter, he didn't get to play much that year. That season coincided with the end of the Korean War and many of the returning players were 23 or 24 years old. Not only were they war vets, they were great big guys. As an 18-year-old startup he learned to warm the bench for a year. Dennis played on what they called the hamburger squad which is the squad that the starting unit beats up on through the week during practice. True to the name, they made hamburger out of them. Yet, without that squad, it would be very difficult for the first team be ready to play on Saturday.

One of his first assignments was for Dennis to gain weight because the coaches felt that he was too small. He had arrived at Carroll weighing about 155 pounds, but within two months they had him up to 170 pounds, a much better playing weight. With the Eisenhower administration trying to deemphasize college athletics and to rein in the number of scholarships, they took on a nanny role and limited the number of substitutions that could be made during a game. As a result, players would end up playing offense and defense. The additional weight was critical for Dennis.

Since his scholarship was insufficient to pay for all of his schooling, Dennis needed to work to augment his resources. He took a job working in the cafeteria of the girl's dormitory where he did dishes for 200 girls, three times a day. His labor earned him his daily meals, something that was very important if he was to gain the weight that he needed. It also put him in a position to evaluate a significant portion of the freshman girls and to think about who he might want to date. Of course, there were times when these young ladies were not at their best or very pretty, such as when they came in for breakfast at 7 a.m. Since he worked with several other young men and rotated between clearing tables, washing dishes, and scrubbing pots and pans, his view would be adjusted based on his assignment, but it was still hard for a young man not to be checking things out.

A particular young lady, one out of the two hundred, caught his attention, and before long he had met the lovely Kathleen Truesdale. He could look at her three times a day while he was doing dishes. Even though dishwashers were not generally who the girls might be attracted to, Dennis was assertive and when he determined to ask her out, that is what he did. She responded positively.

Tuition was $500 per year and the scholarship paid $250 per semester to cover his tuition. The dishwashing job paid for his meals. The money that he had earned and saved during the summer before his freshman year allowed him to meet the financial obligations, including housing costs, of a young student. However, there was little money for books, so for some of his classes he didn't purchase a textbook. Dennis had an uncanny ability to focus on the lectures, and he never missed a lecture. In the case of some classes, such as his history class, he realized that the expectation was that the students would be able to recite back what had been taught in class. In these situations, he shared, "All I had to do was listen carefully and then spit back what I had heard when exam time came." Since he took very challenging courses as a science major, often without books, he found that if he listened carefully in class, took copious notes, and then studied those notes prior to an exam, he fared very well. His ability to take notes and remember lecture content without purchasing a textbook saved him a lot of money. He earned a cumulative A-average for his four years of college.

After the football season, Dennis was on the basketball team where he was a point guard; the quarterback on the basketball court. Since he was focused primarily on setting the offense, and then passing the ball, he didn't shoot very much. His assist total rivaled his scoring. Little did he realize, however, that his basketball career would be short-lived and would conclude at the end of that, his first season.

Basketball games and associated practices took him into the beginning of the track season. As a capable sprinter and long-jumper, Dennis was given the job of earning five points for the team at the meets. A first place individual finish earned five points, a second place was three, and a third place finish earned one point. Though the competition was stronger than in high school, he still regularly contributed to the team total in the long jump.

A side benefit of his athletics came when one of the local fraternities, thinking it would prove beneficial in attracting other members to have some athletes in the fraternity, extended an invitation to Dennis to join. When they offered him membership without having to pay the normal dues, it made sense to have a spot to study or to sleep for a while. It was a logical and no-cost benefit, so Dennis joined the fraternity.

Chapter 13 – Dating and Marriage

Dennis had recognized in high school the importance of setting priorities in his life. He had been busy since early in his high school experience so now, in college, he decided what was most important to him and that was what he pursued.   Determined to succeed, he practiced hard with the sports teams, fulfilled his commitment in the cafeteria, expended the necessary effort in the classroom, and determined to get to know Katie.

Even while going to college, Dennis continued his hunting and fishing as often as he could. As a result, he would often have game or fish to eat. While he and Kathleen were dating, he had shot a couple of pheasants while hunting one weekend. His mother prepared the birds for a picnic for them, a lunch they enjoyed in Frame Park in Waukesha near the Fox River. It was a pleasant lunch and while he doesn't remember if they had wine with lunch, Dennis suggests that if they did, it would have been Ripple as he couldn't afford anything better than something he could buy for $1.98 a bottle.

Katie was a very pretty girl with a strong sense of her own purpose. In other words, she was a free spirit and always had ideas of doing something really different. Her parents had sent her to Carroll College thinking that it would help channel her energies and keep her occupied. Even with her interest in Dennis, she was not willing to be tied down.

The couple dated that first semester of their freshman year but then Katie left school before the second semester began, having decided that she was going to see the world. The money didn't get her very far. The bus ticket she purchased only got her to Cedar Rapids, Iowa where she was hired as a nanny for an individual who did the farm report on the radio in the mornings. It was quickly apparent that this was not a good situation.

The radio equipment was set up in Katie's bedroom. When the guy got up at seven o'clock in the morning, he made his report from her room while she was still lying in bed in the room and his wife was sleeping in their room. When Dennis learned of the situation, he immediately determined that it was not healthy and realized it was time for him to become Sir Galahad and rescue her. On the weekend he drove to Iowa. It apparently took some convincing that she needed to be rescued, but he was emphatic with her that she was not staying in that situation. They gathered up her belongings and loaded them, and her, into his car. When they called her dad, Dr. Truesdale, and explained that she needed to return to Connecticut, he sent her an airline ticket. With Dennis' help, Katie finally realized that she was not in a good situation and she needed to get out of it.

Not content with just rescuing her, while they were still in Iowa City, Dennis proposed marriage to Katie. She responded positively. Of course Dennis hadn't yet told her father that bit of news, but he convinced her to go back home to Connecticut where her parents lived. The gallant knight had rescued the damsel in distress, had pledged his love to her, but then sent her one thousand miles away to her parent's home.

With Katie in Connecticut and Dennis in Wisconsin, they tried to maintain a long-distance relationship, but they it found it to be very difficult. By the end of the following semester, Dennis realized that the relationship was important enough to him that he needed to do something about it. He got into his 1946 Plymouth, another oil burner but an upgrade from his high school transportation, and drove out to Old Greenwich, Connecticut. With each gas station stop he instructed, "Fill the car with oil and check the gas." Instead of the free oil from the station in Wauconda, Dennis purchased oil in five gallon cans because that was less expensive than buying the oil in quarts.

Once in Connecticut, Dennis reiterated his marriage proposal to Katie, informed her father of his intention, stated emphatically that they were going to get married, and he committed that he was going to take care of her. It had to cause the good doctor and his wife to pause as they met this young 19 year-old who wanted to marry their daughter. Dr. John was persistent in his questioning as to whether or not Dennis was ready to commit. Surely he thought the kids were too young to marry, but Dennis figured he was ready. Her father was supportive and loaned them $1,000 to help Dennis finish school, money Dennis paid back shortly after he graduated.

Given the choice as to whether or not they wanted a big wedding or to take the money that would have been spent and use it to start their married lives together, the young couple was in agreement to take the money. A small garden wedding was held at the Truesdale home with the Atlantic Ocean in the background. Dennis' mother and his aunt had flown from Chicago, the first time that they had been on an airplane.

Dennis had finished his first year of college, survived a year on the football hamburger squad, had become the white knight and rescued his sweetheart, proposed marriage, married, got on his black horse (the 1946 Plymouth) to return to Wisconsin, and as he recalls, "We were on our way."

In traditional fashion, they drove away from the wedding with cans tied to the bumper of the car and with a "just married" sign on the back. They honeymooned in Niagara Falls for a couple of days and then headed north and then west through Canada. Dennis even managed to get a little fishing in. The trip across Canada and back into Wisconsin took almost 15 gallons of oil. The money received from Katie's parents was sufficient to get them back to Wisconsin.

Since the marriage occurred between his freshman and sophomore years of school, Dennis still had three years of college to finish. But now he was a married man with responsibilities. Neither of them had a job. It was very apparent that Katie had no intentions of going back to college, but it would have been almost impossible for both to attend school anyway. Dennis still had his scholarship for tuition but there was now a need to add an apartment and food for two to the budget.

Back in Waukesha, even though they had no place to stay, they had a car full of wedding presents, and a bright future. As they looked around for places to rent, they quickly realized that everything that was close to the school was too expensive. Eventually, as they got out of town into the country, they found a place to rent. The owner, Ed Schultz, showed them an upstairs apartment in his farmhouse. The apartment had bathroom fixtures, including a toilet and a tub, but no walls for privacy. It similarly lacked a kitchen sink. He explained that they would have to do their dishes in the bathtub unless they wanted to put in a kitchen sink, which is what they did until they could afford a sink. They now had an apartment that rented for $55 per month, located about 5 miles northwest from the school, with no bathroom walls or a kitchen sink.

Dennis had worked construction the year between high school and college and now worked the remaining weeks before football and classes started again. He had made $1.25 per hour in a similar job before college but now he was making $1.80. The problem was that the job only lasted until the football season started.

Even though the scholarship paid tuition, they still needed money to live on. Since Dennis was heavily involved in sports, the managers at Sears were excited to offer him a job in the sporting goods department. It provided enough to pay the rent and buy food. Katie got a job as a waitress at the Avalon Hotel in Waukesha.

When they could afford to purchase a sink, a friend of Dennis' helped him install it in the kitchen so they didn't have to do the dishes in the bathtub. When Dennis' father came to visit, he helped build a wall around the commode for some privacy.   Each was a welcome addition.

They were doing okay financially until Katie got pregnant and was no longer able to work. So now at 20 years old, as a full-time student, and a college athlete, Dennis was to become a father. Their baby, Debbie, arrived one year after they got married.

Chapter 14 – Married College Sophomore

Dennis continued to attend classes during each summer while in college. He sought job opportunities as he had time, and even played in a summer baseball league in Waukesha, where, he noted, his hitting improved significantly. Marriage certainly brought a new dimension to his life.

Dennis' athletic scholarship was for three sports. During his freshman year he had been on the hamburger squad for football, and although he traveled with the team, his playing time was limited to the last couple of games of the season. He played basketball and was on the track team as a successful long-jumper. As he now juggled athletic responsibilities, classes, part-time work in the cafeteria, part-time work in construction or at Sears, marriage, and other demands, something had to give.

Dennis had mixed feelings when the athletic director approached him and suggested that he was more valuable to the football squad than the basketball team and asked that he focus on football and not play basketball. Although somewhat reluctant to give up his spot on the basketball team, this much needed change enabled him to retain his scholarship and freed up a considerable amount of time during the basketball season.

Dennis started the football season in August and made the traveling team. Yet, as he began his second year, there were still two quarterbacks in front of him and he was not getting into the games. As he watched the season slip away, he was discouraged with the situation. It had gotten to the point where he decided that since he wasn't going to get into the game anyway, why haul his helmet with him? A helmet is awfully hard to fit into the traveling gear bag and is generally the last thing to get packed.

They had a game midway through the season at North-Central Illinois College.[v] Convinced that he would see no playing time, he was sitting on the bench, as usual. As fate would have it, both of the two quarterbacks who played in front of him were injured during the same quarter and were carried off the field. The coach called his name, even though Dennis thought Coach McCormick had forgotten it. Dennis got up, went over to the coach, and had to tell him, "Coach, I don't have a helmet." All the coach could stammer was, "What?" Dennis tried to explain that he never got into the ballgames anyway so why would he bring his helmet? Well, they had to call a special timeout while they looked for a helmet to fit him from one of the other players.

With Carroll down 7-0, Dennis was now in the game. Since all of his practice time had been as a member of the hamburger squad, he was used to calling the other team's plays, not their own. As a result, he only knew about six plays; three passing and three running plays. On the first play he called from scrimmage, he handed off to the fullback who ran for 72 yards before he was caught and tackled on the one-yard line. As Dennis shares, "As I went back into the huddle, I said to these big guys (they were shaving, they were so big, and I didn't even have whiskers), what do I do now guys? What do you think?' Well, this big tackle looked at me and said, 'You take that ball and you crawl right up my ass!' So I called the play which was 'up your ass on two.' After I called the play we broke the huddle. I took the ball, put my head right up against his rear and he carried me right into the end zone. I scored a touchdown on the second play I was ever in playing college football. I also ended up throwing two touchdown passes and we won the game 20 to 7. It was a big thrill, gave me a good start, and I built on that success, not only in athletics but ultimately in business. And that's why I tell the story because it was the basis and the beginning of my success."

Dennis took his helmet to the remaining three games, saw additional playing time, and even helped the team to some success as they tied the next game and won the remaining two games that season.

Many young athletes have an over-developed sense of who they are and perhaps think they are pretty special. Sometimes that leads to them being bullies or having a hot temper. Dennis wasn't overly concerned about his self-importance. He was an excellent athlete but didn't necessarily feel he needed to impress anyone on campus. That being said, he was always looking for ways to improve his performance on the field.

As a 175 pound quarterback and safety in college he had to use his head rather than his brawn because the brawn wasn't there. Yet he was still responsible to tackle 250 pound fullbacks. Since Dennis played as a defensive safety, if the fullback got to his vicinity there was generally no one else to tackle the runner but him. If the runner broke through the line, he was Dennis' responsibility. Realizing that he had to out-think the running back, because he couldn't out muscle him or beat him physically, it required that he consider and determine the weaknesses of the runner. There wasn't a lot of time to figure that out and Dennis would quickly study and make a decision. It generally meant he had to tackle the runner very low as the last thing you wanted to do was to catch him at his thighs. The strongest part of a football running back's body is his thighs. Usually when he bowls someone over it is because they tried to tackle him on the strongest part of his body.

The key for Dennis was to make the tackle and not get hurt since the person making the tackle gets hurt just as often, if not more, than the person getting tackled. He learned early on, through the coaches, to get his head in front of the tackle rather than in back. When he would angle in for a tackle he had to get his head in front of the runner's legs so he didn't catch the brunt of his force. Once he got his head in front of him he could then launch himself from the ground and wrap his arms around the lower part of the runner's legs. That was the best way to make a clean tackle. He had to outthink the big guys, which eventually also carried over into how he might outthink potential customers or competitors, especially the big guys.

Without a commitment to the basketball team, Dennis put his free time to good use with his part-time job at Sears, working in the sporting goods department prior to the Christmas season. They thought that a local college quarterback might do a good job, especially since he knew a lot about hunting, fishing, and athletics.

Since his pay was a minimum wage base plus a 1% commission on the items that he sold, he was fairly aggressive in his efforts to sell. When it required telling a lady just how good she looked in the hunting coat that she was trying on, or how good a winter coat looked on little Johnny, he would stifle the smirk and then work to make the sale. He would generally work three or four evenings during the week with additional hours on Saturday and Sunday.

The sporting goods job didn't last very long as Sears let all of their seasonal help go after the Christmas season, but it was retail experience. He had been reasonably successful but wasn't entirely unhappy when he saw that job come to an end.

Chapter 15 –Merchants Credit Bureau

One day, shortly after his job was eliminated at Sears, Dennis was sitting in the front room of the fraternity house between classes visiting with some of his friends. He found himself wondering, perhaps aloud, what he was going to do next. Tuition was paid and he was attending class, but how was he to provide for his family, especially now that a baby was coming? Little did he realize that he was about to experience a pivotal moment in his life, one that would, because he was there at that particular time, completely change his future.

As the guys were talking, the phone rang. The fellow next to Dennis answered, listened for a moment and then responded, "I am sorry. I am not interested in the job." There was no hesitation as Dennis grabbed the phone away from his friend and said into the phone, "I don't know who you are or what the job is, but I will do it." The somewhat startled voice on the other end of the phone said, "You sound like you mean it and that you're interested in the job. Would you like to come down for an interview?" With a positive response from Dennis, the caller asked how quickly he could be there for an interview. Dennis asked if five minutes would be quick enough.

The office was five or six blocks away and Dennis ran to make sure that he got there before someone else did. The business was located on the top floor of a two-story walk-up near the Five Points area of Waukesha, a somewhat unique area where multiple streets come together just a few blocks from the college. He ran up the stairs into a dark hallway where the sign painted on the frosted glass of the door greeted him: *Merchants Credit Bureau and Detective Agency*. His initial thought was that it looked like something out of a *Sam Spade* type detective show on television. After knocking on the door, Dennis met Norman Anderson, who would become a big part of his life. This was the beginning of a relationship that lasted for many years.

After introducing himself as Dennis Punches and expressing that he was interested in the job, he asked what Norm wanted him to do. Norm's response was that he wanted Dennis to go out and get some business for him and that he was going to teach Dennis the collection business. When Dennis asked how much the job paid, Norm indicated that he would give him one dollar per face-to-face business call that he made, up to twenty-five dollars per week, plus one tank of gas per week, an additional five dollar value.

As they talked, Dennis found out that Mr. Anderson ran a collection agency with just two employees; himself, and a lady who worked part-time doing some typing. Norm explained that he would like Dennis to learn the collection business, but more importantly, he needed him to find more business. In response to the question of how to go after the business and who the potential customers might be Norm indicated that everyone was a potential customer because everyone has personal debts, and many have debts that are owed to them. So therefore, he figured that it didn't exclude anybody. While that thought was sinking in, the next reasonable question seemed to be, "How do I get the clients?" The response was, "Go downstairs.

Look to the left and look to the right. Those are all your customers. All you have to do is persuade them that they need you."

Even though Norm agreed to pay for each sales call, he included the caveat that Dennis had to bring new business into the organization because it wasn't going to do any good to have him making calls if he didn't bring additional business. That was the job.

The final question seemed to annoy Norm. In response to what training he would give, Norm grabbed a bunch of listing blanks, handed Dennis a pencil, suggested that he go downstairs, look to the left, and then look to the right, and get customers, reiterating that everyone had bad debts. It seemed easy enough so Dennis accepted the job offer, they shook hands, and it was time to go to work. Dennis wondered how much faith Norm had in him that he wouldn't even invest a pen in his new employee, but he took the pencil.

Dennis went downstairs and as he looked to the left and then looked to the right, he saw a clothing store and a typewriter store. He realized that everyone in his position had worked that particular group of potential customers. It seemed to make the most sense to go elsewhere to practice. Getting into his car that he had purchased from one of his coaches, a 1949 Buick Roadmaster which got about 10 miles to the gallon, he headed for Hartland, Wisconsin. When he looked up Main Street in Hartland, plotting his next move, he could see a clothing store, two dentist offices, a doctor's office, a plumbing store, a gas station, and a shoe maker shop. There were even a couple of taverns, but since he figured that he couldn't shine shoes again, he decided that he would start with the shoemaker.

Taking a listing blank and his pencil, he made his entrance into the shop only to be met by the din of the equipment. After several minutes of trying to yell his purpose over the racket of the machine, the shoe maker reluctantly shut off the machine and asked Dennis what he was doing. Dennis started with a basic explanation that they would recover money for him by collecting his bad debts and that it wouldn't cost the man anything unless they made a recovery. The shoemaker replied that he didn't have any debts, to which Dennis countered that his boss had told him that everyone had bad debts. After they talked some more the man finally went to a back room, brought out an old cigar box in which he kept all of his receipts, and produced a single NSF check for $10. The check was tattered and had to be at least five years old, and was displayed for Dennis with the explanation that this was the only guy who had ever stuck him.

After being shown the check, Dennis suggested that if he would give the check to him, they would go collect it and bring him back five dollars. The shoe maker couldn't believe that they were going to charge him five dollars to collect his ten-dollar check and said he wasn't going to pay Dennis, or anyone else, five dollars. With that, he put the check back in the box. The competitive juices were working and Dennis determined that he had to get that check. He continued to talk to the man, reminding him that he didn't have anything right now as the check was worthless. Finally, an hour later, Dennis got the check.

Even though they never collected the check for the shoemaker, that first sales call was a success, and while it took an hour and a half, Dennis got the business. The experience taught him that if he was committed enough to what he was selling, and told the customer the truth, someone would buy. By the end of day he had made multiple contacts and had several people signed up in Hartland. The total that day was approximately $5,000 worth of business, with approximately half of those dollars that were collected. Needless to say, this made Norm very happy. And, of course, it made Dennis very happy, as well.

Dennis suggests, perhaps tongue in cheek, that this was how he methodically picked out the future business that he would be in. Perhaps the job was obtained because it was absolutely necessary with a child on the way, but Dennis will suggest that on that day, the Big Guy was looking out for him.

Within two months, Dennis had added two doctors, the Standard Oil gas station, the Jacobs clothing store, two dentists, and was bringing more business into the credit bureau than they had ever seen. He soon received a small raise on his commission. In the evenings, after he had finished doing dishes and eating at the girl's dormitory, he would go back to the office where Norm taught him how to collect on the telephone. Dennis would fit sales calls to potential clients in between his classes during the day to find new business and at night would come back and collect the debts.

Perhaps there is a reason that the collection business had a bit of an unsavory reputation in that time frame. Collectors were bound by some rules but were not above using some tough practices. At the time, it was legal to garnish an individual's paycheck before obtaining a judgment against the debtor. After finding out where the individual worked, they would send a garnishment letter to the employer for the amount owed. That would allow them to take the guy's check while they sought a judgment. Of course, the individual was eager to make payment arrangements so he could get his check released. As a result, a lot of time was spent with the Justice of the Peace pursuing claims in small claims court.

Dennis' on-the-job training included the small claims court part of the business, learning how to make the phone calls, and how to type the collection notices. Dennis accomplished all of this while going to school full-time, keeping close to a straight A average, and maintaining active participation on the sports teams.

His position with the Merchants Credit Bureau in Waukesha was the start of his business career and soon led to a measure of success. Norm was very happy with Dennis because he was making more money; and that allowed Dennis to make more money.

Chapter 16 – Practice Teaching

When improved income allowed Dennis and Katie to afford something better than the $55 a month rent at the farm house, they found a place right on the edge of campus on McCall Street. With two more years of school to finish, a new baby, and moving up the economic ladder somewhat, it felt like the $90 a month rent was tolerable and justifiable. Debbie had been born and the couple soon had another baby on the way.

When Laurie was born Dennis still had a year of school left. He had become the starting quarterback at Carroll College and now had his own cheering section with his wife and two daughters sitting in the stands. Even when no one else would cheer for him, he could count on his family. They enjoyed a fair amount of success during his junior year on the field with the team finishing the year with a 5-3 record. But his final year in school saw the team struggle. As they finished with 2 wins and 6 losses that season, it was good to have Katie and the girls cheering him on.[vi]

As he had in high school, Dennis contributed to the success of the Carroll track team. As a long jump specialist, he regularly jumped 21 or 22 feet, a significant distance for a college athlete at a small school. As his stated job was to get five points in the long jump, Dennis considered it a good day when he could contribute by taking first in his event, something that happened fairly often while participating against small colleges.

In contrast to his experience his freshman year on the hamburger squad, during his final three years playing football the coach tried to keep him away from a lot of contact. His freshman year they made him a battering ram, a piece of hamburger meat. But after that first year, the coach recognized that they couldn't afford to have him hurt in practice. In the games he still had to play both sides of the ball, offense and defense. As a freshman, Dennis made the traveling team for football and was on the hamburger squad but didn't play in many games. His participation on the hamburger squad gave him enough activity to earn him a letter because the hamburger squad played such an important role in getting the first string players ready for the upcoming game.

One of the ways that Dennis made food money during his junior and senior years of college was participating in Friday evening poker games. There was a group that would meet regularly, usually in Dennis' basement. One of the guys worked for a brewery and could get a 24-bottle case of short-fill beer[vii] (the bottles were not full enough to sell) for a dollar; so with abundant cheap cigars and beer, the guys would get together. Dennis had a unique approach to the games, unique from his partners, as this meant food money for him; he was looking for income. He took a game of chance and, as with football opponents, he studied the habits and patterns of the guys he played with. He recognized that the later it got into the evening the more loosely the losers would play. There was a group of six that usually played together so Dennis got to know their patterns and weaknesses and would often take advantage of them. Since it was the family food money that he was using as his stake, he had to watch carefully. During a big night he might win $30, although more commonly it was $10 or $15. He did lose sometimes, but if they played 10 times he would win 8 of those opportunities.

It wasn't all serious business for him though because, as he shares, there were lots of lies told, good stories fabricated, and good companionship shared. He personally found it challenging to decide who he was going to bluff out of a hand. They were playing nickel, dime, or quarter poker with three raises, but no check and raise. So, along with having a good time, Dennis persuaded those six guys to fund his food budget. Even though they didn't like handing over their money to him, they did it.

The group of six guys didn't welcome very many newcomers. They were content to play among themselves. However, there was one evening when a guy showed up who truly was a card shark. Having disclosed that he had tricks up his sleeve, he demonstrated that he could manipulate the cards, shuffling and moving the cards while looking the other players in the eye. He would then deal the cards. When the guys would look at their hand, one of them would be excited because it might contain three Jacks. What they didn't realize was that he had manipulated the cards such that he had three Kings and he knew who had the three Jacks. He wasn't willing to show the guys how he did it but promised not to use such means against them. He even suggested that they pass him on the deal as he just wanted to play with them. After his demonstration, they would never have played with him if he were dealing.

As he neared the end of his college experience, Dennis did his practice teaching at Waukesha High School located on Grand Avenue just a few blocks from the college. When he first came into the classroom, the students, likely sophomores or juniors, were cutting up. Realizing that he needed to quickly take control, he walked towards the back of the room to the biggest kid who was clowning around, Tony Gabrysiak, a 6'2" tall football player, who was taller than Dennis. Dennis grabbed him by the arm and told him to come with him to the front of the room. Tony quickly got up out of his chair and meekly followed. Once at the front of the room, Dennis grabbed the boy by the shoulders, pushed him up against the wall, and while he held him there he told Tony that he was either going to learn something in the classroom or he was out of there. For emphasis, Dennis asked, "Do you understand me? Have you got it?" All this time Dennis had this big kid pinned up against the wall with Tony looking down at him. Tony quickly realized that Dennis was a tough guy and a football player. With the lesson taught, Tony was marched back to his seat and told, "Now sit down and start learning." You could have heard a pin drop in the classroom. Of course Dennis did it for effect. He wanted the biggest kid who was making the most amount of trouble to set the example of the way he was going to communicate with these 30 or 40 other kids. The kids got the message and it was a great experience after that.

Dennis always looked for creative ways to make the learning effective and interesting for the kids. To prepare for their final exam in physiology, part of the biology curriculum, he had them sing to the tune of *Dem bones, Dem bones, Dem dry bones,* modified to use the correct anatomical terms. For example, the patella is connected to the femur... all the way up to the cranium. Dennis explained that because the final was going to be worth 50% of their grade the students had to learn those body parts, know where each body part was connected, and its proper name, starting with the phalanges, the metatarsals, the tarsals, the tibia, the patella, the femur, etc. He knew the approach was different and to this day those kids probably remember singing to *Dry Bones.*

Figuring that a different way of communicating in the classroom would make it more interesting for the kids, it also made it enjoyable for Dennis as he developed his teaching style. He worked hard to do more than just read the next chapter and stay a chapter ahead of the students, something many practice teachers do. He was committed to making a difference for them and for himself. Since he was determined that he was going to help the students to learn, which doesn't always happen with student teachers, he never had a discipline problem. He made it very clear that the students were not going to take advantage of him or lose the learning opportunity for themselves. Successful in his efforts, he received his teaching certificate for secondary education.

During that same time period, Dennis was also officiating in the Catholic high school basketball conference in Milwaukee, working for the WIAA. They paid him $12 a game for officiating but it required that he travel all over the city for games. This was just one of many ways that he found to make a little money to cover the costs of his education and provide for his family. This worked well because it was something that he could do in the evenings a couple of times a week.

Chapter 17 – Struggling with a Decision

As he prepared to graduate from college, Dennis' primary thought was, "Here I go into my teaching career." He had consistently pursued that dream from his days as a high school student. When recruiters came to the campus to interview potential teachers, he was offered three teaching positions: the first at the Kamehameha School in Hawaii; the second for a job in Pewaukee, Wisconsin; and the third in Green Lake, Wisconsin. Excited that he had three job offers, he was less enthusiastic when he learned the starting salary for each was $4,000 per year for teaching plus an additional $500 for coaching. Even though he was a science major, it didn't take long to calculate that this was less than $400 a month.

He was working part-time in the collections business at Merchants Credit Bureau and was making well over $400 a month. He shares, "It didn't take a mathematical genius to figure out that if I could do that working part-time in the collection business, and since the schools wanted to pay me the same amount of money for working full-time, teaching really didn't make a lot of sense. I had to think about it for a while and was torn because I had my mind set on teaching."

While Dennis was doing his practice teaching, there was a big flu outbreak in Waukesha that impacted many of the teachers and students. The school district called and asked if he would teach part-time, not only doing his practice teaching, but also to teach classes for teachers who were sick with the flu. Asked to teach a chemistry class, the curriculum was a little more challenging for him and he found that he was just trying to stay ahead of the kids. But this experience also led to the creation of a good friendship. Charlie Miller, the regular teacher of that class, also filmed the Carroll College football games and took many of the pictures. One of those pictures was presented to Dennis that shows him as a defensive back knocking the ball out of the hands of a receiver.

During their discussions, surprisingly, Charlie, a chemistry teacher himself, strongly counseled Dennis not to go into teaching. They discussed the topic at length with the argument made that Dennis would not be able to make any money teaching, which makes it very hard to provide for a family. $4,500 per year for teaching and coaching was a tough amount to live on. He went on to say that if he had it to do over again, he wouldn't go into teaching, either. Those conversations were a significant influencing factor in Dennis' determination of what he was going to do.

About this same time Dennis also became acquainted with John Taylor as they both attended the Waukesha Presbyterian Church. They became very good friends, sharing a passion for sports and for hunting. Dennis took him to a couple of his secret spots for duck hunting in Oconomowoc, with the two of them getting up before four o'clock in the morning so they could hunt before school, something that was reminiscent of his high school years. They would make it back before seven o'clock in the morning, ready to get the day under way. They each enjoyed the chance to get up and shoot a few ducks, but it also gave them a chance to talk, especially about Dennis' future.

Dennis had completed the first of the two required semesters of practice teaching the end of his junior year and he had another semester to complete in the fall. He was still working in the collection business and was doing well with that. But now, someone he respected was challenging his desire to become a teacher. There was a lot to think about. As a young husband and father with two small children, the need to make money loomed large. He decided that he should complete his practice teaching so that he didn't close the door on that option, but it was definitely time to weigh all options. He was making more money working part-time in the collection business than the schools were offering to become a full-time teacher. He had to look at the responsibilities of a family, realizing that those responsibilities were not going to go away; there were two kids who needed a roof over their heads, to be fed, and eventually to be educated. The influence of his friends would ultimately play a significant part in Dennis' decision not to teach.

In the fall of 1957 Dennis still had one more semester of practice teaching to complete. He had enough credits to graduate prior to the fall football season but was pleased to be invited to play the football season of his senior year. While he was confident in his decision to play that last season, with a January graduation looming, the need to provide for his family was foremost in his mind. He was still struggling with the decision of whether he was going to go teach school or stay in the collections business.

He had pretty much eliminated Kamehameha as a possibility as they only played eight-man football instead of eleven-man. It was apparent that each of the schools, including those in Wisconsin, used the same starting salary level, and it wasn't very much. The decision would not have been nearly as difficult to make if his desire to teach hadn't been so strong.

While wrestling with the financial implication of teaching, Norm Anderson, his boss in the collection business, suggested that he had almost half a year to make a decision about teaching or staying in the business. He further suggested that Dennis should come to work full-time and give the business serious consideration. The school districts would wait for a few months for a commitment and, since the idea made a lot of sense, Dennis stayed in the collection business after graduation while he also worked on a decision. Perhaps most difficult was to give up on the idea of coaching. He wondered, "What if I was to become the next Vince Lombardi?"

With the memories of an excellent biology teacher and football coach, 3 ½ years dedicated to preparing to teach, practice teaching behind him, and qualifications to teach biology, history, English, and chemistry, the classroom held a great draw. He was still convinced that teaching was what he wanted to do with his life even while he worked those summers with the collection agency. Yet he could hardly wait to graduate because he had two children and a wife to support. Come graduation, there was no opportunity to take time off and ponder a decision. He had to stay focused.

Reflecting back on those college days and the decisions he made, Dennis has recently spent some time thinking about his chances of success if he were nine years old now, instead of in the 1940s. Would he be able to accomplish in today's environment what he has done in his lifetime? His initial thought was that the answer would be no, *but on the other hand* (thank you, Tevye)[viii] it may have taken a different form. The role as a bill collector would not likely be something he would start today, although the real estate and other things that he has done might still have happened. More likely is that he would probably have done something in the IT area, which was not even around when he was starting in business. Certainly the product or the service would be different but *his* ability and drive would probably not have changed. He is still who he is, assuming that the same genes and chromosomes all lined up the same way.

This is still a land of opportunity. One way or another he would have gotten to college. He would have taken time to have a family. His aggressive and competitive nature would play out. With the advantages of our country and its opportunities, it is not a place where one should develop a defeatist attitude. It is a place where an individual should figure out what they might do that would make them happy and go after it. The opportunities here still have the potential to lead someone who is willing to work hard to success.

Sometimes you have to make your own opportunity. Even though he expected to be a teacher, Dennis, as a biology major, also had a backup plan. His coursework included pre-med work as a backup to his teaching and coaching, just in case he felt the need to go on to medical school. That led to demanding coursework that included biology, genetics, anatomy and physiology, endocrinology, chemistry, math, and history. There was no slacking in his college experience. He was there to learn and prepare to earn.

Since he attended classes each summer as well as during the normal school year, Dennis graduated from college in 3 ½ years, receiving a BS degree. He was the first of many generations to even go to college from the entire Punches family, and certainly the first to graduate. When Dennis graduated from Carroll College in January of 1958, he had distinguished himself as an excellent student, as an outstanding athlete, as a budding school teacher, as an excellent salesman and bill collector, and as a husband, father, and provider. He added nine college athletic letters to the 16 he had won in high school and gathered many medals from winning the long jump or sprint events on the track. Although he probably has achieved something of a record in the number of athletic letters, he did so while carrying a heavy academic load, working at least one job the entire time he was in school, getting married, and becoming a father twice over. He was a busy man.

Though the decision was made to continue to work in the collection business for a time, he still struggled with abandoning the teaching career. There was still work to be done, options to be weighed, and a decision to be made.

Chapter 18 – Herb's Passing

Shortly after Dennis graduated from college, he made a trip to Eagle River to visit with his father. In spite of a couple of rehabilitation stints for his alcoholism, Herb continued to struggle. In fact, he had recently completed rehab and had moved in with his brother in Eagle River.

It was during partridge season and the lakes had not yet frozen over so they could still fish and hunt; a double bonus for an outdoorsman. The partridge are often seen around the roadways or trails since the birds need gravel to help them with their digestive process. So, when hunting partridge, the normal process is to hunt along those trails and roadways, waiting for the birds to come out of the woods. It is uncommon to see a lot of partridge together, but as they were hunting that morning, they spotted a group of three birds. They stopped the car and Dennis jumped out. When the birds flushed (took off), he shot all three of them and he quickly had his limit of birds. His years of hunting in Wauconda had trained him to be an excellent shot. His semi-automatic shotgun also helped.

They gathered up the partridge, put them in the car, and headed to Catfish Lake, the area where Dennis had been born, just outside of Eagle River. They rented a boat for the morning since neither of them owned one and mounted Herb's little Scott Atwater five-horse motor on the boat. Within 20 minutes Dennis had landed a 25 pound musky. By 6:00 a.m. he had killed his limit of partridge, by 8:00 a.m. had caught a 25 pound musky, and they were in the local tourist coffee shop by 8:30 a.m. where the fish was put on display. What was especially satisfying was that this was probably the most fun that Dennis had ever had with his dad in all of the time that he was growing up. Herb was glad to be there and see Dennis' success. For his part, Dennis realized that he was just the lucky one to catch the fish on his fishing pole.

When Herb fell off the wagon again shortly after that experience, Dennis had to again commit him to rehabilitation at the facility in Winnebago. This was the third rehab process and, while it probably didn't hold much hope, Herb finally conquered his problem. When he left the facility Herb moved to Waukesha to live with Dennis, Katie, and their family. Although he would remain sober for the rest of his life, by that time he had beaten up his body so badly with the booze that his health was poor.

The trip to Eagle River marked a turning point in their relationship. Not only did his dad appreciate and enjoy the day with Dennis, watching his success with the partridge and the musky, but he also knew that Dennis was trying to help him with his drinking issue and his health. Herb's attitude had softened extensively towards Dennis because he had finally accepted him as the leader. He knew that he had fallen out of the leadership role because of his dependency on alcohol and not being able to conduct his own life. Dennis had become the alpha male.

Although the move for Herb to Waukesha to live with Dennis and his family was likely a reason for some concern, and there might have been some hesitation based on the distant relationship that they had as he was growing up, Dennis was willing to take the chance to care for his dad. The couple of days in Eagle River had helped pave the way for an improved relationship.

Herb enjoyed the activity of his son's home. He had lived with them for about a year when he became very ill one night, complaining of severe stomach pains. Still sober, they were not sure what they were dealing with, but Dennis recognized the need to get him to the hospital so they could check him over and determine the nature of the problem. Herb was admitted to the hospital and Dennis returned home, confident that the problem would be diagnosed and treated. However, when the phone rang a short time later, at about two o'clock the next morning, Dennis was informed that he needed to hurry to the hospital as pneumonia had set in, and they didn't expect that Herb would live. Herb died later that same morning of a bowel obstruction. He was only 56 years of age, which, for Dennis, was way too young. It was especially difficult as the relationship between them had finally started to strengthen. A very strong, silent type of man, Herb never complained very much. He would be missed.

Chapter 19 – Athletic Achievement

Over the course of a four-year high school career and a four-year college career, Dennis was an extremely accomplished athlete. In a rare feat, he earned a total of 25 varsity letters between his activities in Wauconda and Waukesha, with 16 high school letters and 9 college letters. His four letters in each of four sports in high school must be some kind of a record as he excelled in football, basketball, baseball, and track. His athletic career at Carroll included 4 letters in football, 4 letters in track, and 1 in basketball. There is little doubt that he would have continued to play for the Carroll basketball team had he not gotten married, but he made that decision and basketball went by the wayside.

There are those who might star in one sport and just be a participant in another, and sometimes they might have a starring role in more than one sport. Dennis was the star quarterback, the point guard on the basketball team, the pitcher on the baseball team, and a consistent winner of the long-jump events, as well as a contributing member of the relay teams for the track team. The collection of letters, emblems, and medals is impressive.

The invitation from the Chicago White Sox ball club was a special honor and, even though he didn't anticipate moving beyond that tryout, he was thrilled to participate. This is a strong statement about an individual's talent that an opportunity would be given with a pro team.

He was a talented athlete who gave his best to his teams. He studied opposing teams and players and expended mental energy learning to be better. He participated when circumstances were not ideal, but he was committed and made the most of his opportunities. These were lessons he would apply not only to life, but especially to business.

During one of those rare moments of looking back, Dennis describes one of the highlights of his football career. He was not very big, only 175 pounds, but he was quick with his feet and with his thinking. This was a good combination for a quarterback, and although his size was a bit of a drawback, his quickness was a critical asset in his role as a safety.

In a game against Whitewater, the Carroll team was on defense. As Dennis had moved down the field while covering his man he could see that the opposing quarterback was going to throw deep to another receiver. That receiver had gotten by his defender and was in full stride running down the field. When Dennis realized that he was the only defender that might be able to make a play he was 30 yards away from the receiver. Not to be deterred he quickly calculated the angle needed to be in a position to defend, and ran as hard as he could. As he approached the receiver he took a quick look back over his shoulder. The ball was right on target. He was gaining ground but it was going to be close. Dennis got to the receiver at the same time as the ball. As he left his feet and stretched out to make a play, he was able to slip a hand in front of the receiver's face and push the ball through the player's hands.

It was a play of a lifetime, saving a sure touchdown. He was not afraid of getting dirty, he took calculated risks, and he played all out. What a delight to ruin what might have been a perfect play for the opposing team.

In 2009, Dennis was inducted into the Carroll College Athletic Hall of Fame for his on-field achievements. His name was added to that wall where the names of these outstanding athletes will be honored for generations to come.

Chapter 20 – Buying a Wounded Business

The conversations that Dennis had with his good friend, John Taylor, were helping him to solidify his life's direction. Oh, how he wanted to teach and coach. He was good at it. He had connected with the kids while doing his practice teaching. He could see that he could make an impact but the realities of providing for a family were such an important part of his decision making process.

As the summer of 1958 approached, Dennis realized that it was decision time. The offered salary for teaching and coaching paled in comparison to his $600 monthly earnings as a bill collector. He figured that he was already $1,000 per year ahead with significant potential for greater earnings. With a wife and two children, he felt he owed it to them to find the best way to provide for them. Teaching and coaching were set aside.

Once he made the decision, he was ready to look at how he might help Norm grow his collection business and create a career for himself at the same time. Dennis was committed to the collection business and intended to be the best collector possible.

Dennis had expanded his sales territory from Hartland, west to Oconomowoc, south to Burlington, and spent more time in Waukesha. Even if some of those stores close to the office had been approached previously, Dennis was now confident that he had the skills to sell to them, and he asked for the opportunity to collect their bills. He had an unusual ability to say the right thing to potential customers, and they responded.

With the amount of business he had sold in Burlington, it seemed the right time to open an office there. They had even started to sell to some businesses that were outside of Wisconsin. While Dennis' selling approach worked, Norm was doing a good job collecting the debts, and the business seemed to be humming along. Dennis noted that Norm's standard of living seemed to be increasing fairly quickly but he didn't think a lot about it because Dennis' was as well. They really seemed to be clicking. That was when it all hit the fan.

During an audit by the state banking department, it was determined that Norm was dipping into the trust funds and using client funds for his personal expenses. He started out borrowing and then paying the funds back, but he was not keeping up. No one is allowed to borrow from trust funds. Norm was in deep trouble. Even though the auditors recognized that Dennis was not involved, and that only Norm was in the trust funds, Dennis was also in a tough spot. The banking department notified Norm that they were going to strip him of his license and force the business to close.

Even though Dennis was required to be licensed to work in the collection business, he had no ownership stake in the collection business. More importantly, Dennis had been the face of the business to most of their business clients, clients who now stood to lose significant dollars because of the breach of trust. How could he again face those clients and convince them that he could guarantee the safety of their money?

With the auditor indicating that they were going to close down the agency for violations, Dennis was faced with the fact that he was working full-time for an organization that might soon cease to exist. As he had often done when faced with a challenge, he stopped and thought about how to avoid a disaster. He determined that there might be a way that he could stop the closure. This competitive 22-year-old got in his car, drove to Madison, and went into the state banking offices. John Doyle, the man who was the head of the collection agency division of the state banking department, had played football for the University of Wisconsin. As they talked they quickly made a connection as Doyle acknowledged that he had heard about Dennis playing football for Carroll since his playing exploits had made the papers.

Dennis asked that they not close the agency and committed that he would fix whatever was wrong within six months. "Just give me a chance," he pleaded. This was pretty gutsy considering that Dennis didn't own the business and really had no ability to change the way things were run. Doyle responded that Norm had to go because of the things that he had done wrong. He took away Norm's license but gave Dennis six months to set things right. Dennis had to make sure that each creditor was paid every penny they were owed.

When he got back to Waukesha, Dennis confirmed to Norm that the regulators were going to take away his license and were going to close him down, but then stated that he was willing to buy the agency, as is. Even with his back against the wall, Norm still had a little fight in him and proposed a fairly outlandish price, thus beginning a round of serious negotiating. A $20,000 number was tossed around and seemed to be where they were meeting.

While he was negotiating with Anderson to buy the collection business, Dennis called two of his Carroll teammates, Bill Kagel and Joe Sydow, along with his brother, Herb, to meet with him in his basement. Much like the Friday evening poker games, Dennis had purchased a $1 case of short-fills beer. He then laid out a plan for building what he called an imaginary company that would one day become Payco. Dennis had a big sales job to complete because now he was selling guys on the idea of going to work with him when they graduated, rather than taking jobs with Johnson & Johnson or Shell Oil. (Apparently, those companies were recruiting the same talent.) He needed to convince them during that planning session in the basement over a beer or two that he could help them make a lot of money. Dennis knew that he could sell, but he also knew that he would need to put together an organization, adding skills in areas where he lacked. His pitch was convincing; several of them agreed to work with him, and the foundation of Payco was laid.

Dennis was fairly confident that he would be able to buy the collection business, but he also knew that he needed an organization if he did get the business. It was still touch and go as to whether or not Anderson would take the $20,000. There was a real possibility that the banking department was going to close them down even if they did resolve the problems. A significant problem was that Dennis didn't have $20,000. There was a lot of risk. But Dennis recalled that someone had once told him in an economics class in college that profit is a return for risk: the greater the risk, the greater the profit. And there was lots of risk here. There were variables over which he had no control. And even though he knew the risk of betting $20,000 to keep the business, he had confidence in himself, especially having had a couple of years working in the business part-time selling and collecting bills. It wasn't the way that he had planned to move forward in the business, but that was the opportunity now.

Dennis and Norm spent a little more time haggling and finally agreed to the $20,000 price. Dennis was a good poker player and had the advantage of having worked for Norm for several years, and now he realized that Norm wasn't bluffing. This was the price.

Now the question at hand was where Dennis could raise that kind of money, especially since he didn't have any assets. $20,000 was enough to purchase half a dozen new cars at the time.[ix] After Norm suggested that Dennis borrow the money, Dennis visited Waukesha State Bank, the local hometown bank, and talked with a loan officer. When the man asked him what kind of collateral he had for a loan of that size, Dennis replied that he had a black Labrador dog and a car. The loan officer was not impressed. Dennis continued to state his case, emphasizing that the business was viable (he didn't talk about the problems with the regulators) and that he was sure he could pay the money back.

The officer wasn't convinced but agreed to talk to his boss, John Davies,[x] the Executive Vice President of the bank. John's son had attended Carroll College and Mr. Davies had watched Dennis play football. John decided that he would go to bat and see if they could loan the money. But when he went to the president of the bank with a proposal to loan money to Dennis, Carl Taylor was emphatic that they could not make the loan because there was no collateral. However, Mr. Davies gave his okay to the loan over the protests of the president. The loan was immediately classified as substandard because there was no collateral backing the loan. If Dennis didn't pay it, they could sue him, but he had no assets for them to collect. This was a pivotal point. If the bank hadn't loaned him the money, the business would be gone. Why Mr. Davies thought it a good idea to provide an unsecured loan to a former football player, Dennis wasn't sure, but he was glad that he did.

With the proceeds of that $20,000 unsecured loan from the bank, Dennis completed the transaction with Norm, who soon moved to California. Dennis now had six months to straighten the company out or it would be closed. It was a real gamble. There was no capital in the business to pay the note back and it was a wounded business, at best. Word was out that customer money had been compromised but all Dennis could do was to fix it.

To begin with, he didn't know exactly what the problem was or how to identify who was owed money, yet his ability to keep the business was dependent on figuring it out. He worked day and night to straighten out the records and determine who money was owed to.

Realizing that he needed some help, Dennis hired Ray Foley, a Carroll student, as a part-time bookkeeper to help him find and fix the early double-dipping problems.

It was very apparent that one of the clients to whom money was owed was Mobil Oil. Prior to the current challenges, Dennis had traveled to Kansas City and worked hard to establish a relationship with Jim Fox, the collection manager at Mobil. Jim had agreed to let them collect in Illinois, Wisconsin, and Minnesota. This represented a major win for Dennis and the business, especially after they had collected a significant amount of money. While Norm and Dennis were negotiating the sale of the business to Dennis, a check had been sent to Kansas City to remit money collected for Mobil, but the check bounced! Norm had dipped into the Mobil trust account and there wasn't sufficient money to cover the check. When Dennis realized what had happened he got on an airplane and flew to Kansas City to meet with Jim.

When they met in the office together, Jim said simply, "Your check bounced." He expected Dennis to take what might be considered a normal approach, which would be to make all kinds of excuses as to why the check bounced, stating either a mistake was made in accounting, or some other reason. Dennis acknowledges that he knew he was dealing with a smart cookie and so he asked Jim, "Do you know why the check bounced? It was because there wasn't enough money in the account to cover it." Well Jim started laughing, completely caught off guard by the comment. Dennis continued, "Jim, let me make it right. I'm in the process of buying the boss out and I will make sure this is covered. But please don't take away the business." Jim appreciated the honesty and the sincerity and was willing to give Dennis a shot to resolve the problem. This was a pivotal moment because Mobil Oil constituted one-third of the business. Jim appreciated Dennis' efforts to make things right and gave him a shot when it was so desperately needed. Mobil would remain a client for many years, for as long as they issued their own credit cards. Dennis breathed a big sigh of relief. That was a close call!

The other clients who had been impacted were not quite as easy to identify but, after studying the records, Dennis finally determined that Norm had been charging interest on interest, a practice which was illegal. Luckily, as he had taken money that he shouldn't, Norm noted on each of the creditors' cards a "TT", which meant taken twice. Since that indicated where the problems were, they picked out all of the cards with the TT notation and then went to work figuring out how much money was still due to the creditor. While they worked on resolving the problems, they also continued to work the business, collecting money as they had committed to do since they were still selling new business. Dennis used the profits they made to pay back the individuals who had been shorted.

Instead of taking six months to resolve the problems, he had things resolved in 90 days. With the money paid back, Dennis was ready to talk again with the regulators. Once again, he drove to Madison where he expressed his appreciation to John Doyle for giving him a chance to fix the business. Dennis extended an invitation to Mr.

Doyle, "Send the auditors back to review the records because we have them cleaned up." After the subsequent review, the auditor simply said, "The kid has done a good job."

With the boss gone Dennis was now 100% owner of the Merchants Credit Bureau with a $20,000 unsecured loan owed to Waukesha State Bank. It wasn't long before Dennis changed the name of the business to Payco. Regular payments were made to Waukesha State Bank, showing that Mr. Davies' trust in Dennis was well founded. With hard work, Dennis was able to find additional business for the company and the growth pattern was established. But now the business was his. He no longer had a boss. He had an opportunity to make of it what he would.

Not content with the status quo, soon Dennis was making enough money that he felt it was time to purchase a home. As they had often walked the area surrounding Carroll College, Dennis and Katie enjoyed the beautiful, well kept homes, and especially appreciated the stately elm trees that lined either side of the street, forming an elegant archway over the street. They had often expressed the wish to live in the area. Now that this was a possibility, they found the home they were looking for when one, just a few blocks from the college on Windsor Drive, became available. Dr. Woodhead had put the house up for sale and when Dennis was able to persuade Wauwatosa Savings that they could afford to pay the mortgage, they purchased the home. Their first house, located at the corner of Windsor and Charles, cost $23,500. Here they would live for the next 10 years.

Chapter 21 – College Scout

Dennis had his hands full with a new business and with his young, growing family. He was heavily committed and he knew that he was bound by time constraints. But when an opportunity came to be the scout for the Carroll football team, this was a chance that he couldn't pass up.

Lisle (Liz) Blackbourn had been the head coach of the Green Bay Packers for three years (1954-1957) but resigned at the end of the 1957 season after a disappointing 3-9 record. He had previously coached the Marquette football team but now he was being paid the balance of his contract by the Packers and had time to devote to another endeavor, without the demands of needing a paycheck. He was recruited to coach the 1958 Carroll College Pioneers.

Since Dennis was still in the area, Coach Blackbourn reached out and invited him to take a volunteer position as a scout for the team. He was asked to travel to the various schools against whom they would play, observe, and report on their play. As Dennis had played four years as a college quarterback and defensive safety, he had a unique ability to look at the strengths and weaknesses of opposing teams. In spite of the time this would demand, Dennis not only saw it as a way to give back to the football program but also to learn from one of the best coaches in the business.

Dennis had been the beneficiary of many college scouting reports, particularly as a quarterback, but now he was expected to provide those reports. Coach Blackbourn provided a specific format with which to diagram the plays, discussed the things that he was looking for, and then sent Dennis to Illinois, Minnesota, or elsewhere in Wisconsin to observe the upcoming week's opponent. Not only was he expected to diagram the plays, Dennis was expected to give his opinion about the strengths and weaknesses of the team.

Those games were played on Saturdays so Dennis would travel to the school where he would watch the game, returning either Saturday night or Sunday morning, depending on how far away the city was. He would finish his scouting reports on Sunday and then meet with Coach Blackbourn on Monday to review the information. Although they used the same format as in the pros, they lacked the advantage of pictures or video, relying instead on what Dennis could remember and describe. His reports were thorough and helped the coach understand the patterns of offensive plays, including such things as how often they ran to the strong side, or how many passing plays they would attempt. This would allow the coaching staff to build their offensive and defensive plans around the way the opposing team played.

Coach Blackbourn was not only receptive but also highly appreciative of Dennis' insights about the teams and would spend a couple of hours each week with him discussing the scouting reports. As Dennis would return with his diagrams, Blackbourn would ask him questions about what he had seen and drawn. He would then ask for Dennis' opinion. "As a quarterback, what would you call? How would you attack this defense?" They analyzed the player roster to assess the size and speed of the line. They spoke of how aggressive a defense might be on a pass rush.

Dennis quickly showed that he knew the importance of each of those issues as he returned each week with a good understanding of the team he observed. They developed a good rapport and the coach valued his opinion. Even though he provided great scouting reports, Dennis won't take credit for the team's success that year. He does, however, take satisfaction in having contributed. The team won the conference championship that year with a record of 6 wins and 2 losses.[xi] It was a great experience to be involved.

Dennis states emphatically that he learned more about the game from Coach Blackbourn than he had in the previous eight years as a player. Of particular importance was what he learned about communication. The coach commanded a respect from the players. When he spoke, everyone listened. If a player did something wrong, they soon knew about it because the coach told him what he did wrong. But then they were also taught what needed to change. Coach Blackbourn could be very intimidating and many a young ballplayer was the recipient of a verbal barrage when they failed to learn the lessons the coach was teaching. Dennis adopted some of those communication skills as his own and applied them over the years in his own leadership experience.

One of the most valuable lessons came as Blackbourn discussed the idea of "getting caught in the garbage." If a player missed a block, was not where he was supposed to be, or wasn't paying attention, often the result would be that someone would hit him and knock him down. Coach Blackbourn called that "getting caught in the garbage." When that happened he would point out to the offender that he could avoid that if he paid attention, made his assigned block, and was where he was supposed to be. Dennis not only applied the concept personally, but would also use that lesson as he taught those associated with him. He was often heard to remind people, "Don't get caught in the garbage of life."

The scouting experience came at a price. Even though his expenses were reimbursed, there was no other remuneration for the time spent, which was extensive. Yet, in a way, it provided for him a chance to have a coaching type experience without becoming a coach. It was especially sweet to gain that experience with an NFL coach. Dennis was willing to give the time and was a better man because he did.

Chapter 22 – Can Thinking Bring Riches?

With a $20,000 business and an unsecured $20,000 loan with the local bank, Dennis had things straightened out with the regulators and was ready to go to work. His first order of business was to elect himself president and CEO. As he shares, "Since there was no one else to vote, I got the job and I have never had a promotion since. I decided that I was going to grow the business and, no matter what I did, it was going to be the biggest, and the best in the country. That was my goal."

Early in his business career, Dennis had read a book that was given to him called *Think and Grow Rich* written by Napoleon Hill in 1932. This book focuses on the success characteristics of individuals such as the Carnegies, the Vanderbilts, the Rockefellers, and others who had made huge fortunes and had become very successful. Hill studied the common traits from each of these families and men to try and understand what made them so successful.

After extensive review and thought, Hill came to the conclusion that each of these individuals was focused on ***qualifying*** and ***quantifying*** their objectives. Not only did they determine what they wanted to accomplish, they also determined the time-frame in which to accomplish the goal. It wasn't enough to just have the goal.

Additionally, as a person worked towards a specific goal they most likely would face some stumbling blocks. In fact, it was a given that there would be many such deterrents to success; the question became how an individual would deal with those stumbling blocks. Some individuals are tempted to give up. Others might repeatedly run into it, never seeming to figure out a way around it. Others will find a way around the stumbling block, maybe even using it to their advantage, but either way they move beyond it. The key was to achieve your objective, never abandoning what you had started out to accomplish, and in the timeframe in which you planned to accomplish the goal.

As Dennis read the book he realized that not only had he already experienced plenty of stumbling blocks, he seemed to be a master at encountering them. He had determined that they were not going to stop him from succeeding. In spite of all of those stumbling blocks, Dennis realized that, as with the objects of Hill's study, he had learned to work his way around them. For aspiring individuals who wanted to get ahead, and who had some talents, they needed to understand that in spite of roadblocks the opportunities were boundless.

In a retrospective review, Dennis recognizes that it may be more difficult in today's environment than it was in 1955, and it would certainly take different forms of services and goods today. But the important thing is that the opportunity is still here in this country. In spite of political and environmental challenges, though not particularly healthy for the aspiring entrepreneur, it is still the best business climate in the world in which to succeed. In a world that is quickly devolving to a society that identifies with taking instead of developing, personal growth, motivation, and success are possible.

In *Think and Grow Rich*, Hill speaks of the desires of successful individuals and the practical steps that they have taken to succeed. Here follows a portion of the book that Dennis focused on to develop his own direction for gaining riches.

"The method by which DESIRE for riches can be transmitted into its financial equivalent, and consists of six definite, practical steps…, fixing in your mind the exact amount of money you desire. It is not sufficient merely to say 'I want plenty of money.'"

"First - Be definite as to the amount." [For Dennis this is the quantitative.]

"Second - Determine exactly what you intend to give in return for the money you desire." (There is no such reality as 'something for nothing.') [Dennis defined this as the qualitative.]

"Third - Establish a definite date when you intend to possess the money you desire." [Dennis established an initial goal to make $1 million by the time he was 30.]

"Fourth - Create a definite plan for carrying out your desire, and begin at once, whether you're ready or not to put this plan into action." [Dennis wrote out his plan and carried it in his wallet.]

"Fifth - Write out a clear, concise statement of the amount of money you intend to acquire, name the time limit for its acquisition, state what you intend to give in return for the money, and describe clearly the plan through which you intend to accumulate it."

'Sixth - Read your statement aloud, twice daily, once just before retiring at night, and once after arising in the morning, AS you READ, SEE and FEEL, AND BELIEVE YOURSELF ALREADY IN POSSESSION OF THE MONEY." [Dennis regularly read his plan.]

Dennis acknowledges that he viewed his situation as one where he had the opportunity, but he realized how critical it was for him to desire to rise above the mediocrity in whatever he set his mind to do. He succeeded in doing this by insisting he play ball with the older boys, with building a shoeshine box and heading for the local tavern, by telling his 8th grade peers that they were not going to keep him off of the basketball team, and in his audacity to tell Norm Anderson that he didn't know what the job was but that he would do it. In each of these settings, it was his determination to excel that led to his success.

It cannot be overemphasized that Dennis felt that the critical part of *Think and Grow Rich* was the idea of quantify and qualify. He wrote on a piece of paper where he wanted to be and by what time. At least three or four times a week, he would remove the piece of paper upon which he had written those goals and reviewed them so that he would stay focused. He viewed everything else as supportive between points A and B. An example of one of those goals was, "You are 24 years old and you want to make $1 million by the time you're 30." He kept that sheet for a long time and wishes that he still had it, but it fell apart after many years of handling. But that was a serious objective for him to make $1 million by the time he was 30 years old. By the way, he missed the mark by a year. It wasn't until he was 31 that he made his first $1 million.

A major driver for each of the studied individuals was their focus. Dennis had a minor in chemistry in college and this caused him to often think in the quantitative and qualitative. He found himself comparing his business situations to chemical equations, recognizing that in chemistry he had to balance the chemicals in order to get them stable. Much like creating a stable compound, he looked to see how he could establish balance to create opportunity. He would look at the quality of what he was doing in the business, would set a timeline for what he wanted to accomplish, and he would always put the numbers to it. Business objectives didn't exist for him without the time and the objective; he kept those in order and they were in his mind all the time. He regularly asked: "Do I have the quality? Do I have the appropriate quantity?" Those measurements helped set the bar for growth and focus.

He quickly realized that business growth doesn't occur as a nice clean slope.

Rather, company growth more often acts with a slope disrupted with peaks and valleys, which represented ups and downs in the business performance.

Since he didn't want the peaks and valleys, he worked hard at achieving consistent growth without sliding backwards. With a determination to avoid any financial losses, he saw that his business followed a pattern of strong growth, with periodic plateaus of minimal or no growth, and subsequent strong growth.

With a consistent determination to grow the business, Dennis recognized that they would grow, reload for growth, reset the bar for growth, and then take the growth. When he saw that they might level out, he would reset the bar, without necessarily waiting for them to reach the goal, and get ready to grow again. They were vigilant in avoiding the big hits and the losses as they grew.

Dennis always carried a piece of paper in his wallet that had his quantitative and qualitative goals for where he had set his bar, and he looked at that paper fairly often. He also found that what was written on it changed regularly as he met and then adjusted his goals upward. Often he would adjust the goals upward and set the new goal before he had achieved an existing goal, taking advantage of perceived opportunities but also continually challenging himself. He always wanted to know where they were going.

Chapter 23 – Personal Business Philosophy

Dennis often reflected back on his experience of being under anesthesia and starting to surface before they were done with the surgery. He recognized that the associated dream was meaningful to him and that progress up the ladder was accompanied by intense pain. Applying that experience to his personal objectives in life, he knew that he had God-given talents that he needed to use. He wasn't sure how far up the ladder he could climb, but he knew he wasn't at the top of the ladder, either. There was still plenty of opportunity for him to achieve. Those reflections drove him all of the time.

Dennis couldn't help but look at the sequence of events and realize that there was a greater power at work beyond his own. As he shares, "If you look at the close calls, including having to buy the boss out, convincing the state bank regulators not to close the business down, and covering a bad check in Kansas City for a third of the business, as those things came together and I had a chance to think about them as the pieces fell in place, I had to stop and thank the Big Guy for helping us through that. I also recognized that these were some of the God-given talents that I had and if I didn't cut corners, since the easiest thing to remember is the truth, smart people would buy what we were selling. You don't have to con them, you just have to tell them what you're going to do, and go do it."

Other changes were not necessarily philosophical; rather, they were quite practical. Because he was so young he bought a pair of glasses, even though he didn't need them to see, and a hat, to make him look older. As a 20-something-year-old he was telling 60-year-olds how to run their collection departments with their bad debts. They couldn't help but wonder what this kid knew. He was willing to try different things to change their perception and improve his credibility.

Dressing for success wasn't just limited to Dennis, either. He tried to pattern his team members who were out calling on potential clients after the IBM sales people. At the time the IBM team represented the pinnacle of those that were making sales calls. They always had on a suit, a white shirt (never colored), a tie, and their shoes were shined.

As he built his sales team, Dennis regularly gathered them for sales meetings on Saturday mornings. One of his top salespeople came in to one of those meetings wearing a blue shirt. He had a tie on, but it was with a blue shirt. Dennis was stunned, and then aggravated. "What do you think you are doing with that blue shirt? Go home and change and don't ever come into this office again unless you have on a white shirt and a tie." The man went home and changed, and was never seen in anything but a white shirt again while engaged in Payco business, at least not until it became fashionable and more acceptable to wear a colored shirt. And only then after Dennis agreed that it was okay to do so.

Since they were in a business where people thought that they were shady, Dennis was determined that they needed to dress differently such that they had a chance to break out of that mold. While acknowledging that there was nothing wrong with being a collector of bills that were legally collectible, they didn't want to fit the image of the typical bill collector. They chose to change the image, especially to their clients for whom they were doing business.

Another part of taking advantage of the opportunities in this country is to be surrounded with good people. Dennis recognized a chance to bring people into the business that he trusted, that were smart, and that had talents and skills which complimented and supplemented his own. He recognized that many in the collection business had kind of stumbled into the business. The competition was still fairly slim, meaning very few of the leaders had college degrees.

With a chance to make a difference, he determined that they needed to wear white shirts instead of colored, and to be surrounded with talented, college-educated individuals. It was his intent to step it up a notch for the whole industry. There was a reason that he invited two teammates from Carroll to the very first planning meeting to encourage them to join him, as well as going back to the same source for similar talent.

During the early stages of the business, Dennis realized that there were several things that he had to learn that he didn't really enjoy doing. He was selling, producing (collecting), accounting, and even cleaning. These were not skills that he had developed in his biology classes. But the discipline that he learned in biology, as well as his other coursework, showed that he could learn and do what he needed to do. There was no one else who knew how to do those functions so he figured he had to learn, even if it meant sweeping the floor at night.

What would cause a young man to take significant risk with a wounded business and a large obligation to the bank? Some might consider this a display of chutzpa, but Dennis acknowledges that it was a calculated risk, supported by confidence in his own abilities as well as those of the teammates he chose. He also recognized that by creating a situation where he had no choice but to succeed, how could he fail?

When looking at opportunity, sometimes we get lost because we are still a country that is brimming with opportunity, and we fail to make a choice and get underway. The story is told, referring back to *Think and Grow Rich,* of a great warrior. The man had to make a decision that would ensure his success on the battlefield in spite of the fact that his men would be greatly outnumbered against a superior foe. After he unloaded his men and equipment from the boats in which they sailed to the enemy's country, he gave the order to burn the boats. The choice was now to succeed against the enemy, or perish.

Dennis made decisions based on the opportunity that presented itself. He quantified and qualified his goals, recording them for regular review. He changed the face of the collection business to the public eye. He was focused on the success of his business.

A critical part of his personal philosophy was embodied in the idea of "do as I do, rather than as I say." He figured that if he set the example, his staff would do what he did and refrain if he refrained. He realized that he couldn't do something and expect that his people wouldn't follow the example.

As he became more keenly aware of the fact that he was bound by time and space, the business demands required that he put a sales organization together. It also quickly became apparent that he had to take steps to control expenses. Their new salesmen wanted to fly first class, stay in the nicest hotels, eat the best food, and enjoy the best booze. One day he called all of them into his office and told them that he was going to show them how to get sales without spending very much money.

Dennis purchased a ticket for $18 for a seat in the caboose on a Soo Line train that stopped in Waukesha and went on to Minneapolis. The caboose on the back of a freight train was a nice place to sit and it was fairly common to have passengers. When he got to Minneapolis Dennis found an office building with a telephone on the wall in the hallway. When he asked the landlord how much they would charge to put a small desk in the hallway from which to work, the response was $50 or $100 a month. Dennis protested that they wouldn't be there very often (which ultimately wasn't the case) and that the price was too high; so they negotiated a lower amount.

After getting a hallway office set up, he went over to the YMCA for lodging where he found barracks-type accommodations for 10 or 12 men. Although he put his wallet in his shorts to make sure that no one stole from him during the night, the wallet was only six dollars lighter for staying there to sleep. A nearby coffee shop provided a pretty good meal for five dollars. The whole trip to Minneapolis cost less than $50 for a couple of days of work.

While in Minneapolis, Dennis interviewed Neal Sparby, selling him on the idea that he was going to sit in that hallway and make sales calls. Neal was working for Johnson & Johnson at the time and Dennis was planting the seed that he could be wildly successful if he went to work for Dennis and Payco. Eventually Neal became president of the company but this was a big leap from a solid organization like J&J to move to an up and comer, Payco. Dennis also made a sales call to Northwest Airlines on that trip, confirming them as a customer.

Upon his return to Milwaukee, Dennis presented his expense report to the three or four sales guys that were on board at the time, each of whom worked part-time, and asked if they really thought they had to have lavish expense accounts to succeed. He had traveled over 600 miles, while spending less than $50. Not only did he interview and hire someone to run that office, he made sales calls in Minneapolis, walking up and down Hennepin Avenue, and successfully added a significant client.

He wasn't telling them that they had to stay at the YMCA, eat at the coffee shop, or ride in the caboose, but he was trying to get across the message that they could succeed without spending a lot of money. There was a clear message, "Get your expenses under control. If I can do so, you can, and you will!"

During another sales meeting early in the life of the business, the sales people suggested that Payco had cornered the market in Milwaukee, and there was no additional business to be booked. Of course, Dennis didn't buy that argument so he asked for a telephone book, closed his eyes, flipped the book open, and placed his finger on the page. The listing where his finger rested was Roto-Rooter Sewer Cleaners. He told them, "I am going to call Roto-Rooter and I will bet you that I will get some business." Within a week he had made a personal call to Roto-Rooter, then located on Bluemound Road, and came away with the accounts of people who didn't pay when they had their septic tanks emptied or cleaned. At their next meeting he said, "So, you have the whole town sold? If I can go into a phone book with my eyes closed and make a sale in Milwaukee, the market is not wrapped up."

While he was trying to impress upon them there was still work to do, he also acknowledged that because the salespeople were commissioned based on the business that they brought in, there were types of work that they might choose to overlook, such as Roto-Rooter. With debts that were relatively small, the commissions would be small, as well. While the salespeople looked for "elephants", the big deals, many smaller businesses, such as Roto-Rooter, had great potential as money makers for the business and the salespeople. Since many organizations didn't even send out collection notices, they were missing some fairly easy collections. Dennis was able to show them that by collecting most of the debts for Roto-Rooter with just a collection notice, at a 50% rate because they were small balances, they generated some very good fees. They were collecting the amounts for just the cost of a notice, roughly 25 cents.

As the sales people followed Dennis' lead, they saw significant success. There were often times when the salesmen made more than he was making. When they had a good month, they got paid! In fact, there were months when Dennis had to hold his own check because they didn't have enough money to cover payroll, a normal challenge with a growing company. But Dennis recognized that this was a timing issue of the cash flow because of the growth. When people questioned why he would hold his check, he would remind them that eventually there would be a big payday for him.

The idea of quantifying the goal, of qualifying the opportunities, the challenge of training salespeople to be frugal and effective, the effort to hire good staff, and the intense focus that Dennis would put on achieving the goals of the business, were constantly in play. Dennis never lost sight of what he was trying to accomplish and, though he could be flexible, he was unrelenting in moving the business forward towards achievement of his objectives. It wasn't good enough to develop a business philosophy. It had to be one that would lead them to success, and it had to be followed.

Chapter 24 – Building a Business

It was touch and go as to whether or not the business would survive as Dennis worked with the clients to resolve the trust issues that had been created by the former owner. After Norm took the $20,000 purchase price from Dennis and moved to California, it must have been disconcerting to think about the potential consequences. If the banking regulators didn't allow him to continue the business, he would be out the money and would have no way to pay it back. But rather than focus on the negative aspects, he chose to focus on correcting the problems, and then worked his tail off to do just that.

Dennis was quick to recognize that he needed to surround himself with good people to help him achieve his goals. He had included his teammates Bill Kagel and Joe Sydow in his early stage planning meeting. After he had purchased the business, he invited Bill, a former tackle on the Carroll College football team, to go to work for him. Bill was ready to graduate from Carroll but had not, as yet, received another job offer. Dennis was able to convince him that they had a great opportunity to grow the business and make some money. Bill became the first employee that Dennis hired and did collections part-time. The two of them would sit at the phones at night and collect bills. Soon another guy from Carroll heard about what they were doing and came over. He caught on quickly and was really good! So now Dennis had two part-time employees to work with him. They used multi-part, snap-out forms and initiated a manual bookkeeping system, so they could do what they needed to without secretarial assistance. With Dennis selling and two employees to help with the collections, they were making some money. Even after paying expenses, including payroll and payments to the bank, Dennis was making close to $1,000 per month.

Even though he brought other individuals into the business, Dennis was adamant that he would never have a boss again. He was determined to take and maintain control of his situation, which meant keeping a majority position in the business.

During his efforts to clean up the business issues, Dennis had little choice but to leave the business at the second-floor walk-up in Waukesha. It didn't make sense to make a change just then, but he really didn't have time to think about it, either. And he certainly had to keep the office where it was until he had the okay from the state banking department that things were straightened out.

After the purchase of the business was complete and he had satisfied the regulators, Dennis moved the business to Milwaukee, sharing space with Bernard Seligman, a Jewish stock broker. The business had expanded beyond Waukesha County and they were now doing work for clients from West Bend and Burlington. Sensing that the time was right, he determined to sell into the Milwaukee market, and as such, it made sense to move their office to Milwaukee. The business was doing well but was still very demanding on Dennis' time. He would sell during the day and then come back to the office to assist with the collecting at night.

To say that the new space in the First Wisconsin Bank Building was compact would be putting it mildly. The Payco space measured only about six feet by twelve feet. Feeling that they couldn't yet afford desks, Dennis acquired some old doors to which he connected legs to make tables for them to work on. The tables were not very stable and would shake when someone worked on them, but when they were pushed up against the wall it helped cut down some of the movement. There was hardly room to move. Six phone jacks were installed along the wall by the tables with six phones soon following. After purchasing some secondhand chairs from Northwestern Mutual, the office was equipped.

Connected to this little Payco office was Mr. Seligman's much bigger office that seemed quite spacious in comparison. It measured about ten by fourteen feet. Since he never came in to the office on Saturdays, the Payco team would take over his office. It was impressive for a debtor who came in to work out a payment plan to see Dennis sitting behind Mr. Seligman's big desk.

Saturdays were a prime day for collecting since most people were at home. Dennis required that his team, including himself, work on Saturdays. They were in business and were collecting money. With several smokers counted among the collection team, and with the door of the little office usually closed, it was truly a smoke-filled room. When the door was opened the smoke would billow out. It had all of the appearance of being a scam operation, but that was the beginning of the office in Milwaukee.

During these early days, Dennis was offered positions with Shell Oil Company and Abbott Laboratories. Not only was the offered starting salary less than he was then making, he also felt that those job situations would be far too competitive. He figured that the other guys in similar jobs were probably smarter than he was and wondered why he would want to compete with them when he was already set up in a business. He was thriving in a business that was one of two enterprises that no one else wanted to go into: the first was as an undertaker, and the second was as a bill collector. The more he thought about it, the more appealing he found his business to be. Not only was there a lack of competition among collection businesses, but he also realized that he didn't have to compete against the best minds of the world in other industries. He certainly didn't want to own funeral homes so that seemed to leave one option; and he already owned that business. He turned down the job offers.

It wasn't long before Dennis realized that he needed to create a one-stop shop for collecting bills - one single organization that could collect bills from all over the country. The sale of collection services to a major local entity quickly brought that idea home and was a turning point in the business.

Dennis had a couple of guys selling for him that had anticipated going to work for NCR coming out of college. Dennis recruited these two hot shot Marquette graduates away from NCR and sent them to California to develop that business. One of these two had uncovered a potential lead with Clark Oil, an organization that was headquartered in Milwaukee. Dennis took the sales lead and made an appointment with the individual who was then their controller and treasurer. In a departure from the standard approach in the industry, Clark had made the decision to honor all major credit cards, including those of their competitors, at their gas stations. The decision proved to be a nightmare for them. They had gathered up hundreds, if not thousands, of small account balances that were not being paid. Dennis offered to take the credit card bills, committed that he would get some money back, and offered a 33% fee structure. The controller was thrilled to turn over those boxes and boxes of unpaid accounts.

Dennis made his people work day and night on those stinky little $20 and $30 balance accounts, generally the equivalent of a couple of tanks of gas. They started with mailed notices and got a good enough response from that notice mailing alone to pay for the whole deal. In fact, most of the money from the Clark debtors came as a result of the notices being mailed. For those who had balances of greater than $50, or who had not responded to a collection notice, a phone call would be made. In those days, the collectors would call collect, something that today would likely land a bill collector in jail. They found it quite amazing just how many people would accept a collect call on a bill that they hadn't paid. Even if the debtor declined to accept the collect call, the collector would just call the person back. A lot of those accounts were paid without the debtor even requesting a copy of the charge, just to avoid the nuisance. Most knew what the charge was anyway and figured that they would rather just send the $30 to get the collector off their back. This one big account was a turning point in the business as it drove significant growth and profitability.

At the same time, Dennis decided that if the oil companies were going to start putting out a whole bunch of credit cards, they were going to have challenges collecting all of their debts. When the oil companies started closing down their regional and local offices and going to large computerized credit card centers, Dennis could see the logic that they would also need somebody on the tail end to help collect the bad debts. There wasn't any reason that it should not be Payco. Each time one of them opened a credit card center, Dennis tried to be the first guy at the door. His sales pitch was consistent, "Let me handle that business as I know you're not set up to handle it at this point. Give me a chance." Many of them did.

Chapter 25 – Oil Companies

After selling the Clark Oil account, Payco quickly outgrew their space with Mr. Seligman. They moved the office to the Wells Building at 423 E. Wisconsin, just up from Water Street. Even had there been room for file cabinets, in those early days they couldn't afford them. They had found that their files would fit nicely in shoeboxes. In fact, to measure their capacity and their effectiveness, when they would ask a collector what he was working on, he might respond that he had two shoeboxes. To move the office, everybody picked up their shoeboxes and marched four blocks down the street to the Wells building. While the tables built from doors didn't make the move, neither was this the time for extravagance. Once again they purchased used furniture from Northwestern Mutual that cost almost nothing, but this time they graduated to desks. Dennis and his team were becoming masters at building out an office for the least amount of money.

With the increasing popularity of credit cards, even before he had purchased the business, Dennis had started visiting the credit card centers as they opened, with the first being Shell Oil in Tulsa, Oklahoma. After buying the collection business and experiencing significant growth, Dennis had chosen to personally call on national accounts primarily from a cost perspective. They were already paying salesmen more than Dennis was making, which was fine because it meant that the business was successful. But the oil companies also wanted to work directly with the individual who was running the business so it was very key, early on, that Dennis make those calls.

Unlike today's sales environment that is built around RFP's (request for proposals), which require that someone go through three layers of people to get to a decision maker, Dennis' approach was to hit it straight on, going right to the head guy and asking for the business. He would work with the manager of the credit card center who had the decision-making power as to whether or not to put them on as a vendor. And, as Dennis will kiddingly suggest, "It was just like shining shoes. How could you turn down a cute little kid?"

A critical function with the sales process to the big oil companies was that it required a lot of entertaining. The guy from Shell Oil said, "It takes a lot of whiskey to sell gasoline!" That meant that lunch started at 1130 a.m. and was finished at about 330 p.m. After a trip back to his office where he signed a few checks, he then got ready to go to dinner with the vendor. That was how one sold. As a salesman, if you weren't willing to entertain in that fashion, they wouldn't have anything to do with you. Not only was it a three martini lunch, it moved right into a three martini dinner.

The second major customer that Dennis pursued was Mobil Oil in Kansas City. Dennis had established a good enough relationship with Jim Fox that when the Merchant's check bounced, Jim was still willing to talk about recovery. Jim was impressed with Dennis' approach, as he describes, "You didn't BS me. You gave me the straight story." Of course, if Jim had said no, it would have been devastating to the business, and in fact may have spelled its doom since he made up 30% of the collection business at the time.

With Shell as their first oil customer and Mobil a close second, after Dennis purchased the business he added Clark, Exxon, Conoco, Phillips, and Skelly. He had a regular call route as they each opened their centers. His whole logic was that, as they shut down their regional centers and went to the processing centers, they were going to need somebody to do the collecting other than the credit card center. These guys were not trained collectors. Even though most of them had some college experience, they were not bill collectors.

The big difference between being a bill collector and someone who is not is that the second person just gets on the phone to ask a delinquent customer to please send some money. The bill collector, on the other hand, will call and say, "Pay or die!" No! Not really. But it is critical for a collector to help a debtor understand that *his* bill is the most important of all of their obligations. When Dennis would do a class with his collectors, he would say, "When you get that debtor on the phone, your bill is the most important bill he has. It is more important than his rent or the food on his table and you are number one. If you can't sell the fact that you are the most important bill to be paid, you are not going to make it as a collector." Now, it stood to reason that they couldn't do that all of the time, but each collector knew what the goal was. The statistics showed that if the debtor owed money to ten organizations, he probably only had money to pay six or seven. The goal was to be high on that list of six or seven, if not the top one, and certainly not one of the three that were left out. That was the whole philosophy. Some people can do collecting and some people can't.

As he worked with the oil companies, Dennis could see and recognize the coming credit card boom. American Express cards were gaining popularity about the same time. The growth of Payco was stretching not only Dennis' ability to meet with all of the sales prospects, but also to manage the day to day of the business while he continued to sell. He called Joe Sydow, another guy with whom he had played football, and hired him to be a salesman. The business was still growing because Dennis was still selling, and now he had some sales help.

Additional growth required yet another move. There was an office building that had formerly housed a grocery store. The building had a basement with a large open space but it lacked windows. As they looked at the space, thinking that it was a good layout for the business, Dennis went to work on the landlord. Looking back at it, he laughingly stated, "We decided that the employees would be moles and would never see daylight. In the wintertime, on short days, they came when it was dark and they left when it was dark. There were no windows to look outside so there was nothing left to do but work."

Dennis was only somewhat amused when the landlord tried to tell him that he wasn't charging enough for the *lower level* of his building. Dennis pushed back, "What do you mean your lower-level? You mean your basement that still smells like vegetables?" They went round and round and eventually Dennis had cut the best deal that he could for his moles. With almost 100 people working in that basement, it served their purposes and was one of the many reasons that they made profit for 25 years. They controlled expenses.

Chapter 26 – Adding Leadership Talent

The growth of the business put increasing demands on Dennis and his team and it was time to fill out the leadership team. Recognizing that his sales skills and vision for the company were most valuable to the organization, Dennis sought someone else to manage the people. He had just the person in mind.

Joe Treleven had been the quarterback of the Carroll football team three years in front of Dennis and was now working for Wisconsin Bell. He had a really good job and was slated to become an officer. Dennis and Joe met in Omro, Wisconsin where Dennis shared his vision of the business they had up and running. The consummate salesman, Dennis was eager to tout the positive prospects of Payco. He shared, "We're going to grow this company and it will have a lot of people. This is a skill that I don't have, managing and organizing lots of people; but you do. I want you to join us." The timing was critical as the Bell System wanted Joe to move to New York but his wife didn't want to go. Joe responded by asking if he would get his name in the listing when they made the Fortune 500. When the response was positive, he further asked if he could do the article when the company grew to that point. With agreement on that point as well, Joe agreed to leave a very secure job at Wisconsin Bell and joined Payco, even though his wife thought he was nuts. With Joe on board, it felt like a significant people management burden was lifted from Dennis' shoulders.

The growth demands on the leaders of the business also justified some administrative and clerical help. Dennis hired Susan Mathison, a Pius High School student in Milwaukee, as a part-time clerical worker. She would go directly to Payco after school and do some typing or whatever else was needed. When she finished high school, rather than beginning college right away, she joined Payco full-time. Dennis was traveling extensively and needed someone to make sure he received timely information, kept an eye on things, and let him know what was going on. But there was no such thing as having a personal assistant; Dennis shared her time with two other business leaders.

Susan would later return to school, attending Alverno College, something that Dennis strongly encouraged. In fact, the company agreed to pay part of the cost of her education. She earned a bachelor's degree and later a master's degree. She was very devoted to the organization and made a significant contribution, eventually becoming a vice president of the company as the head of human resources. When they realized that she had great potential, they were careful not to hold her back. When the need for a human resources department was evident, Susan was a natural fit. But that also left an opportunity for someone as Dennis' assistant.

Beverly Wortman had just moved to Milwaukee from South Dakota, where she had worked as an assistant to a bank president. Susan hired Bev to assist Dennis, Joe Treleven, and their controller. Although they were confident that she could do the job, no one quite anticipated the professionalism, organizational skills, or the capacity for work of this soft-spoken woman. She was up to the task and soon showed the ability to handle the demands of all three business leaders. It has been stated that she did the work of three women, keeping up with the CPA on the finance issues, assisting Joe with people issues, and keeping track of Dennis, who, as he would state, was always screwing things up in her schedule. Bev would remain in that position until they sold the business and she was a key contributor to the long-term success of Payco.

Joe did well running the operational side of the business; he was an excellent people manager with an uncanny knack for detail. He managed the collections portion of the business, developed the operating budgets, and became the business historian. He was able, through his cryptic note taking, to develop a log of events and decisions. If there was a question on something that had been discussed, he would simply pull out his notebook, refer back to the event in question and state, "we decided thus and such on March 15th."

Within a fairly short time, Dennis felt that it would be a good move to make Joe the President of Payco. That would allow Dennis to focus on the sales side of the business, but Joe didn't want to be president, and declined. In many organizations, that would have ended the working relationship, but Dennis recognized and respected Joe's value to Payco. Instead of President, they named Joe the Executive Vice President. Although Dennis made it a point to show his people that he was their partner in the business, the operation of the business was all funneled through Joe. If someone wanted to have something other than a casual conversation with Dennis, they had to start with Joe.

With Joe on board Dennis felt like the organization was taking shape. He had Bill Kagel who knew the collection business and had been with him for a couple of years. Joe Treleven was now on board and capable of managing a large group of people. Joe Sydow was selling. Ray Foley, who had originally been hired as a part-time bookkeeper, was also in a full-time position with the business and would eventually move into an IT role. He was critical to the initial success of the business. Dennis was personally running the sales group and he felt like he had all of the pieces, most of which were filled with individuals from Carroll College.

To help solidify the relationships and tie his leadership team to the business, Dennis distributed 49% of the ownership of Payco to his leadership team. He carefully considered the impact of each position to the business and distributed the shares based on his impressions. There was significant subjectivity to the effort, but, since he owned the shares, he also had the right to do with them as he saw fit.

Chapter 27 – Leadership Challenges

Dennis consistently worked hard to recruit and surround himself with good people who had the talents and capacity to do the job. Though few would have the drive and focus that he possessed, he still made efforts to hire those who were aggressive and talented.

Dennis had recruited Joe Treleven from Wisconsin Bell, a major feat. Joe was very capable yet had a unique trait: he was not one to take praise for doing his job. At one time Dennis thanked him for helping the business meet their financial targets and suggested that he had done a good job. Joe replied that he already knew that they had been successful and he didn't want, or need, anyone to tell him that he had done his job well, or otherwise. He was so self-confident in his abilities that he didn't look for, or want, praise. He only wanted to know when he was not on the right track. Similar to Dennis, Joe had outlined his own goals and he didn't need someone else measuring them for him.

Unfortunately, Joe's operational capabilities did not extend to the sales side of the business, something Dennis found out the hard way. Dennis used to call him *"Dead Right"* because of an experience that they had together. Needing to make a sales call to Gimbel's Department Store in New York, a significant client for Payco, Dennis asked Joe to accompany him on the visit. The credit manager/controller wanted a rate cut for the work they were doing for the retailer, a cut that would have been a significant hit to their revenue. Dennis took Joe along because he felt he needed some backup support on the numbers in explaining why the price cut should not occur.

After the customer presented his request, Joe explained, in no uncertain terms, how the price cut was not sustainable, and in the process backed the poor customer right into a corner.

Dennis quickly called a recess to the meeting and invited Joe out of the room and into the hall. Amazed at what he had heard and seen, Dennis told Joe, "You can't approach the situation that way. You have to give him a little win somewhere." Joe replied, "You are either dead right or you're dead wrong." Dennis could only respond, "We don't want to be dead at all so please don't be dead right." While he had to acknowledge that Joe's argument was dead on, they still needed the account.

The two men returned to the meeting room and were able to salvage the account, coming to a reasonable solution for both organizations. There was little doubt that Joe would have maintained his being right and they would likely have lost the account. Dennis learned the lesson and never again invited Joe to accompany him on a sales call. He found that it was highly preferable to invite someone from the accounting department.

Another experience was particularly disheartening to Dennis as it impacted not only an employee relationship, but also a friendship. Dennis had hired a jock right out of school from Carroll to be a salesman. Joe Sydow was an excellent football player, a running back who was the fastest man on the team, and an All-American. Since Dennis was the quarterback and responsible to call the plays, Joe had to run the plays as called. Sometimes Joe had complained that he wasn't getting the ball enough as the running back, but he had no choice but to run the plays that Dennis called.

After getting him on board, Dennis gave Joe an opportunity to develop his sales skills. As a big athlete, he garnered attention wherever he went, and since some people were naturally attracted to him, his stature allowed him a measure of success. Because people wanted to be around Joe, they were willing to give him business which ensured that they would see him again. He was able to achieve some early success; success that ultimately covered up some shortfalls in his work.

As Joe was one of the original four players at the beginning, Dennis had given him almost 19% of the ownership of the business. With a long-term view of the company, he had hoped that Joe would make a consistent, long-term effort.

Unfortunately, the trust was, to a large degree, misplaced. Dennis came to realize that Joe wasn't a very good salesman and, in fact, perceived him as lazy. Dennis was able to overlook that for some time as he figured that as long as Joe could call on the people who looked up to a jock, he could bring in enough business to pay his own way. What he also realized was that he wasn't going to change Joe or his attitude.

As the type of person who takes pride in people liking him, Dennis was puzzled by the dislike Joe began to show for him. Unwilling to accept Dennis' leadership, Joe would often push back, fighting Dennis on decisions, questioning things, delaying things that he should have done - almost always because those decisions had come from Dennis. Over time Joe became a great source of contention in the business as he voiced his displeasure over one thing or another to anyone who would listen to him. He could always point out a fault in a plan but never had a better idea to put forward for consideration. The truth was that Joe couldn't accept Dennis' leadership, and there could only be one leader.

The rift finally got big and bad enough that Dennis told Joe that they were going to have breakfast the next morning. From where they sat at a Marc's Big Boy restaurant, they could see a *For Rent* sign in the window of the building across the street on Wisconsin Avenue. Dennis had had enough and knew that the relationship couldn't be fixed. He pointed out the sign and told Joe that not only was he going to set him up in business, he could compete directly with Payco because it was obviously the only thing that was going to make Joe happy. Dennis was the leader and wasn't going to change, and since Joe had decided that he wasn't going to follow his lead, Dennis gave him 30 days to decide if he wanted to compete or just leave. Dennis encouraged the competition, excited about the prospects of putting on the gloves. But either way, Joe was leaving the company. Within 30 days he was gone.

In spite of Dennis discouraging the action, Joe determined to sell his ownership stake in the business for $200,000, a stake that would have been worth close to $20 million if he held on to it through the sale of Payco in 1996.

But the most important lesson was that the man had become a significant impediment to the success of the business. He was a stumbling block. They had to figure out how to get around the impasse, and Dennis was not willing to put the success of the other team members at risk because of this one individual. Sometimes you have to cut someone loose.

Chapter 28 – American Express Opportunity

With a solid organization in place, and with the credit card boom of the early 1960s occasioned by the advent of the oil cards, American Express, and Visa, it was time to develop a nationwide presence. Dennis flew to Los Angeles, rented a postage stamp sized office, and hired a part-time person. He then flew to New York to open a similar office. With those two locations he could advertise that they were a coast-to-coast operation and Dennis could now legitimately sell the concept that they could collect anywhere in the United States. This was certainly true even though they were doing all of the collecting from one location. Since the collection calls were done with a long distance call anyway, it made little difference, except perhaps to the client, where the collector sat.

The next big opportunity that came along was American Express Credit Card Company. As AMEX got into the business they were sending out lots of credit cards, in many cases without pre-qualifying the recipient. They were generating a lot of bad debt and Dennis was determined to get on the list to help them collect those bad debts. The company contact Dennis was working with was several layers down in the American Express organization and not a decision maker. However, when Dennis found out, through his contact, that the treasurer of American Express would be in Chicago for a meeting, he asked his contact to help him arrange an appointment with the treasurer in Chicago. Dennis would drive down to meet him.

Although staff members in New York were actually the ones that had the authority to approve American Express Partners, what better way to get an opening than to visit with the treasurer? With an appointment granted, Dennis drove to Chicago to the American Express office on Michigan Avenue. After waiting some time for his appointment, as Dennis walked into the meeting room he was greeted with, "You have 15 minutes, because I have another meeting coming up!" Dennis quickly realized that he had only a few minutes to sell the treasurer of American Express on Payco's capabilities, an opportunity that would not likely be repeated. The pressure was on.

As he jumped into his normal presentation, Dennis quickly realized that he was not getting through to the man. While struggling to determine what direction to take the conversation, the treasurer stopped him and asked him where he was from. When Dennis informed him that he had lived in Island Lake, Illinois the man replied that he had a property in Island Lake and went on to say that his son had worked for the water meter reading company. When Dennis asked if the man's son was named Joe, the response was positive. Dennis continued, "I worked with your son. We worked together reading water meters." Well, everything in that meeting changed. The 15 minute meeting expanded as they talked about the good old days in Island Lake. The outcome of the meeting was that Dennis had a referral to the staff in New York that boasted the treasurer's blessing to handle the Chicago business. This was another pivotal experience in the business.

After visiting with the treasurer, Dennis took one of his staff and they drove straight from Milwaukee to New York, rejecting the idea of spending the money on a last-minute airfare. They had the blessing of the AMEX treasurer but now Dennis needed to sell the collection department on the idea of giving them the business. They drove all night long, arriving at about 7 a.m. and checked into a flea bitten hotel in Manhattan, sharing a room to save money.

Dennis made his nine o'clock appointment and was able to sell the credit department on the capabilities of Payco. While the blessing of the treasurer was the key to his getting an appointment in New York, he knew that he still needed to sell them on the concept because there would be resentment if they were simply told that they had to give him the business. The credit team recognized, and appreciated, Dennis' efforts to give them a say in the matter, and they were willing to give him a chance to show what he could do. He felt that it was important to go out to their office so that they could see who they were dealing with, that he was a good guy, and that Payco really could handle the business. It was also apparent that an appointment would not have even been granted in New York had it not been for the intervention of the treasurer, and the treasurer would never have given his blessing had it not been for Dennis' acquaintance with the treasurer's son.

American Express started Payco out very small, sending limited amounts of business. Even though the early amounts were small, Dennis made it a point every month, no matter how much the check would be for, to fly out to New York to hand-deliver the money that they had collected so that he could show their results. Every month he would take them out to lunch or dinner, whichever they preferred.

This was a critical operating procedure that Dennis implemented; Payco didn't mail the checks. They were to be hand carried and delivered, and personally by Dennis if it was a large account. On other accounts, the salespeople would take those checks and walk in and hand-deliver them. He realized that if they had money for someone, that person would always take time to see them. The American Express checks weren't very big at first but grew from $2,000 or $3,000 per month to the point where Payco was earning $1 million a month in fees. That level of fees meant that they were collecting and delivering $2 million or $3 million per month for American Express.

This started a long-term relationship with American Express, a relationship that Dennis has jealously guarded and nurtured. He carries an American Express credit card showing that he has been a member since 1960. His Australia business now handles all of American Express collections in Australia.

The business growth soon justified opening offices in Indianapolis and Minneapolis to accompany the presence of their coast-to-coast offices in Los Angeles and New York. That number would grow to about a dozen offices, doing approximately $2 million per year in fees by the mid-to-late '60s.

Chapter 29 – Additional Bench Strength

As the growth of the business supported it, Dennis created a team of seven individuals to run the various aspects of the business. He was the ringmaster and visionary rolled into one. He had the vision for the business and a laser-like focus on its success.

Dennis surrounded himself with a leadership team that included six other individuals to which, when Dennis included himself, he referred as the magnificent seven. These were the core leaders for the business. They were talented and driven, and most importantly, they bought in to the vision that Dennis had sketched for them. They saw the potential of the business, but, as importantly, they bought in to the idea that Dennis could lead them to success. There would be some changes over the years in that group of seven but each was handpicked by Dennis. Those that replaced one of the original seven had worked themselves up through the ranks of the business and had shown that they were leaders who could get the job done.

Dennis was the CEO and the resident visionary for the organization. He recruited Bill Kagel right out of Carroll College and taught him the collection business. Bill would eventually manage the team of 2,000 collectors and 200 managers. Joe Treleven, the Executive VP, was hired from Wisconsin Bell and ran the operations side of the business. All of the organization would report through Joe, and if someone wanted access to Dennis, it started with Joe. Pat Carroll was Dennis' protégé in the sales and marketing arena and was in charge of large accounts, sales, and marketing, although Dennis would always keep a finger in that pie. Neal Sparby was a former Johnson & Johnson employee and was recruited to head the IT function. Susan Mathison started as a part-time administrative assistant while still in high school and would ultimately lead the HR function. Al Keely, a former marine and their resident disciplinarian, handled the commercial and outside business ventures. A Carroll graduate, he was well known for his spit-shined shoes, immaculate dress, and commanding presence. Dennis would never let people say that they worked for him; rather, they worked with him. He would say, "You are my partners. Yes, I get a bigger slice of the bread, but you still get a slice."

As the business grew, the seven needed other leaders to help accomplish the goals of the business. Dennis identified another group to supplement the magnificent seven, which, using a football analogy, were his go-to team. A football coach always had a group that he knew he could depend on in certain situations to move the ball. If it was 4th down and they had twelve inches to go to gain a 1st down, there was a go-to squad that he would send out that would muscle their way forward for that 1st down.

This particular group of 20 allowed Dennis to address issues facing the business and give the group marching orders that would change the status quo. After going public, Payco would tally one hundred and three quarters without a loss. Yet, there were times when the business started to plateau and wasn't growing very fast, or sometimes, hardly at all. The business was still doing okay, but Dennis perceived that they were getting fat and lazy (the business – not the 20). He would call this group together to review the situation, to talk about how they were going to move back to growth, and reminded them that some of them would not be there the next year. He was candid in his comments and questions, such as, "Look around and realize that you are only as strong as your weakest link. Is the person next to you carrying their weight? Is the person next to you going to help you or hurt you? Here is the money to encourage you to get to the next level and the payouts will be set on the performance of the company, that which you impact, and even though you don't have complete control, you are the go-to team. The money won't be equal between you. But look around you and see who's not going to be here next year."

By the time he got to this point, Dennis had seen what was happening to the performance of the individuals so he already had a pretty good idea of who might not be there the following year. Sometimes he intended to intimidate, but he wanted to help his team realize that they were only as good as the weakest link of those among them. He did not want them tolerating substandard performance from their peers.

There were multiple opportunities during the life of the business to use the talents of this go-to team. Sometimes he had to gather the group to address a specific problem, but rather than wait until there was a problem, Dennis implemented annual meetings to develop direction with them. He would gather them for planning meetings which would also include some fun and games with the intent to develop a cohesive group. They each knew their status in the organization, which was important to them.

Dennis was determined to keep away from the bureaucracy that often develops in large organizations. He never wanted his leaders, or his staff, to feel like they had to develop fiefdoms or sit at a specific desk to be recognized or to succeed. He never wanted to be "Mr. Punches" to the team. He saw himself as a teammate and asked people, throughout the entire organization, to call him "Dennis". He felt that if he kept it personal enough people would feel that they were individuals and not just a number.

The compensation philosophy at Payco was built with a couple of very key components. The first was that the pay plans intentionally provided insufficient income for an individual to live on their salary alone. Incentive plans were in place for all staff members that required them to produce and then rewarded their production. It wasn't enough to be busy, each had to produce. If they did, they were well compensated. The second component was the absence of across-the-board salary increases. Dennis thought that the first element should be sufficient to motivate the staff and was completely unwilling to reward behavior that didn't benefit the business. His outlook created a little bit of friction between him and Joe T., but he was emphatic that in such an environment the weakest link continues to hold down the entire organization. Even at the collector level the incentive plans allowed them to significantly impact their compensation and there were many months when collectors were making more than managers. "Across the board raises encourage complacency," he would argue, "while incentive plans drive the wanted behaviors."

The desire was to develop hungry, assertive collection people. It wasn't necessary that they have a college education. Payco developed, with assistance from Wonderlic, a specialized test that helped them find aggressive individuals. They wanted to make sure that they avoided the Fibber McGee[xii] type of individual who, as a salesman, would knock on the door of a potential customer and then say to himself "There's nobody home, I hope, I hope, I hope!" Payco went to great lengths to weed those types of individuals out of their recruiting pool.

Collection calls were most affective between the hours of five and nine p.m. which was generally when a collector could get the breadwinner on the phone and could work out a payment plan. It wasn't a matter of just harassing someone and telling them to pay their bill. The collectors would often have to work with people and their budget to help them figure out how to pay something on the bill. While the people would often make excuses as to why they couldn't pay their bill, it was up to the collector to help establish that *this* debt was the most important one for them to pay, outside of feeding their children. Their job as collectors was to get to the top of the list of the bills that an individual would pay.

The collectors heard their share of sob stories and excuses, but one story about a debtor's conversation with a collector stands out. When the collector reached the man, the debtor said to the collector, "I have a system for paying bills. I take all of the bills that come in at the end of the month and I put them in a hat. I'm not prejudiced. I pull them out one at a time and pay them as long as I have money. When I run out of money and there are still bills in there, I can't help it. And if you call me one more time, I'm not even going to put your bill in the hat."

Not only were the debtors creative in their excuses, the collectors had to be creative to keep pace. In the days before the banking laws were changed such that this would no longer be legal, Payco had an office in Chicago. A really sharp collector was working an NSF check for about $2500 that was owed to Northwest Airlines. Noting that the check had been drawn on a bank on Michigan Avenue in Chicago, which was very close to the Payco office, he took the check and ran down to the bank. Once there, he presented the check for payment to see if the funds were in the account. When the teller said that there were not enough funds to cover the check, he asked how much the account was short. Without thinking, she replied that it was short $72. He quickly pulled out his wallet, gave her $72 to deposit into the account, and then requested payment on the NSF check. He cashed the check, collected the $2500, and received his commission on the collection.

Chapter 30 – Family Life & Changes

Dennis had kept up a very busy pace from early in his life. His principal in high school had made special accommodations for his schedule because of demands at home, academics and athletics at school, and his work obligations. Even though he was on an athletic scholarship at Carroll College, Dennis was driven to complete college as quickly as he could and attended school year round. The scholarship only took care of his tuition so he had to work for living expenses, expenses that quickly grew as he married and had a family.

After graduation, his frenetic pace continued as he poured his efforts into the business that he had purchased. He had immediately set goals as to what he wanted to accomplish with the business, and those goals required his time and attention. He was selling during the day and collecting money in the evenings. Saturdays were prime time for collection activities so his work schedule was often six days per week.

The business was responding to his efforts and a normal decision for a young couple that had seen some success was to purchase a home. The commitment to buy a home on Windsor drive was significant, but, similarly, the purchase of a business was a significant decision. As Dennis contemplated providing for his family, he also took on ownership of four four-family apartment buildings in Waukesha. The time demands of this venture were fairly limited but still required his attention as he found and qualified renters, maintained the buildings, and dealt with the normal maintenance and repair issues. The combination of activities kept him busy.

Perhaps recognizing some of his own approach to life, Dennis likes to tell the story of his daughter, Debbie, as a two or three-year-old. One evening supper included peas and, by the end of supper time, the peas remained on her plate. He took a common fatherly stance and demanded that she eat them. When she refused, he told her that she would sit there until she ate them. After a couple of hours, with intermediate peeks into the kitchen to make sure she was okay, Dennis returned to the kitchen to find Debbie fast asleep with her face planted in the peas. She never did eat them. Strength of will was apparently an inherited trait.

Debbie and Laurie had been born while Dennis was still in college. Skip (Dennis II) and Emma Lou were born after his graduation. During the busy time of starting a business, and with Katie pregnant with Skip, they made the commitment to purchase their home in Waukesha. Even though Emma was supposed to be a boy, so they would have two girls and two boys, it didn't work out that way, and with just two years between each of the four children, they quickly had a houseful of children. It seemed like all was going well. Dennis found it hard to believe what a change he was experiencing as he reflected on his humble circumstances while in high school and compared those to being a successful business owner, husband, and father.

Even though he was very busy, he still tried to spend as much time with his family as he could. He was determined to be a better dad than was his own. They looked for things to do together, and, as they grew up, the children learned to hunt and fish. The girls especially liked to go fly fishing with him. They would take his Winnebago camper and go fishing on the Tomorrow River near Waupaca, Wisconsin. They would stay the night, catch some trout, and cook them for breakfast the next morning.

The family also developed a passion for skiing, frequenting the slopes in the various areas of Wisconsin. One year for Christmas, when the children were still quite young, Dennis shared Christmas cards with the children. Each envelope had a single letter written on the front, except for Emma's; hers had two letters. After a few puzzled looks, the kids finally realized that they needed to look at all four envelopes together. After lining up the envelopes in order the letters spelled ASPEN. The cards contained train tickets with passage from Chicago to Colorado, including sleeper car accommodations. Dennis felt that the kids would not likely have a chance to spend an overnight on a train unless he made it happen.

Even though the children were still quite young, they were quick learners. Once they arrived in Colorado, Dennis enrolled the two youngest, Skip and Emma, in ski school. As the ski runs closed for the day, Dennis headed over to the hill where they held the ski school to pick up his children. To his horror, they were nowhere to be found. When ski school had ended early that afternoon, the two of them simply headed home with a couple of kids that they had met on the ski hill. Dennis made a quick call to the sheriff to try to track down his children. Luckily, the parents at the home realized they had two extras and called the sheriff to report they had the kids.

Several years of success in the business helped the family to prosper. Dennis received an offer from someone to purchase the apartment buildings in Waukesha which netted a $60,000 profit, an amount that he quickly divided up into four education trusts, $15,000 for each of the children. Although it was hard to leave their lovely home in Waukesha, the family found, and purchased, a parcel of 15 acres in Wales, Wisconsin. This was a secluded area in the beautiful hills of the Kettle Moraine Forest, and here they built their dream home.

Dennis continued to espouse the concepts found in *Think and Grow Rich*. He saw in his own situation how an intense focus on what was important in business would propel him to success. As he read the stories about Rockefeller, Vanderbilt, Schwab, and Carnegie, he recognized the consistency in their approach. Each had a personal success roadmap and was diligent in following it closely. What he would later come to realize was that the book didn't deal with the intimate details of their family lives and never discussed the impact of business commitments on the family.

What he did recognize in his own situation was that as the business grew, he and Katie grew apart. Not only was he spending most of his time on the business, it became apparent that their life goals were different. Dennis was working six days a week and then traveling on Sunday to get where he needed to be to make a sales call on Monday morning. Outside of their vacations or long weekends to hunt or fish, much of his family interaction occurred as they attended church together on Sunday mornings. They would put a pot roast in the oven before they went to church so it would be done by the time they got home and would eat dinner about one o'clock as a family. After dinner, he had to start thinking about getting to an airport so he could fly out and be ready for Monday morning sales calls.

Although the selling aspect of the business took most of Dennis' time, and he was no longer doing collecting at night, when he was in town he would still to go to the office and check on the crew at night to make sure that everybody was working and productive. As they began opening multiple offices, initially in Los Angeles and New York, and later in Minneapolis, Indianapolis, and Chicago, this meant that he had to spend time making sure that the staff was trained and understood the goals of the organization. The Chicago business opening meant getting up at four o'clock in the morning, driving down Highway 41 from Milwaukee (I-94 had not yet been built) to the Loop in Chicago. He would work all day and then drive home, arriving about nine o'clock at night. There wasn't energy to do much else besides go to bed. But that was what was required to get a new office started. He recognized if he didn't stay focused every day, it was difficult to expect the level of success that he wanted.

Dennis could see that he and Katie were on different tracks. The more he focused on succeeding in business and providing a good living for the family, the more she retreated from those things. She was not at all interested in material things. He would insist that she purchase nice clothes. They couldn't talk about the business as she had no feel for making money, and, frankly, she wasn't interested. In fact, after her conversion to another church, her goals were quite the opposite as she wished to have them get rid of all of their material wealth that they had acquired and go to Burma as missionaries.

The pain of having his own parents divorce was still fresh in his mind even though it had happened almost 25 years earlier. That experience had caused him to make a significant resolution that he would never let that happen to him. He shared, "Come hell or high water, I was never going to get divorced." But now he found himself heading down a much different path than his wife. He didn't like it but he wasn't willing to give up his dreams of a successful business, and Katie wasn't going to be happy pursuing wealth. The more he moved towards material things, the further away she moved. The split became wider and wider. They didn't argue or have shouting matches. There wasn't time for that.

A watershed event occurred for Dennis that seemed to bring the whole issue into focus. He had set a goal early on in his career to make a million dollars by the time he was 30 years old. He had grown the business to the point where they had taken Payco public (see next chapter) and the brokerage firm, Loewi and Company was throwing a luncheon in his honor to celebrate. Dennis had made his first million dollars with the combination of salary, gain on real estate transactions, and the $400,000 or $500,000 that he picked up in stock proceeds as they went public and he sold part of his ownership. It was a big day for him.

He had been in New York to meet with American Express and make other sales calls, as he did once each month. His flight back to Milwaukee was delayed by fog and they had to cancel the luncheon on what he perceived as one of the biggest days of his life. Unable to celebrate with business colleagues, he got home that evening and told Katie of the wonderful thing that had occurred. When he told her that he wanted to buy two tickets to Jamaica and go celebrate, just the two of them, without children, she made it clear that she didn't want to go and would rather donate the money to the church. Dennis was so angry that he went without her.

When he got back from Jamaica, he could see that they had hit a fork in the road. It was right there in his face and he knew the only way he was going to save his marriage was if he went to Burma and became a missionary. And that wasn't going to happen.

They made valiant efforts to work on the marriage, including several sessions with a marriage counselor. Even that failed as after the 3rd session the counselor told Dennis that the marriage was not going to survive since they were on such divergent paths. Even then, neither of them wanted the divorce, but neither saw a way to accomplish the goals of both. They were married in 1955 and divorced in 1971. Dennis was 36 years old.

The divorce was amicable, if there is such a thing. But, as Dennis will share, "Divorce creates two years of absolute hell, the first year leading up to the divorce and the second after the divorce." Katie turned to her father, Dr. Truesdale, for guidance through the divorce process. As a scientist for DuPont, he was extremely intelligent and was willing to carefully consider all implications. Dr. John had recognized challenges with his daughter's goals in life, many of which predated the marriage. He had appreciated Dennis and his willingness to rescue his daughter from a very difficult situation, but now he was trying to look out for his daughter's best interests.

Wisconsin was a community property state and Katie was entitled to half of anything that Dennis had. Recognizing that a split of his Payco stock with her would eliminate his position of control in the company, and would similarly eliminate his ability to have the business flourish, he talked with Dr. John to try to avoid that situation. He committed to give Katie all of his cash resources and the home they had built in the Kettle Moraine Forest, if they would leave the stock intact. With the stock ownership intact, he would be able to continue to grow the business and would be in a position to best provide for Katie and their children. He was able to convince Dr. John that it would be in everyone's best interest, and especially that of his grandchildren; Dennis' children. Gratefully, John listened and never pursued the Payco stock. John and Dennis created a gentleman's agreement between them that Katie would not pursue the stock if Dennis continued to take care of the children and her. Dennis was true to his commitment, was never late on a payment, and worked hard to make things tolerable for his family.

After the divorce, Katie stayed in the area, living in the home in Wales for a period of time before it was sold. Dennis subsequently purchased a home in Dousman for the family where she and the children lived. This gave him access to his children and he made significant efforts to spend time with them, especially during vacations and holidays. He made special effort to find places that he wanted to expose them to, often in Europe. Depending on their ages and interests at the time, Dennis would take all four of his children to Europe or might take two at a time. The trips allowed them to be exposed to many of the prominent landmarks in Europe. They stayed in castles in Austria with lots of discussions about history. They spent time in France and a lot of time in England. They were getting exposure, as children, to what was happening in the world. They enjoyed such trips on a regular basis, something that others might experience as a single trip of a lifetime to Europe. Rather than travel first class, they generally stayed in a bed and breakfast, or a two-story walk-up type hotel. Dennis wanted the children to have an opportunity to see what life was like for the people living in that country rather than staying at the Ritz. They grew up with an appreciation of what was going on in each of the countries that they visited.

Convinced that this was a way to give back to his children, Dennis felt that travel was one of the greatest educational parts of one's life, especially to be exposed to why people think the way they do, to their governments, to their food, and to their entertainment. For example, when he realized that they didn't understand the game of cricket he took them to see cricket games, with similar experiences with rugby and Australian-rules football. As they got a little older, Skip spent a year in Switzerland learning French, which would later be used in his ministry in the French Cameroon. Two of the girls also spent semesters abroad in Europe.

Katie would subsequently remarry and moved to the Seattle area in the state of Washington. Dennis fought that move because he knew it would make it more difficult to see the children with her half-way across the country. But she gained the approval for the move and was gone. The three older children were already in college so Emma was the only one who moved to Seattle with her mother.

With all four of the kids living out of the area, Dennis worked on plans as to how best to spend time with them when he had the opportunity. They continued to plan hunting and fishing trips together and they also continued to ski. A key element of the plan to spend time together was to purchase a home in Vail, Colorado.

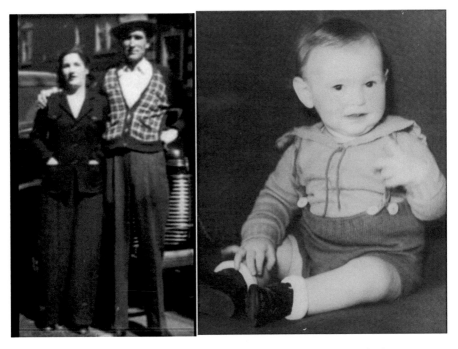

Dorothy & Herb Punches – Dennis' Parents   Dennis as a little one

Dennis – Planning his next move   Bob, Dennis & Herb (Bob & Dennis had been boxing)

Pat, Bill, Dennis

Wauconda Varsity Letter

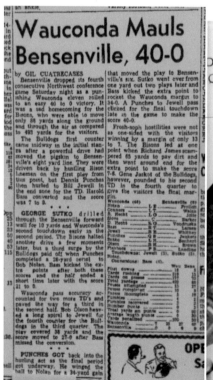

Wauconda Mauls Bensenville, 40-0

by GIL CUATRECASES

Bensenville dropped its fourth consecutive Northwest conference game Saturday night as a punishing Wauconda eleven rolled to an easy 40 to 0 victory. It was a sad homecoming for the Bisons, who were able to move only 88 yards along the ground and through the air as compared to 493 yards for the visitors.

The Bulldogs first counter came midway in the initial stanza after a powerful drive had moved the pigskin to Bensenville's eight yard line. They were driven back by hustling Bison linemen on the first play from this point, but Dennis Punches then hurled to Bill Jewell in the end zone for the TD. Harold Bass converted and the score was 7 to 0.

GEORGE SUTKO drilled through the Bensenville forward wall for 10 yards and Wauconda's second touchdown early in the second period. The Bisons halted another drive a few moments later, but a third surge by the Bulldogs paid off when Punches completed a 26-yard aerial to Bob Nolan. Bass kicked the extra points after both these scores and the half ended a short time later with the score 21 to 0.

Wauconda pass accuracy accounted for two more TD's and paved the way for a third in the second half. Bob Olson heaved a long spiral to Jewell for the fourth counter for the Bulldogs in the third quarter. The play covered 38 yards and the score moved to 27-0 after Bass missed the conversion.

PUNCHES GOT back into the hustling act as the final period got underway. He winged the ball to Nolan for a 34-yard gain

that moved the play to Bensenville's six. Sutko went over from one yard out two plays later and Bass kicked the extra point to rocket the Wauconda margin to 34-0. A Punches to Jewell pass clicked for the final touchdown late in the game to make the score 40-0.

Frosh-soph hostilities were not as one-sided with the visitors winning by a margin of only 13 to 7. The Bisons led at one point when Richard James scampered 65 yards to pay dirt and then went around end for the extra point to make the score 7-6. Gene Jaskot of the Bulldogs, however, pounded to his second TD in the fourth quarter to give the visitors the final margin.

Dennis delivers a pounding

Den Punches
Quarterback
Stu Slove
Center

Stu Slove & Dennis

A favorite target for many years Dennis in Waukesha during College

Wedding Day – Kathleen & Dennis Dennis during college

Herb & Dennis - duck & goose hunting   Siblings- Herb, Shirley, Patsy, Bill (f), Bob, Dennis

Defensive stop for Dennis (#10)

Carroll Football – Dennis as Quarterback

Wauconda & Carroll Athletics

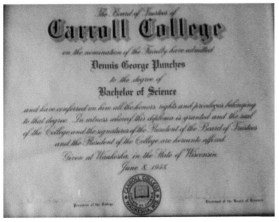

Carroll College Diploma

Dennis after college Graduation

House on Windsor Drive in Waukesha

House in Wales – In the Kettle Moraine Forest

Laurie, Skip, Debbie & Emma – in Aspen, CO   Dennis, Emma & Skip - Aspen

Dennis, Emma, Debbie (b), Skip (f), Laurie & Katie

F

Castle in Austria Where Dennis & The girls stayed   Dennis – about 40 years old

Laurie, Dennis, Debbie, Jack, Emma, Skip   Dennis – The Curly One

Dorothy & Dennis   Dorothy & Jerry Jensen (he took good care of mom)

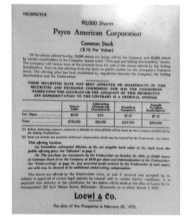

Fishing on the Tomorrow River – Waupaca   Dennis & Bill Kagel – the founders of Payco

Initial Public Offering (IPO) Prospectus   Payco Brookfield Headquarters

FRIDAY, DECEMBER 31, 1989

MONEY & INVESTING

The '80s: The Decade Investors Cashed In

20 Winners

	CLOSING PRICE		
	12/31/79*	12/8/89	GAIN
Presidential Life	$0.18	$19.25	+10,771%
Circuit City Stores	0.26	21.38	+8,108
Mark IV Industries	0.20	14.75	+7,387
Mylan Labs	0.35	24.00	+6,721
Hasbro	0.33	20.13	+6,507
Limited	0.54	34.00	+6,177
International Dairy Queen	1.54	45.50	+4,880
*Payco American	0.46	21.75	+4,646
Marion Merrell Dow	0.84	35.50	+4,107

Payco at #8 of Top Performers – Decade of 80s   Hard at work at 50

Beverly Wortman – Trusted Assistant

The Big Payday – Payco sale proceeds – November 1996

Wayne Player, Dennis, Gary Player

Dennis with Gary Player

Dennis at the Masters Tournament with good friend, Gary Player

Dennis working on his swing   Dennis with Grandchildren on the slopes

Family Ski Trip

Those are a little bit short, guys! (Dennis & Skip)

Grandpa Dennis at Christmas Time

Let's go fishing   Dennis with a dolphin

One Lucky Punch – 65' Hatteras – Purchased 1997

Enjoying the Boat   Robbie & Dennis

Dennis G. Punches Sports Complex at Carroll College

Dennis presents $1 million to Frank Falcone of Carroll College

Helping Fund Athletic Facilities at Carroll

Carroll College Hall of Fame Induction

Tsunami Relief Golf Outing – Greg Norman, Bill Clinton, Dennis, George H.W. Bush

Debbie, Dennis, Laurie

Dennis at Westmont College
Santa Barbara, California – 2005

John Pearce & Dennis – Collection House is on a roll

North Star Resort   North Haven Resort

Trophy Northern Pike   Master Angler Certificate

Dennis - Master Angler - 43" Northern – Utik Lake

Beaver Float Plane

Dennis at North Haven in the Conference Room

John Taylor & Dennis - Hunting in South Dakota   Dennis, John (seated), Bill Kagel

Russian Commander's Hat – Dennis in the Ukraine

Dennis' Children & Spouses

Karen, Skip, Jack, Debbie, Dennis, Laurie, Peter, Emma, David

Family with Angela

Angela & Dennis

Alice, Dennis, Stacy

Angela, Dennis, Alice

Debbie's Family

Evan, Amy, Candace, Debbie, Jon, & Jack

Laurie's Family

Laurie & Mikey   (Mikey's & Kelli's Wedding)   Kelli & Mikey

(l to r) (b) – Ryan, Jeff, Peter, Mikey (f) - Katie

Skip's Family

Danielle, David, Dustin, Nate, Karen, Skip

Skip, Dennis & Nate

Emma's Family

(b) Billy & David, (m) Heather, Emma, Jami, (f) Kylie

Billy, Kylie, & Heather (Kylie is Dennis' Great-grand-daughter)   Jami & Grandpa Dennis

Dennis & Angela

Chapter 31 – Publicly Traded Company

As noted, Dennis had distributed a significant portion of the ownership of the company to members of his leadership team with the goal of uniting them in the business. He often told them that they were like the *Brementown Musicians*, the fairytale written by the Brothers Grimm in which the animals got together to form a band. The duck played the flute, but not very well. The pig would play a horn, and so on. If you would listen to them separately, they were horrible. But when they were all together they thought they sounded just wonderful. Dennis likened his team to that group of animals and suggested perhaps they were making a lot of noise, and maybe it didn't always sound very good, but he thought they were going to be successful.

As the business grew, they continued to fill in their organization with quality people who had the skills to drive business success. They had set the goal of creating the first nationwide collection company to provide one-stop shopping so that the big companies like American Express, Visa, the oil companies, and other such national companies could go to one place and get service across the country. In the period between 1962 and 1970 they had opened at least a dozen offices across the country, from coast-to-coast, and not just the postage stamp sized offices originally opened in New York and Los Angeles. They were the only company that was able to provide that one-stop shopping for collection services.

Since the business had grown dramatically with a model that was unique in the industry, and they were doing about $2 million per year in fees by the late 1960s, Dennis felt that it was time to take the business public. He approached Blunt, Ellis, and Loewi, who were the brokers in Milwaukee who were bringing out most of the new stock issues in that time period. Dennis made an appointment and shared that he wanted to take the company public, the first publicly traded, pure collections business in the U.S. But Loewi wasn't buying the story. He insisted that such a public offering would never fly, first of all because people would not want to buy stock in a collection company, and, second of all, they were too small. Dennis replied that he didn't buy the first argument but asked for a definition of being "big enough." Loewi responded that they needed to have about $5 million in annual fees; then they could talk. Dennis told him that he would be back.

As Dennis describes it, "I felt like I had been sent to get the broomstick from the witch in *Wizard of Oz*. But guess what, I got it." There was a need for critical mass, and, once he understood what he needed to do, this was a goal that was quantifiable and to which Dennis could attach a timeframe.

Dennis had developed a long-time friendship with a man by the name of Dick Horn who was running a collection business in Columbus, Ohio. Seeing an opportunity to generate the critical mass, Dennis suggested to Dick that they consider merging their two organizations. While Dick thought that might be a good idea, he had already started negotiations to sell his business to a conglomerate and had an offer in hand. Dennis pled with Dick not to sell his business until they could meet in Chicago and he could share with Dick his vision of the companies coming together.

Once together in Chicago, Dennis presented his plan as to how they could grow to a critical mass of $5 million in annual fees and could become the first publicly traded collection company in the U.S. Dick was somewhat reluctant, hesitating because the offer to buy his company was for $2 million. Dennis implored him not to sell the business, sharing with him that he thought Dick could do much better than that. Dennis was convincing and Dick bought the story. Ironically, the business that had extended the offer for Dick's business declared bankruptcy a short time later.

Dick came to Milwaukee to look at the Payco operation. At the time, they were running pretty smooth with approximately 50 people on the telephones. During that visit, as they sat at the bar at the Karl Ratzsch restaurant, Dennis sketched out an organization on a napkin and talked of how he could see that a combined company would work. Sensitive to the perception for Dick's employees, Dennis suggested that Dick be the chairman and he would be CEO and president. Having a sense of continuity would help the employees avoid feelings that Dick sold out on them. Dennis wasn't concerned about the "big man" title; he just wanted control so he could continue to grow the business. Since he knew Dick's organizational structure, he sketched out where everyone would fit in the combined organization.

Dick had recently undergone a throat operation and had lost half of his larynx so he spoke like the Godfather. In his deep, scratchy voice, Dick said, "Okay Denny! If I do this, will you show me the good life?" When Dennis responded that he would, Dick was convinced. They each signed the deal as it was recorded on the napkin. This set in motion the plans for the merger of General American Credit and Payco, which would ultimately be named Payco American. The organizations were about the same size but didn't compete much with one another as Dick was located in the Ohio market and focused on the eastern part of the U.S., and, even though Payco had an office in New York, their concentration was more in the western U.S.

Even with the combined numbers of the two businesses, they were not quite at the combined $5 million in fee revenue so they continued to run the organizations separately, each focused on increasing revenue, performing well, and getting ready for a public offering. Within a few quarters, they felt that they had the critical mass and Dennis determined it was time to go back to Loewi and Company. Combined, they were at the $5 million in annual fees, even though they had not yet formally merged.

Milo Schneider at Loewi indicated that they were preparing to take out a bunch of new IPOs and said, "We'll see what we can do." He then gave what, to Dennis, seemed like unique advice. After telling him what kind of team he needed to put together, he asked what kind of car Dennis drove. When he responded that he was driving a Chevy station wagon because he had children, Milo told Dennis that he had better not drive up in a Lincoln Continental or a Cadillac "because it's not good for the shareholders."

They prepared the initial offering, made final plans to merge the two companies, and all was going well. Payco and American General had each performed well for many quarters. However, just before the offering date, Dick's company had a financial hiccup and lost enough money in the quarter that it would have a dramatic negative effect on the stock price. The impact was such that they couldn't merge the companies and take them public on the combined results. Both Dennis and Dick were distraught. They had worked so hard. Dennis could see the work going for naught and Dick was wondering about the $2 million that he might have claimed from the other sale.

The only thing that Dennis could see to do was to proceed with the offering with only the Payco performance. With the securities regulations that were in place, he could no longer commit in writing that he would buy Dick's business. But Dennis had made a commitment to Dick and vowed to be true to his word; he just couldn't put the commitment in writing. "Trust me," he told Dick. "We will do everything we committed to do. It just won't be until after the public offering." Dennis then moved forward with preparations to take Payco public.

They took the company public in 1970, the first company of its type to be listed on the stock exchange. With the sale of 90,000 shares at eight dollars per share, they raised almost three quarters of a million dollars. Loewi and Company took 10,000 of the shares as their commission and fees for the public offering. While not all of the proceeds belonged to Dennis, as he had shared ownership with his team, it was a good start towards his goals. However, even after the public offering, Dennis still owned 51% of the Payco stock, maintaining his control of the organization and its future.

Dick soon got the performance of General American straightened around and they moved forward with the merger. Dick was shown the good life, became the chairman, and Payco American had the combined performance of two strong organizations with the critical mass that they had hoped for.

Shortly after the merger, the stock market went into the dumps. Payco's stock price dropped from the $8 per share initial offering price to just one dollar per share. This didn't make any sense since the cash book value was four dollars per share. They could liquidate the company for four dollars per share but the market only valued them at a dollar, one of the unexplained vagaries of the capital markets. Dennis often thought of the sage advice that he had gotten from his SEC attorney from Grand Rapids, Michigan who told him, "Run the company the way the company ought to be run. Put on the blinders and don't be caught in the up-and-down of the quarters or events that will occur. You stated the basis of your earnings-per-share, so stay focused and make those targets." Dennis worked with his team to stay focused and they kept making money.

In the midst of the market downturn, the Loewi organization determined that they would no longer hold IPO shares from Payco, or anyone else, for that matter. They were liquidating their shares, including the 10,000 shares of Payco stock that they had taken at an $8 price. When Milo approached Dennis and informed him that they were going to sell those 10,000 shares, Dennis realized that it was impossible at the time to get a block of 10,000 shares, and he certainly didn't want to see the market price driven down even more. Surprised that Loewi was bailing out, Dennis didn't hesitate to tell Milo that he would purchase the shares, buying the 10,000 shares for $10,000. That was a pretty good bargain considering that Dennis ultimately sold them for $144 per share.

Chapter 32 – Student Loan Business

One of the human assets of the merged companies that came from American General was an employee who was a very good motivational speaker. As they discovered his talents, the Payco team started using him throughout the combined organization. One of the concepts that he taught was the idea of focusing on a synonym called SOPADA, which stood for subject, object, present situation, action, delivery, and accountability when working on projects or processes. After Dennis used the concept to organize their sales process, he encouraged use of the concept in many other parts of the organization. Dennis will still go through that process today when he wants to organize himself for a project. It provided a way to analyze a business element, focus on its strengths, fortify it where weak, move it forward to achieve its objectives, and hold people accountable for the results.

Payco American had been publicly traded for a couple of years, had weathered the initial downturn in their share price, but was still so small that it was difficult to generate much interest in their shares. They were just above the pink sheets.[xiii] They had merged with American General, opened new offices, and operated profitably; yet no one seemed to care about the organization. It required that they look at all aspects of the business, many of those reviews incorporating the SOPADA approach.

Several years after going public, they reached the 10th year of a sales cycle, one originally started by American General. They had been working with the United States government to get the collection of delinquent student loans out of the hands of the bureaucracy. The Justice Department, by law, was the only group, prior to Payco's involvement, that could collect student loans. But, as Dennis shared, "There weren't enough attorneys and people in the Justice Department who knew what they were doing to even start an appropriate collection process. They had the wrong people trying to do the collections."

As is the case anytime the government is involved, nothing moves quickly. While they recognized the importance of continuing to seek the government business, as Payco continued to pour the money into the lobbying effort they had to question the potential value. The change made a lot of sense but it was difficult to get politicians to bite the bureaucracy. It wasn't until a downturn in tax collections that there was recognition in Congress that this was the right thing to do. In the meantime, Payco management questioned with every budget cycle whether or not they should continue, because it was an expensive sales process. There was never a sales meeting held where they didn't talk about what was happening with the government, if they had made any progress, or whether or not they should continue. They knew there was gold at the end of the rainbow, if they could hold on long enough. They regularly followed the SOPADA review process, but they were running out of patience.

Through the services of a lobbyist, Payco was finally able to gain the attention of a Republican congressman from Ohio to be, as Dennis would describe, their Rabbi to preach their story to the House of

Representatives. He sponsored a bill which would allow the government to go outside of the Justice Department to service student loans, arguing that it could be done much more effectively and efficiently. The Payco team was on board to help write the bill.

After passage of the needed law, Payco was given an exclusive opportunity, on a trial basis, to go head to head against the government employees acting as collectors. The trial period was slated to last a year with a $93 million contract, a huge contract at the time. Payco was required to report their progress on a monthly basis in order that their information could be compared to the success of the government employees. Even though the trial period was supposed to last a year, by the end of six months the government collectors cried uncle as they were not even close to what Payco was producing. Payco then had an exclusive on all of the collection work for the remaining six months of that first year trial.

Payco America received the first government contract to be an independent organization to collect government debt. It was a proud moment as they were recorded in the Congressional record for their stellar performance. That was truly a milestone in Dennis' business career.

All of a sudden the marketplace recognized the potential impact of student loans to the Payco business, began to put the numbers to it, and, recognizing that Payco had the inside track, the light came on with investors. After recognizing what a great opportunity this was, the investors drove up the stock price.

Payco's activities in the student loan collection business also attracted the attention of Kidder Peabody, a national broker organization. They contacted Payco, informed them that they liked the business model, and then started pushing the stock. Their activity helped move the price from a multiple of eight or nine times earnings to almost 20 times earnings based on what they saw in the model and what the Payco team was accomplishing. Kidder Peabody sponsored a trip to New York for Dennis to do "dog and pony shows" setting meetings with the analysts from each of the brokerage firms, as well as potential investors. While Dennis took along his CFO to back him on the numbers and to make sure that he got the story straight, it was his own charisma that engaged the analysts as he was able to tell the story as the founder. That was what they wanted. They wanted to know who really had the understanding of the business and the ability to drive it forward.

The student loan business continued to be a significant portion of Payco's business for several years. However, ultimately it became so competitive that the profitability disappeared. The need to back off of their student loan activity was as apparent as their efforts to get in. If the business would no longer sustain profitably, why should they pursue it? It was easy to see what was happening. After Payco would make a bid on a contract, competitors were allowed to review that bid. Those competitors would under bid the price whether it made any financial sense or not. Since there is little logic for a public company to sell at a loss or very little profit, Payco backed off of the business.

They were the profit pacesetter, having become the largest collection agency in the U.S. They were okay to let someone else take the loss.

Chapter 33 – Worldwide Growth

Dennis and his sales team quickly made up for the loss of the student loan business with additional credit card collection work. American Express was a significant client, and they would also add Visa, Citicard, and MasterCard. Hospital Corporation of America, the largest hospital chain in the U.S., became a very good contract. Payco functioned differently than many of the other collection companies in that they had a broad view of the kinds of businesses that they could collect in. They were as comfortable working utilities as they were credit cards or hospitals. They had the capability to develop verticals in each of those areas and then trained their salespeople to be specialists. If the work they were trying to sell was in the medical arena, the salesperson needed to understand the business since they would be looking at patient information, insurance, and the related information. It was no longer a matter of just saying, "We'll collect your bills."

Another selling point was the quality of their facilities which made it easy to bring in customers or potential customers to demonstrate the organizational capabilities. They had come a long way from the second story walk up in Waukesha. The corporate headquarters building in Brookfield on Executive Drive was a real showcase. After encouraging his team to participate in the ownership of this new building, Dennis moved forward with the construction project to build a 60,000 square-foot building which, when completed, was fully leased by Payco.

With offices in the United States, Mexico, and Puerto Rico, when American Express asked Dennis to go to Japan to help set up and manage their credit and collection systems on their AMEX cards, this unique outsourcing arrangement spoke volumes about the esteem with which American Express held Dennis and his Payco team. American Express set up the office but it was run by Payco staff under a management contract. The top individual at American Express for credit worldwide, Ray Larkin, became a very good friend to Dennis. One can imagine this happening after working together for so many years. It quickly became apparent to Dennis that they could not make any money running the business in Japan so Ray committed to increase their U.S. business. Payco had the reputation of being able to set up and run the collection systems and AMEX needed Payco's help in Japan. The relationship was also such that Ray was invited to sit on the Payco board of directors.

The experience in Japan taught Dennis a valuable lesson in efficiency. He observed that the Japanese workers would take a piece of paper, hustle across the room to drop the paper on someone else's desk, and then hustle back to their own desk. There was a flurry of activity but very little accomplished. Dennis and his team studied all of the movement, what was accomplished with the activity, and developed a regimen to improve the business. They implemented the Payco model which reflected their work ethic and workflow, aided by the value of their software and their collection system. There was also a need to understand that in their culture the Japanese will often repeatedly say,

"Yes, yes, yes," and then close with a "no." Staff had to be trained not to accept that "no."

One of the biggest gambles the organization took was moving to a Hewlett-Packard/Ontario Systems IT platform. HP provided the hardware and Ontario Systems helped to develop proprietary software for Payco. Dennis signed a $35 million purchase order for IT equipment and systems, a contract value almost equivalent to the net worth of the company. Technology was an area Dennis felt they had to address if they were to stay a notch ahead of their competitors. They had to take this next step.

Even though it required a lot of hard and smart work, the system implementation was successful. They were on the hook for $35 million but paid it off fairly quickly with the systems paying dividends through the growth and effectiveness of the business. Payco became a cornerstone customer for Ontario Systems as they implemented a mainframe with dumb terminals, a predecessor to personal computers. With two thousand collectors bouncing in and out of a single mainframe it was a significant IT environment. No one else in the collection industry was willing to make that kind of commitment.

A valued feature of the system was that if an individual had missed a scheduled payment that they had negotiated, within 24 hours a notice would pop up on the screen of the collector. The system provided the contact information and the payment history so the collector had all of the necessary information on the screen to make a call to the debtor.

The collector had to take corrective action because the notification would not go away until he took approved steps to resolve the issue. He could not address other issues until he had addressed that particular situation. This was considered low hanging fruit. The hard work had already been done in coming to an agreement with the debtor. They couldn't afford to let this easy money slip away. The computerization changed for the better the way they did business and significantly accelerated their growth.

In December of 1989, The Wall Street Journal presented Dennis with a plaque that highlighted the top performers out of 4,000 listed companies during the ten-year period from 1980 through 1989. Payco was the eighth best investment that an investor could have made over that 10-year period. The stock came out during the IPO at $8 a share and eventually went to $144 a share, with much of the growth during the '80s. It was a great testament to the well run organization, Dennis' vision, and his efforts to keep the team focused on their growth. Payco performed between the seventh best investment, International Dairy Queen, and the tenth best, Walmart. They were in some pretty good company over that 10 year period.

Of the five IPO issues that were brought out by Loewi at the same time, Payco was the only business that survived; the other four failed. Even though the share price dropped as low as $.75 per share, Dennis and his team knew they were on solid ground. They had a good business model and their customer base was strong.

The Payco team eventually expanded to include 4,000 employees with 200 district managers. By 1996, the business had grown from several thousand dollars in monthly fee revenue to over $200 million in annual revenue generated from 42 locations in 4 countries.

Although it was sometimes a bumpy ride, they stayed focused on the business and kept making money. By the time they finally sold the business, Payco had achieved 103 straight quarters of profits. They never had a loss in a quarter. Of course, in the public market sector the gauge was each quarter's performance. They had to live from quarter to quarter. It was important enough to them that sometimes Dennis would hold his check to make that number. He might catch some grief over that but he was looking long-term and knew that the big pay day would come only as they consistently performed.

Chapter 34 - Cruise Control? Never!

Dennis clung tenaciously to his goals while growing the business. Though the items on the sheet of paper in his wallet changed with the phase the business was in at any given time, he was focused on success for himself, and for the team that he had built. Taking the company public was a stepping stone to that success. His recognition of the need to tie his team to the organization through ownership and incentives was part of that focus. As with the ladder in his anesthetic induced dream, sometimes the growth and decisions were painful, but he was determined to continue up the ladder.

He had survived several disruptive experiences in the business: the threat of the banking department to shut down Norm Anderson, and by extension, Dennis; the failure of American General to meet their financial targets just as the business was to go public; the potential impact of diluting his position by having to split the shares in his divorce; the stock price doldrums that occurred right after going public; and the struggle to keep all of the right management talent in the appropriate slots.

Prior to the Payco IPO, Dennis had distributed 49% of his ownership stake to his management group, the magnificent seven. With varying levels of responsibility and potential among those seven individuals, he divided the shares consistent with how he saw that he needed to. Absent specific objective criteria, Dennis will admit that the process required significant subjectivity as he divided the ownership.

However, as he was confident in his team and was comfortable with the way they worked individually and together, he quickly had a picture in his mind of how the ownership should be split. For the most part, those decisions paid long-term dividends through the concerted efforts of the new ownership group.

During the 25 years following the Payco IPO, Dennis and his team led Payco through consistent growth. They achieved 103 straight quarters of profitability, stellar performance for a publicly traded company. Once Dick got American General back on the financial track, Dennis fulfilled his commitment and they merged Payco and American General to become Payco American. They now had the desired critical mass. It was fairly easy to see the impact of developing and maintaining trust with clients, with management, and with staff members. Dennis had long since determined to keep his word in the big commitments, but he was also tenacious in keeping his word in the small detail, as well.

Some thought that he was a workaholic, but that wasn't true. Dennis regularly found time to do things that were important to him, such as all kinds of outside activities including boating, hunting, fishing, skiing, and golf. For many years he had felt that he couldn't play golf unless he had a customer with him. He had spent many hours working with the oil companies and the credit card companies, which also included extensive entertaining and time on the golf course. But in this phase of his life, he found golf to be personally rewarding.

By the late 1980s, the Payco business was running well and profitably under the daily leadership of the magnificent seven. Even though Dennis continued to travel extensively in his sales role, there was less demand on his time to be at the corporate headquarters in Wisconsin. With his children engaged in their own lives away from the Milwaukee area, there was even less reason to hurry home to Wisconsin. In spite of praying for snow when he was hunting as a teenager, the snow and cold now held little attraction.

Dennis made the decision to move to Florida and become a resident in about 1990. Although he can name a number of reasons for the move, the weather and the lack of a state income tax were important deciding factors. He soon realized that there were great opportunities for fishing in Florida, and what really caught his attention was saltwater fishing. He had always been an inland or freshwater fisherman, but now he had a chance to pursue a great variety of wily and large fish. Over the years he would purchase a series of different boats, seeking those which would bring comfort and fishing success. That interest in boats would bring him into contact with Robbie Durston and would eventually result in hiring Robbie as his full-time boat captain.

When the constraints of time and space again helped him to realize that he needed to focus on his most important clients, he made the decision to move other clients to another member of the sales team. Entertainment was still part of the mix and fewer clients meant more personalized attention to them, but it also freed up time for Dennis to relax and enjoy some personal time as well. He never lost sight of the need to pay significant attention to the head of American Express.

That individual knew that Dennis would be in his office at a drop of the hat since they represented $12 million of annual revenue and were the most profitable client that they had. Frankly, the organizational change was beneficial to the client base as well as to Dennis.

Joe had the operation running like a Swiss watch. Dennis could count on his magnificent seven. He would also call on his go-to team many times over the years to address things such as complacency in the organization, to help kick start changes that would get them off of a plateau and growing again, and, at other times, to clear unproductive staff from the team. Although he was sometimes an intimidating figure, and had no reluctance to intimidate, he worked hard with this group of 20 individuals to keep Payco on track and growing.

Dennis constantly had the feel for the business and where the company was going. He regularly met with the marketing people, discussing where their next opportunity was coming from so that he could help determine what the company's next move should be. It was a fine-tuned machine, probably one of the country's best, well-run, organizations at the time. The entire staff knew the direction they were headed and could see that the results were coming in.

Yes, there were some disappointments, some unfulfilled expectations, and a downturn in profits along the way. Once in a while they would struggle with a plateau of earnings. They always managed to make a quarterly profit, but sometimes the profit wasn't where they had planned or needed it to be. He would call his go-to group together and they would go to work to address the issues. Dennis had no reluctance to put them "under the glass", but he also put the incentives in place to reward their improved performance. They could always have a conversation with him if they felt he wasn't being fair, and he would listen. He constantly preached that they were only as strong as the weakest link. This caused team analysis of strengths and weaknesses but also caused individuals to look deep into their own motivations for success. The cream rose to the top and the others found it more palatable to go to work somewhere else.

Dennis displayed his distinctive management style. He was engaging and forthright. He set the goals and attached the rewards. He expected, demanded, and rewarded performance. He was not above intimidating staff members but that was only done when absolutely necessary - and he decided when it was necessary. His personal goals drove the business goals, which might sound backwards, but it was through those goals that he showed the team where the company could go and needed to go.

With the growth of the business, many individuals within Payco experienced personal growth as they moved along career paths, with promotions to supervisor roles, to assistant managers, and to managers. By the early 1990s, there were 4,000 employees, 200 management staff, and the magnificent seven. They had 60 individual licenses and many other regulatory entities with which they worked. Employees were spread throughout the United States with others in Mexico, Japan and Puerto Rico. It was amazing to realize that the genesis of all of this was the little collection agency in the 2nd floor walkup in Waukesha.

Throughout his career at Payco, all of which was as the CEO, Dennis was careful about how much money he took out of the business. He was the largest shareholder with a controlling interest, but his philosophy was to take a reasonable salary and expect the big payout at the end of his career. Additionally, as he controlled his own salary and spending habits, he was better able to control the spending by his sales team and other management and staff members. If he didn't take a lot of money, no one else was going to, either. Of course, there were still sales staff that made a lot of money, oftentimes more than what Dennis made, but that was based on their sales successes.

Salaries were a function of providing a decent standard of living and, as was the case with the incentive plans for the collectors, Dennis felt that he needed his team to be hungry for the big payout at the end. His largest annual salary while at Payco was only about $250,000. His senior leadership team made less than that but still made good salaries. Even though they likely could have made significantly higher salaries in other organizations, he sold them on waiting for the payout. He continually preached, "Follow my lead. We will keep plowing the earnings back into the company, creating a stronger balance sheet and making us much more attractive, besides growing to critical mass." His guys bought into the idea of a big payday at the sale.

Even though Dennis had still held 51% of the business at the time of the IPO, he subsequently took some money off of the table to diversify his interests, mainly in real estate purchases. As the stock split several times during the history of the company, it allowed him to reduce his holdings below 30% of the business by 1995. Yet, as the largest shareholder and CEO, he was still in a position to guide where the business was heading.

Chapter 35 – Sale of Payco

The venture capital (VC) community had grown dramatically and there was a lot of money invested with organizations that looked to purchase well-run companies that had the potential of making significant short-term gains. Payco was a mature organization, prominent as the recognized leader in the collection industry, and profitable. They soon garnered attention from the venture capital community. Dennis was approached by several VCs to inquire about the willingness to sell the business, with one organization out of San Francisco that appeared to be quite interested. Since the numbers they proposed exceeded that of any of the other VCs, they were clearly the organization to work with. These were unsolicited inquiries as they had not put the business on the market. Soon there was an offer on the table to have Payco be acquired by a company called OSI, with the acquisition to be funded by the VC firm.

As the leaders of a publicly traded company, Dennis, his board, and his management team were obligated to do that which was in the best interest of the shareholders. With Dennis as the CEO, Chairman of the Board, and as the largest single shareholder, he personally had much at stake. But he was also deeply concerned about the team with which he had surrounded himself.

After the initial VC contact, Dennis looked at his staff, and especially his leadership team. He realized that he would soon turn 60 years old. Joe T. was already 63, and the rest of the guys were all close to 60 years of age. In fact, of the magnificent seven, there was only one that was not in that age group. As he considered each individual, their age, their personal goals, and their continued commitment to the business, he realized that he was going to have to build a whole new organization again when those guys wanted out, no matter when that occurred. By this time, they each had plenty of stock. As Dennis had taken opportunity to divest some of his stock, they had also sold some of their stock. As he describes them, "They were getting to be pretty much fat cats." While that gave him a certain measure of pride, the question that kept running through his mind was, "Can I count on them to stay another five or ten years?" The answer seemed to be a resounding "No!" And, although he could probably keep the team together for another 3 to 5 years, he felt he would really have to push to make that happen. Frankly, he decided that if he was in their shoes, he would likely be looking at his own exit strategy before long.

He also had to be honest with himself, as the boss, and the largest single shareholder, Dennis was eventually going to get the lion's share of the value of the business. There was a big payday ahead for him and the rest of the shareholders. He felt that it was time to seriously court a buyer. Even though he had come to the conclusion that the others were ready to be done, he gave them a chance to voice their own opinions. A couple of them felt that the sale was premature but the majority thought it to be the right time. As he would share, "it was a collective agreement but I pushed it."

Annual revenues were now over $200,000,000. The business was a far cry from the days of spending an hour to talk the shoe maker out of his $10 check. Dennis had built a business plan with a couple of buddies over a case of short-fills in his basement and spent years of hard work and focus on the business success. Payco was a business that had several distinctions: the first coast-to-coast collection business presence, the first one-stop collection service, the first publicly traded collection business, the first business to be awarded government collection business, and now, as it was to be sold, the $155 million purchase price was the largest paid by a VC up to that time. It was amazing to realize that the business was about to be sold for $155 million.[xiv]

Admittedly a bright and capable student, Dennis will claim that he was no rocket scientist; a science teacher, yes, but a rocket scientist, no! He was a focused overachiever, determined and unrelenting in his pursuit of success. And, as he confirms, therein lays the opportunity that still exists for the entrepreneur today. But that entrepreneur has to be willing to pay the price.

Normal protocol when working with VC's is that they want some continuity with the management of the business. By having employment agreements in place with the senior leaders, it provides a safety net for the new leadership team. Sometimes, as was the case with the Payco sale, in spite of having such agreements, the new team really doesn't want any involvement of the prior leaders after the sale. Dennis was insistent that the VC protect the team, but he was still amazed at how little interest they had in how the business had been run. The checks were signed and distributed and the new management team was in place.

Dennis realized that his personal financial future was secure and, since he had a three-year employment agreement, expected that he would be busy for a period of time. He was named as a special advisor to the CEO of OSI and was a member of the new board of directors. Since the new CEO had no collection experience, Dennis expected that he would have a chance to do some training, but the new CEO had no interest whatsoever in talking to Dennis. The man declared that he was in charge and he would run the business as he saw fit.

Acknowledging that the thrill of counting his money wore off in just a couple of days, and since the CEO had no interest in his input, Dennis found himself in the position of watching newly minted MBAs poke and punch at the business without the benefit of knowing anything about either the business or the industry. It was frustrating to see bad decisions made and, even more so, that no one cared for his opinion or that of any of the team that had built the company.

In spite of his role as a board member and his three-year retainer, it only took one board meeting to bring things to a head. The CEO and the VC representative made it very clear that they were running the business and the board meetings. As that first board meeting was called to order, these two individuals sat at the table carrying on a conversation while Dennis and the rest of the board members just sat there. No one else was invited into the conversation and the discussion was carried on in low tones such that no one else could hear their discussion.

Dennis had already experienced the frustration of watching some of his key employees eliminated, of sitting in his office with no ability to make a difference in the business, and of being cut off from key customers with whom he had worked for years. And now, he sat in a board room watching these two individuals talk without any regard to the other board members. He wasn't happy!

While the two guys continued talking Dennis picked up his chair from where he was sitting at the far end of the table and moved it over right in front of them so he could face them. As he sat down, one of them asked what he was doing. Dennis replied, "I couldn't hear you and it is obvious that if I had something to say that might be worthwhile, you wouldn't be able to hear me. So I just thought I would move my chair over here to where I could hear better."

Three weeks later they asked to buy out his contract so that they could get rid of him. As he described, "I was a pain in the ass but I could see what they were doing to this company. We had one hundred and three quarters of profit without a loss. I had put my entire life into building the business. I couldn't stand it!"

They eventually got rid of most of the employees in the company that were over 50 years of age, in the process eliminating almost every individual who had historical knowledge of the business. Although they did their financial due diligence, there was never an effort to spend any time with Dennis to figure out how to run the business. Their 25-year-old MBA's were turned loose with their three ring binders that supposedly contained how to run the business. How frustrating it was to see them treat the employees as a bunch of robots, expecting that all they had to do was press the buttons and the robots would collect the money. The human element was gone.

In spite of all of his good intentions to be there for his employees, ultimately Dennis was not able to do that. He no longer had control of the business. It was a lesson well learned. And that lesson hit home as the business was sold and changes were made. He couldn't do anything about it.

Chapter 36 – Help from Bev

Prior to the acquisition of Payco by OSI in November of 1996, Dennis was responsible for 4,000 people and, as he states, "They all got paid before I did." After the acquisition he found himself responsible for only three people - himself and two others. Even though his role in Payco had been reduced to something that was mostly symbolic, he had the proceeds from the sale of his Payco stock to manage as well as the other assets that he had accumulated. Those consisted mainly of real estate that was scattered through California, Ohio, Wisconsin, Florida, and Arizona, and included apartments, commercial buildings, and warehouses. He still owns much of that same combination of assets. It was very apparent to Dennis that he needed help as he knew that he wasn't going to be able to stay on top of the detail of this tremendous number of assets.

Beverly Wortman had worked as Dennis' assistant at Payco. As was the case in many of the expense control measures he implemented, since Dennis determined that no individual executive would have his own assistant, he shared Beverly's time with two other individuals. When Dennis and Bev talked about Payco being sold, she suggested that their paths were about to part ways as she didn't see that he would need her any longer. Dennis responded quite vigorously, "Are you crazy? Do you think I'm going to let you go? You have run my life for the last 14 years. You aren't going anywhere except with me."

Dennis had come to rely on Bev's attention to detail, her calm demeanor, and her friendship. With the formation of Payback LP, a holding company formed for most of the endeavors in which Dennis is involved, Bev was hired to assist him in the details.

The two have developed a tremendous relationship. Dennis is an early riser and is generally early to the office. Bev has found that she works better if she is on a 10 a.m. until 7 p.m. schedule, giving crossover time when they are both in the office but also quiet time for her after Dennis leaves for the day. Of course, she is always available to him by phone and they speak often.

Over his business career, Dennis has developed the ability to quickly determine if he wants to participate in a business transaction and will often make an on-the-spot decision. As he makes deals and business transactions, he is most interested in the general concept and structure and leaves Bev to work out the details. She makes sure that he doesn't overlook important details and Dennis will state emphatically that, "She has saved me more money on big transactions than you can believe. She is the detail person. She knows everything that I do. She spends my money like it was hers and I like that." Beverly is frugal and has helped Dennis to be so, as well, but now, as he has shared, she is leaning the other way. She reminds him that he is 77 years old and that he should spend some money.

Bev has a contract to work for Dennis until five years after his death. He depends heavily on her to assist him in running his hundred million dollar enterprise. As the Executive Vice President of Payback

LP, she tracks real estate activities, assists Dennis in the details of the business deals he engages in, assists him in his personal travel arrangements and scheduling, and manages the staff that has since been hired to assist with the resort business that will be discussed in another chapter. As importantly, she is a good friend.

Chapter 37 – Buying a Hatteras

Since moving to Florida, Dennis has owned a succession of boats - both fishing and sail boats. He has enjoyed the diversion of salt water fishing and the beauties of the East Coast of the United States. With a process common to many boat owners, Dennis also thought about buying a bigger boat.   He had already progressed through various sizes, but the time had arrived to buy the boat of his dreams.

Shortly after Dennis sold Payco, he decided that it was time to buy **THE** boat. Knowing that no one was going to buy it for him, he sought out and purchased a 65 foot Hatteras Sportfish. This boat is a wonderful combination of fishing boat and luxury yacht. He had ready cash for which he had worked very hard and now it was time to use some of that cash. It was something he wanted for himself, he had the resources, and he bought it.

When it came time to buy a boat, Dennis had never been on a Hatteras. He had been to a couple of boat shows and had walked through the new and used boats. When he did see a Hatteras he decided that someday that would be the boat he would buy. And now that he had the money he didn't have to ask anybody.

Some years earlier, Dennis had become acquainted with Robbie Durston who had been the captain of a friend's boat. When that individual got rid of his boat, Robbie needed a job and went to work for a couple of years at Payco. After Dennis sold the business, he hired Robbie to work full-time helping him with his Florida real estate.

With the decision made to find a Hatteras, Dennis put Robbie to work looking for a 65 foot Hatteras that he could buy. It took almost a year of looking before they found the right boat in Puerto Rico. When Dennis saw the boat, it had a brand-new $7,000 fighting chair that was still in the box. This, along with other signs, suggested that this was a boat that had not been abused. Dennis and Robbie looked the boat over carefully and determined that it was the boat that he wanted to buy.

Though somewhat hard to find, the market suggested that a used 65' Hatteras would sell for about $1.8 million. Personal circumstances of the former owner made him eager to sell the boat, and Dennis was able to purchase it for $1.1 million. He invested some additional money in renovations and was thrilled with his purchase. Dennis and Robbie enjoyed a pleasant cruise returning from Puerto Rico past the Turks and Caicos and through the Caribbean. The trip also gave Robbie, the new captain of the boat, time to get to know the vessel. As a qualified 100 ton captain, he is one of a handful of people who are qualified to operate a boat that is 65 feet long and weighs 180,000 pounds (90 tons).

Not ones to just ride around in the boat, as that would be a waste of time, they go fishing. An early riser, Dennis will buy the Wall Street Journal and the local newspaper and will be on the boat ready for departure at six in the morning. With Robbie piloting the boat, along with a part-time mate, they go out, set their lines, and fish for several hours, returning by 11 a.m. Dennis reads the newspaper until there is a fish on, usually a dolphin, a wahoo, or occasionally a sailfish. The flat-nose dolphins are delicious eating so those come back to shore on the boat. The others are generally returned to the water to be caught another day.

With a boat that he enjoyed, the right crew for the boat, and time to enjoy it, Dennis entered a lot of fishing tournaments and had a lot of fun fishing in the Bahamas. He spent enough time in the area that he eventually purchased a building lot on Grand Bahama Island and built a home. He splits time between that home and his home in Jupiter, Florida, always welcoming his children and grandchildren to come and enjoy as often as they can.

Dennis still enjoys the boat today. He recently had new motors put in the boat along with having the interior redone, so it is like a brand-new boat. When he built the house in the Bahamas, he took the boat down there but travel challenges made it a little bit too inaccessible so he brought it back to Florida. During the months that he lives in Florida, if the weather cooperates, he will use it a couple of times a week.

With a 60th high school class reunion approaching, Dennis hopes to gather the remnants of his high school classmates in Florida for some time on the boat. With only 60 students in their graduating class of 1957, there are only 22 or 23 that haven't *"slipped off the dish"*, as Dennis will say, meaning they haven't died.[xv] He shares, "I'm working to plan an event and invite them down to Florida, use the boat, and get as many of them together as I can for the 60th reunion." He sees that as a good use of the boat.

Chapter 38 – Money Counted – Now What?

When Dennis sold the business in 1996, which was a big move for such a young man, he decided that it was time to retire. He was 59 years old, had worked very hard, had developed extensive outside interests with horses, golf, skiing, and real estate, and thought it was time to do the things that he really wanted to do. That lasted almost a week before he realized that he was bored. The pursuit of a Hatteras boat was a great diversion but he still had some fire in the belly. He also recognized that it was a belly which had gotten a little bigger through years of business entertainment and travel. He made a decision that, with the urging of his good friend and fitness buff, Gary Player, he was going to lose some weight and get back in better shape.

Even though he was bored, he really never anticipated getting back into the collection business. A common feature of acquisition agreements is a non-compete with the executives of the acquired business. Dennis had agreed with OSI and Payco at the time of the acquisition that he would refrain from competing with them. That didn't seem to be a problem to him because he had no intention of starting again in the collection business in the U.S.

It was about this time that a friend from the collection industry, who resided in Australia, gave him a call. John Pearce knew that Dennis had sold his business. When Dennis picked up the call, he heard John say, "G'day, mate. Why don't you come here, down under?" John laid out a business scenario but Dennis struggled to muster any excitement about getting back into the collection business, especially so far away. But John was insistent. Dennis finally said, "I'll tell you what I'll do. I've never been to Australia so I will come down and take a look, but please understand, I'm not promising you anything. I think I've had enough and I don't need to go halfway around the world to do the same thing again."

Dennis flew to Australia and, as the two of them looked over the business, he realized there was an opportunity. His creative juices started flowing and he saw some potential. He spent some time thinking about what they might do, sketched out a plan, and acknowledged that his interest was tempered by the location; but he had to admit that he was interested. However, he also questioned if he could really do this again.

Realizing that he had nothing to lose, Dennis presented his plan to John, sharing the objective and the timeline. He had already established the quantitative and the qualitative goals. Old habits die hard! But that was a natural extension of his thinking. Anticipating that he might get some reluctance from John, Dennis stated that if John agreed with him on the approach, he was interested. Otherwise, he had no interest. John was quick to reply, "That sounds like a good plan, Mate!" They ended up doing a rollup and Dennis, in his words, threw some money at it. Several times over the subsequent months Dennis went out on a limb and took some more shares in the business, Collection House.

Dennis had realized that he wasn't willing to turn his assets over to another individual or business and expect them to pay the level of attention that he would to growing those assets. As he described it, "If I was going to make a lot of money going forward, it was still on my nose." As he realized that he still had the ability and the willingness to help lead another organization, and that he had an opportunity to make a significant amount of money, he had to make the decision whether to fail or succeed. But it was going to involve some risk to make it happen. He wasn't content with letting a stock broker play with his money.

He took a big risk in Australia when he provided a $10 million bridge loan to the company, a loan for which he was personally obligated. No one else had been willing to front that kind of money in Australia for the business. Dennis served as the chairman and John was the CEO. With the proceeds of the loan, they started buying companies and getting the critical mass together, the same way that he had done at Payco.

When they took the business public in 2000, it was the most successful IPO in Australia that year. Dennis had become a major shareholder in what had become the largest collection company in Australia and New Zealand over a period of two short years - a position that the business still holds in the market. Dennis and John also became the two largest individual shareholders in that public company. Dennis was right back in the collection business, this time down under.

Dennis seemed to be destined to keep his leadership skills active in the collection business. He had met a gentleman during a trip to Europe, a Swede by the name of Bo Gorannson, who was in the same business in Europe. They became good friends and Bo asked Dennis to be on the board of his company, Intrum Justitia, which is the largest collection company in Europe. At about the same time, Bo became a member of the board of Collection House. The friendship and the relationship have been good and have given Dennis a chance to learn a lot about the European culture, especially their business culture, in the years of his involvement in those ventures.

Growth didn't come without challenges. John decided that he no longer wanted to be the CEO and they went through a succession of three different CEOs, none of whom seemed to be able to get the business headed in the right direction. Two of them were bankers, conservative in their thinking and misguided in their view of their role as a caretaker of the business and, as such, were unwilling to rock the boat. But this wasn't the conservative phase of the business. It was time to rock the boat and give it a chance to grow.

As Dennis observed the performance of each of the three CEOs, he realized that they were each taking the business in the wrong direction. As the largest shareholder he knew he had to do something. Rather than let them sink the business, he became the hatchet man and personally fired them. Finally, on the fourth CEO selection they found the right guy. He had grown up in the industry, working in IT in one of the businesses that they had purchased. This individual had subsequently made a successful move to operations and quickly grasped where the business needed to go.

One of the growth strategies that they employed was to diversify and purchase a couple of complementary businesses. One was an evaluation company similar to Fitch that looked like it had a lot of promise. In Australia, all credit reporting is negative, with reports made only when someone doesn't pay their debt. After pumping a lot of money into that little business, they realized that it was not going to fulfill their expectations and they eventually sold the business at a loss. They subsequently bought a commercial credit bureau that competed with Dun & Bradstreet. When the opportunity came to sell the business, they chose to do so and made a nice profit.

After those experiences, Dennis suggested that they get back to making money doing what they knew how to do. It was time to regain focus. He had become the master of focus as he grew Payco and now realized that it was time to get rid of the distractions at Collection House. He again shared the vision of focus on collecting money, buying receivables, and getting back to the appropriate profit margins on the business. He was the proponent of getting back to their model and staying with it; that model being the original plan that he had sketched out in his early meeting with John. The result of the refocusing effort was to see a phenomenal growth in the business and a resultant stock price increase.

Dennis had also learned a valuable lesson at Payco with their IT commitment as he saw the positive effect that it had on their growth.

One of the stellar features of Collection House was their proprietary software system that they were developing, called *The Controller*. It was by far the best such system in Australia. They were several phases into the development of that system when Dennis got involved and they subsequently invested additional money to upgrade the system. That proprietary system was one of the things that Dennis saw of value in the organization. His assessment was correct in that their systems made a huge difference in their business development.

A dramatic difference between Payco and Collection House was in the sales approach and environment. While Payco had about two thousand customers, Collection House only had about thirty. Payco had pursued the commercial market, the retail market, the consumer market, and the utilities, each of which was a profitable segment. Now, at Collection House, Dennis had to learn the nuances of having only thirty customers. He insisted that they know each of the decision-makers for their clients. In this environment, everybody used requests for proposals (RFP) and review panels. As a result, the sales force demands were different than in the U.S. They needed to focus on a small sales force and a larger service force to support the clients. Dennis adapted well to the change and was an important player in the discussions with several major clients.

When Collection House was working with Telstra, the major Australian telecom business, one of the panel members challenged Dennis as to his potential contribution. This individual had previously experienced a situation where John had gone over the man's head to his boss. He was still smarting from that encounter and was not leaning favorably towards giving the business to Collection House. Thinking that he would needle Dennis a little bit, he asked what he, being from the United States, brought to the table. When Dennis responded, "I have 30 years worth of mistakes that I don't need to repeat," the man burst out laughing and Collection House landed the business. Dennis made the necessary adjustment to the environment, albeit in a somewhat unorthodox manner.

Dennis had taken a significant financial position in the business. At the time of the initial public offering the stock came out at about $.35 per share. There had been some volatility in the share price, and at one point when the share price got down close to $.30, someone offered Bo $.30 per share for his block of stock and he determined that he wanted to sell his shares. In fact, he was quite adamant that he was going to sell. When Dennis found out he called Bo and tried to talk him out of selling the shares, arguing that the basis and infrastructure of the business was sound and that the current situation was just a blip in the market. Bo was not to be deterred. Dennis decided, that with Bo determined to sell his shares, he would personally extend an offer of $.35 per share, which Bo accepted. Dennis didn't want to take advantage of someone, especially a friend, and made his best effort to talk him out of selling. However, in good conscience he wrote the check to Bo for his shares. They are still good friends and Bo has done well financially, but Dennis suspects that Bo still looks periodically at the stock price for Collection House and questions his decision.

Similar to the situation with Bo, one of Dennis' former partners from Payco had purchased 500,000 shares of Collection House stock at $.35 per share. When the stock value hit $.75 per share, the individual determined to sell his shares. Dennis realized the potential negative impact of dumping that many shares on the market at the time so he went to all of the directors, telling them that the individual wanted $.75 a share, the market price at the time. After he gave each of the directors a chance to commit to purchase some of the shares, two of them agreed to take 100,000 shares each. Dennis determined to buy the remaining 300,000 shares at $.75 a share.

The efforts to regain focus on collection activities paid off for the business in its profitability which positively impacted the stock price. The share price grew past the $.75 per share, traded at close to $2 per share in July of 2013, although it has slipped back to $1.85 per share in late September of 2013. His inability to convince his friends not to sell their shares worked to Dennis advantage as he now owns shares worth significantly more than what he paid. The company also committed to paying an annual dividend that, for Dennis, has been a source of significant positive cash flow back to him personally. Since he still owns fifteen million shares, the dividend is significant.

Even with strong leadership in place, Dennis has determined that while he remains the largest shareholder, he will keep an eye on the business and protect his interests. He has taken a less significant role, stepping away from his responsibilities as chairman of the board. Not only did he learn from his mistakes of the past, he has determined to avoid new ones. He will remain vigilant with his investment.

Chapter 39 –Business Lessons

For many years, Dennis carried a piece of paper in his wallet that had written on it his quantitative and qualitative goals for where he had set his personal bar. It was an important piece of paper that he looked at fairly often. The paper, and what was written on it, changed regularly as he met and then adjusted his goals upward, something that often happened prior to achieving an existing goal. But he always wanted to know where he was going.

As he learned from his pain dream and climbing the ladder, he realized he had many God-given talents that, if used correctly, would help him ascend the ladder. He has always been motivated by the thought that he had not yet reached the top of the ladder because, as he states, "I would already be a zillionaire." The vision of the ladder was a driver for him. The focus was to use the talents to their best possible outcome.

Although he no longer carries a sheet of paper in his wallet, the qualitative and quantitative objectives are etched in his mind for almost every venture in which he is involved, including Collection House and other activities.   He recognizes the thresholds and objectives for each, and anticipates his exit strategy, as appropriate.

At 77 years of age, in spite of some physical challenges, he is grateful that he is still sound of mind. Remaining active in his projects has kept his mind engaged and healthy, and because he has been engaged and healthy, he continues to enjoy the pursuit. Dennis will suggest that he doesn't know where the next opportunity will take him, but, as long as he is healthy, he will stay focused in the business world. Those pursuits will complement his philanthropic efforts.

Perhaps one might consider that Dennis has gambled on some of the projects with which he has been involved.   Long ago he even established his quantitative and qualitative approach to gambling. He describes the concept, "If you consider the gambling experience of most people, they will set a limit on how much they're willing to lose but very few will set a goal as to what they expect to win. I maintain that it is much more important to focus on what you are willing to win. Those who set a limit on what they will lose often focus solely on that and start out with a negative approach.

"When I go to a Casino I know what I am willing to lose but I determine in advance how much I will win, generally doubling my money, and I quit when I achieve that goal, no matter how much I have taken to the casino. I don't believe in luck, or in runs of luck. But I do believe in the discipline of knowing how much you will win before you quit.

"Most individuals who double their money will then continue to gamble and give back not only their winnings, but also the money they had taken in originally. I've watched this all over the world, including Monte Carlo. My contention is that if you don't know how much you're willing to win then don't go into the casino and gamble because you are going to give money to the casino."

One evening Dennis went into a casino and lost 13 straight hands of blackjack, which is almost unheard of. Unwilling to blame rotten luck, he recognized that it was simply how the cards fell. He quit because he was within the loss parameters that he had set. Similarly, many times he has doubled his money and left the casino while still winning. He will also apply this concept to a stock, setting a stop-loss point as well as a growth limit.

One of the most important lessons that Dennis learned was that you can't learn while you are talking, so he worked to become a good listener. That included listening for the salient bullet points from the person who was talking and formulating that into how he might motivate them to do business with him. He had two poignant experiences that drove this point home. The first situation was when he met with the treasurer of American Express. Acknowledging that he was failing in his attempt to tell the man why he should do business with him, it was only after Dennis was willing to listen that he found some common ground with the man. The second experience was noted as he responded to the attorney for Telstra, sharing that he had brought 30 years of mistakes that he didn't need to repeat. He had listened carefully and responded in a way that was a bit out of the ordinary. And it worked. Instead of responding with a self-flattering, long-winded dissertation, he took a self-deprecating approach that helped them win the business.

It is critical to be an engaged listener. That requires thinking about what the other person is saying. In a sales environment you need to listen to understand so you can respond appropriately, but too many are busy talking or thinking about the quick response that they don't listen to understand. Especially challenging is the individual that Dennis calls a "topper", one who is always thinking about how he might top or better your comment. It is better to listen to understand.

As a manager, Dennis consistently tried to lead by example. He wanted to show his expectations by the way he did business rather than having to explain each step in doing things his way. It was that *lead by example* approach that allowed him to come up with the idea of going to the phonebook and blindly picking Roto-Rooter as a potential customer. It was a subtle but powerful message to the team showing which way he wanted them to go. Many other managers would have said, "Do this, go here, and do it my way."

A salient feature of the Payco customer service that Dennis advocated was taking a check that represented the money collected for their main clients and hand delivering it to them. He wanted their clients to be able to see that they were successful for them in collecting their money. When showed specific results, it made it easier to ask for more business. Inevitably, a couple of the salespeople had a hard time understanding the importance of the approach, would stuff the check in their briefcase, and eventually mailed the check. Dennis felt strongly enough about it that if leading by example didn't work, when he did find out, he would call them on it. They would be given an opportunity to get in line, and those who did things his way were quite successful in their sales efforts. Those who resisted soon realized that their lack of success was telling. Dennis left it up to them to get on board but was not reluctant to encourage them to find something else to do.

The team from American Express welcomed Dennis to their offices when he brought their checks. It is hard not to get excited over multi-million dollar checks. But not every client was an AMEX. The controller at St Joe's hospital in West Bend was the client contact and looked forward to Dennis' visits. It was important to her to see him personally in her office, visit with her over a cup of coffee, and talk about their business. It wasn't good enough to make a phone call or send someone else to see her. As long as he made the call, he had the business. He used that example with his sales staff to help them see how business could flow from such a personal touch.

Dennis, for the most part, was a good judge of people, in spite of struggling with his salesman friend from Carroll. He made the decision to hire key teammates that would fill in skill areas that he lacked. As the company grew, he had to depend more and more on his teammates. As part of the effort of selecting people with the right skills, he also chose people who would follow his lead. As Dennis will share, "These were people who understood what I meant when I grunted." He didn't have to beat on them about doing their jobs. He was able to share his vision, help them to see how their role fit in that vision, and move forward successfully.

One of the downfalls of the Payco management team was that they were all about the same age. They had grown up in the business together, made decisions together, and made money together. They had Dennis' confidence and his trust. At one point Dennis tried to bring in a fairly high-powered individual from Shell Oil who, on the surface, appeared able to help them drive the business forward. He was a miserable failure as he was mostly interested in his personal growth and in climbing the corporate ladder. The only corporate ladder Dennis cared about was the one from his dream that kept him moving forward in spite of frustration or challenge. Feeling that he couldn't trust a new young team like he could the magnificent seven, he didn't make that move and, as a result, there was no succession plan in place. At the time of the sale of Payco, his team was ready to step aside. In retrospect, it probably wouldn't have mattered because, in spite of their employment agreements, the former management team was all pushed aside anyway. But he acknowledges that he could have done a better job in developing the next group of leaders.

Chapter 40 – Life Lessons

By the time Dennis had graduated from high school, he had learned much from the school of hard knocks. But life wasn't done with him yet. There were more growth opportunities and challenges ahead. What life had taught him in those early years was emphasized in his anesthesia dream: life is hard, it can be painful, you have to keep moving up the ladder, and there will be God-given talents that you must use. Those talents were special skills and abilities that he could hone and strengthen if he were to use them, but if he didn't take advantage of them they would be gone. His psyche would not allow him to leave them unused. He was successful as a student and as an athlete and had developed basic philosophies as to how he would live his life. There were additional lessons to learn and he had developed a mindset that allowed him to accept that he had more to learn.

Several of life's greatest lessons were emphasized during his college years. The first such lesson was that Dennis came to recognize and accept that there was a higher power that influences and assists us. As he shares, "Far more than just having Jupiter align with Mars, there will be times when something occurs that has to have a better explanation than coincidence. There is a spiritual direction that, if heeded, will lead us to greater things than we might accomplish of our own accord." Dennis was willing to accept and acknowledge it in his life. His life would be completely different had he not been in the fraternity house the day Mr. Anderson called about the job at the collection agency. He would not enjoy the association with his children and grandchildren had he not felt the need to go rescue Katie in Iowa. There really is a higher order in life.

The second lesson was that there were boundaries of time and space that he could not exceed. He was constantly on the go and the activity was intoxicating. He was a full-time student, a respected athlete, a husband, a father, an employee, and an individual. There was so much to do and only so much time to do it in. He had the same amount of time as anyone else but was willing to learn the lessons of how to best use that time. He had to learn to prioritize his efforts, use his time wisely, refuse to allow others to waste his time, and make every minute count. That is not an easy formula, especially with a family, but he became a master of managing time.

The third lesson was that life drops stumbling blocks in our way. Dennis is extremely competitive on the athletic field and in business. It is critical to learn early on that one shouldn't expect clear sailing every day. Sometimes the path seems wide open and great progress is made. Most of the time as you work towards an objective, there will be a stumbling block that will appear out of nowhere between you and that objective.   With knowledge that the stumbling blocks will come, an individual can, and must be prepared, to deal with them and use them to help achieve his goals rather than let them stymie success.

The fourth lesson is that with the competing demands on our time, attention, and lives, we must work on each of the multiple aspects of our lives, including intellectual, physical, emotional, and spiritual, to retain a semblance of balance. If one was to focus too much energy on any one aspect, his entire life will be out of balance.

The fifth lesson is the importance of education. As the first of the Punches family to attend and graduate from college, he recognized the value of his education and the opportunities that it opened for him. He vowed that he would not be alone in being educated; he was setting a new expectation for the Punches family, starting with his own children. A college education was not optional, not for his children or for his grandchildren.

Other lessons were also well learned, some of which will be discussed in the following chapters, along with amplification of some of the above noted lessons.

Chapter 41 – Stumbling Blocks

Lesson three, as noted in the previous chapter, suggests that life presents stumbling blocks. As a successful athlete, Dennis will often use sports analogies to emphasize a point. In talking about life's stumbling blocks, he shares, "As an athlete you learn to train your body, working hard for an objective. That training includes effort and pain but that effort and pain makes you stronger. That strength prepares you for the contest.

"As you are running a race, let's assume that a whole bunch of big boulders fell from the sky. They are not in a perfect line, but are scattered all over. As you run your race you come up against the boulders, often one at a time, but sometimes they are stacked against each other. The bunch of boulders is almost like a maze. You are not the only runner that has to deal with the boulders; every runner in front of, and behind you, has to deal with them, too. The difference is in how each runner chooses to approach the boulder. Some will run into the boulder, back up, and run in to it again, repeatedly banging up against it. Some will determine how to climb over the boulder, while others will seek a way around the side. Some of the runners will simply sit down and give up after they get past the first boulder when they see another in their way. Those boulders represent life's stumbling blocks."

Stumbling blocks, although generally viewed as an impediment to achieve our goals, can be the very things that give us the strength and courage to move forward in our lives as we struggle to overcome them. Sometimes we need to mount a stumbling block so that we have an elevated view of what lies ahead, opening to us a vista of the possibilities and of the decisions that need to be made.

Dennis recognized the need to allow his children to face stumbling blocks in their own lives. In a controlled environment, you can often let them start out with smaller ones. He made sure they had chores to do around the house. They attended the public schools. Though he didn't fix their problems for them, he listened to them when they were frustrated or disappointed by a teacher or a friend. He encouraged them to look at the problem and then consider what might be an appropriate resolution. As they talked, the children were often able to develop their own solution.

He didn't have to conjure up too many challenges; life seemed to generate a sufficient number. They had to learn to surmount their own challenges and to gain their own strength. He was there to encourage, and sometimes to show the path through the boulder field, but he didn't clear the path for them. He didn't want them to be like the children whose parents smoothed their path, cleared all barriers, provided the private school, enrolled them in the best college, paid for their advanced degrees, but left the child helpless against the difficulties of the real world when they were finally required to face challenges on their own. It is more than a Darwinian theory of survival of the fittest. It is real life. Life is tough, and those who have learned to deal with tough challenges are best prepared to succeed. This interaction between Dennis and his children became more difficult after the divorce as he had less involvement with them during the week. But recognizing the importance of growth opportunities, he did his best to direct them towards some boulders in their lives.

Even now that his resources are significant, Dennis has interaction with those he cares about and will provide financial assistance. But he helps them see the need to work for that which they receive and to take responsibility. It shouldn't be as easy as just asking for the money.

Chapter 42 – Keeping Balance

The fourth lesson, although intuitively learned, was painful when he became focused on the value of keeping balance in life. Recognizing that there are multiple aspects of life, each of which demands attention and nurturing to grow, an individual must spend time in each area that he wishes to improve. Different researchers may vary the labels, but for purposes of this discussion, we suggest that the principle areas are intellectual, physical, emotional and spiritual. As we consider those four areas as being distributed around a square or rectangle with the frame attached at a single point, the frame will not hang straight unless the areas are equally balanced.

Intellectual Physical

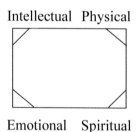

Emotional   Spiritual

While completing his education, and continuing after he purchased the business, the demands on his time were significant. As he worked to build a business he took time to play some evening baseball, to hunt and fish, to surround himself with intelligent and thoughtful people, while he not only provided for his family but also did his best to spend time with them. Perhaps, at times, his family drew the short straw. But he also dealt with the effects of religion dominating the thoughts and activities of his wife. She had been converted while they were living on Windsor Drive in Waukesha. Although he thought that a move to Wales would allow her to distance herself somewhat and develop more balance, that didn't happen.

As he contemplated divorce, Dennis did a personal inventory. At age 36 he was the CEO of a publicly traded company, he had already made his first million dollars, and he was committed to his family. He was trying to keep his life in balance. He nursed the relationship along for some time but then felt that he had to choose. To stay with his wife meant stepping away from the other things that were important to him. He could see himself having to focus too much time and energy in the emotional arena to save the marriage and that would have tilted it dramatically away from all other areas of his life. It was about this time that a phrase from the Rudyard Kipling poem, "If" came to his mind. Kipling had written, "If all people count, but none too much."[xvi] He determined to choose his ability to make a living and support his family over focusing on the emotional and spiritual that would have been required to keep the marriage intact.

Dennis shared his feelings about maintaining balance. He said, "I really began to understand this concept of balance in life as I got closer to the divorce. My personal life was very balanced at that point. Each of those areas was very important to me, including having started a Presbyterian Church in Waukesha. I certainly believe in the Big Guy. And I continue to work on all four areas. They really came into focus for me as I watched my wife go out of balance."

The experience was a poignant reminder to carefully watch that square to see not only where he was, but also his children, and to make necessary course corrections. If he was too weighty in any one area, the review at least let him know that to be the case, whether he tried to fix it at the time or just recognized that he would need to address it at some point in the future. After all, as he suggests, "There are times in our lives when we will be heavily weighted in one area to the detriment of another."

Dennis also observed his staff and especially his management team. If he saw them focused too heavily in a given area, he would try to help them see the need to get back into balance. That sometimes meant encouraging them to take some time away from work to devote to other aspects of their lives. Other times, he would see something wrong in their performance and, as he observed, the problem became apparent as to what was out of balance.

In retrospect, Dennis observes that he did little physical training outside of the normal sports seasons because he was involved in so many sports. But one thing that has helped him maintain balance in the physical arena is that his high school coaches put the fear of death in him with their stern warnings about smoking or drinking. They told him, "I don't care who you are or how good you are, if I catch you [smoking or drinking] you are out of here!" The experiences of watching his father struggle with alcohol also influences his behavior. Dennis has never smoked in his life and, though he will drink a little wine or maybe a little vodka, he never drinks to excess.

Chapter 43 – Listening to Understand

Dennis suggests that he is an intellectual parasite, although the phrase may sound harsher than his intended meaning. To keep his intellectual self strong he surrounds himself, or tries to spend time, with people who add something to his understanding. Confirming the cliché, "You can't learn when you are talking," Dennis engages people who are bright and successful. He enjoys spending time with those who might add perspective or understanding to his life. That doesn't mean he always agrees with everything that is said, but he acknowledges that even at 77 years of age there are people who can help him go, "Wow! I never thought of that." He avoids the people who seem to stutter, "I, I, I, I, I," as well those to whom he refers as "toppers." It is bad enough to have to listen to someone who wants you to understand just how important they are, but even worse to listen to someone who, no matter what you say, seeks to "top" your story with one of their own.

Dennis realized early in his life that he needed to be careful about choosing to whom he was going to listen, from whom to take advice, and how to choose what part of that advice to accept. He became a discriminating listener, determining what would be valuable to him, and then storing it away for future reference.

When he combined those two ideas, seeking out intellectual individuals and then being discriminating about what he took from their thoughts, he realized that there were many who had influenced his life. He will forever be grateful for individuals like his high school biology teacher who was also his football coach, coach Hailey; Norm Holz, another high school football coach; John Taylor, a good friend from Waukesha; and Coach Blackbourn, the former Packer coach and truly a mentor for Dennis. From each of these individuals, Dennis garnered ideas and approaches that helped make him who he is. These were valuable life lessons.

Two particular life lessons came from Coach Blackbourn. He taught Dennis about not getting caught in the garbage when you aren't paying attention to what you are supposed to be doing or what is going on around you. He also showed that there were times to be intimidating in your approach with others, most notably when you wanted to make sure that there was no way for them to misunderstand what you were trying to share with them. Each concept would be shared with Dennis' children and his work associates. His go-to 20 team was a special target of his intimidation, but also the recipient of his invitation to not be caught in the garbage. He expected them to do their jobs well, and, if they were the weak link, to have them go away and do something else.

Chapter 44 - Politics

Dennis' political leanings reflect his effort to keep balance in his life. He experienced the nanny state of the U.S. government as he was a college football player. Regulations imposed by the Federal Government on the ability of a coach to substitute players stemming from its efforts to regulate scholarships and money spent on sports, meant that Dennis, as a college quarterback, was required to play offense and defense. It is almost unthinkable now to consider having your starting quarterback in the defensive backfield as a safety taking on the other team's running back or trying to provide pass defense against a wide receiver.

Having been raised in a staunchly Democrat family, his father and family having been the beneficiaries of the New Deal era policies, it might follow that his political leanings would be similar. However, absent an unplanned interaction with a local Milwaukee judge, Dennis' thinking might have been much different.

During the campaign leading to President Kennedy's term in office, Dennis attended a wedding reception at the home of a judge by the name of Stauff. During the evening, the judge invited Dennis to his study for a conversation about the upcoming election and asked who Dennis expected to vote for. When Dennis replied that he really liked this Kennedy guy because of his charisma and personal leadership traits, the judge was quick to respond, "Wrong! You know nothing about his platform or what he owes in terms of favors granted during his campaign." He then went on to explain that no matter the personal capabilities of the candidate, they are beholden to those in the political machine that helped get them elected. You have to look deeper than the personality; you have to consider the platform and who he owes. Leadership doesn't just come out of charisma or because someone has the ability to have "words fall trippingly from his tongue[xvii]."

Dennis' father grew up worshiping the ground that FDR walked on. Yet, as a blue-collar union worker, Great Depression survivor, and CCC worker, Herb was politically lazy and wouldn't even go to the polls. Although Herb was willing to talk about what was going on, he wouldn't do anything about it and never voted. Another take away from the conversation with Judge Stauff was that once you make your decision on a candidate, go cast your vote.

The conversation brought about a significant and lasting change for Dennis in his political philosophy and helped him become the true conservative that he is today. As an entrepreneur he sees the need to have the freedom to build a business, to provide a valuable product to the community, and to provide meaningful jobs. It bears fruit in his desire to help fund the campaigns of those that will support those conservative values. Not only does he vote, but Dennis also sends money to support the campaigns.

Because he was tutored and challenged by Judge Stauff, Dennis also takes time to talk politics and the process with others. For example, if he is in a taxicab in New York, he will challenge the driver, not trying to sway him to a particular political party or viewpoint, rather to help him see the importance of involvement in the political process.

Perhaps his greatest frustration in this effort is dealing with mugwumps. This term dates back to old English politics where an individual wouldn't make a decision on where they stood and were described as having their mug on one side of the fence and their wump on the other. It is better to make a decision and stand behind that decision.

He tries to avoid the groups who will discuss politics, growl about their disagreement over policies and approach, but do so primarily within a forum of like-minded individuals. Dennis calls this *preaching to the choir*. He finds he has much more influence by taking time to visit with someone with whom he might make a difference, showing them the importance of engaging in the process.

Dennis describes himself as an arch conservative. He learns what is behind a candidate, looking beyond their personality. He challenges people in their political thinking, and he refuses to preach to the choir, recognizing that he is much more effective if he teaches instead of preaches. He uses his influence and money to back those who will make a difference. And he votes.

Chapter 45 – Importance of Education

The fifth of Dennis' life lessons that we discuss here is the importance of education. His dad, Herb Punches, only had an eighth grade education. His mother, Dorothy, married at 15 years of age. Grandparents and great-grandparents were not well educated. There was no money for college for Dennis' older siblings. His athletic scholarship was a game changer for the Punches family. Perhaps Dennis could have been content with his own scholastic success, but that was not to be. He was determined that his would be the last Punches generation that had limited college graduates.

It is hard to ignore that Dennis had a positive attitude, and, while he was regularly placed in challenging situations, he moved forward with confidence, no matter what. Whether it was forcing his way on to the baseball team with the older boys, finding a way to provide for his family when his father was sick while still making good marks in school and lettering in four different sports, or working multiple jobs during college to complete his education, he was determined to succeed. The athletic scholarship went a long way towards allowing him to complete his college education as it paid his tuition, but there were far more demands on the wallet associated with education than just tuition.

Since he had children while he was still quite young, his educational pursuit was very fresh in his mind as he started to consider what part education would provide in their lives. As a young business owner with the many obligations of a business venture, a homeowner with a mortgage, and a myriad of expenses associated with raising a family, his personal goal of changing the educational direction of the Punches family was lofty and for a time felt out of reach.

With all of those financial demands facing him, Dennis had taken a calculated risk by buying rental properties. He was a busy man but saw an opportunity to make some long-term gain on real estate. When the time came to sell his four four-family apartment buildings in Waukesha, a sale which provided a net gain of $60,000, it would have been easy to invest that back into other real estate, push it into the collection business, pay down a mortgage, or spend it. But Dennis saw the importance of educating his children. The $60,000 was split four ways and became the corpus of four separate education trusts to which he would make additional contributions to bolster their value. With additions made by him plus the interest paid on the accounts, those trusts would each grow to exceed $200,000 by the time the kids were headed to college. This wasn't the only decision that could have been made, but, to Dennis, it was the most important decision that he could have made at the time. He was changing the future. His children would have college educations.

It wouldn't be enough to fund just one generation. Long-term change meant that succeeding generations of Punches, would also need to be educated. Career success in the collection and real estate industries allowed Grandpa Punches to fund similar education trusts for his grandchildren. It was that important to him. His financial stability made the funding of those trusts somewhat less onerous or challenging to him, but it still speaks to his insistence that a Punches family member will be educated.

Lack of education doesn't necessarily mean that an individual will not be able to provide an adequate living for his family, nor does having an education assure that they will provide well. But Dennis is regularly in situations that allow him to see how education, or lack of it, impacts our society. Many of the minority populations still lag in receiving a college education, whether as a result of financial constraints or lack of interest. But lack of education for those populations plays a significant role in their situation in our society. He sees the defeatist attitude. He recognizes the unwillingness of the uneducated to live by appropriate societal norms. He watches their aggressive behavior. Though he sees the negative impact in society, there is a limit to what a single individual can do to change the approach for good. However, he does see the value of planning and preparing for the education of his family members and he takes an active role in that funding.

After helping to fund the education of a minority student, he was dismayed when the individual returned to a similar menial job as he held before receiving an expensive four-year degree. Change can only occur if the person is willing to change.

Not all of one's education comes in a classroom. Dennis wasn't able to bat in a ball game until he was almost 10 years old. Though he rowed the boat so his dad could fish, he spent much time learning about fishing before he ever held a pole. Much of his education was of a practical nature, which also comes into play as he looks at and assesses our current education system. And, although education is a key priority for him as he interacts with his family, he knows there are challenges to its value.

Recognizing the need to keep his brain active, Dennis took an Erhard training session, a mind-training program intended to help participants look inwardly. The weeklong program was in a strictly controlled environment - classroom setting, no bathroom breaks during sessions (except with doctor's orders), a four-hour session in the morning, and a longer session after lunch. His first takeaway was developing the commitment to keep the little deals. If you make a statement, such as "let's do that sometime," then make it happen. The other takeaway was in the statement, "God created you to be happy, so why not be happy?" Dennis was happy to adopt the approach of "if you want to drive your enemies crazy, be nice to them."

A voracious reader, Dennis will reflect back on poems that have made a difference in his life. He continues to read and quote poets such as Robert Frost and Rudyard Kipling. Two of those poems are Frost's *Stopping by Woods on a Snowy Evening*[xviii], and Kipling's *If*.

Other reading has included novels but also quite a number of what could be considered personal development books. A Richard Bach book, *Illusions,* touches both of those areas. Dennis recognizes in himself the willingness to let go of the rocks and branches in the stream, even if it means that he will be banged around going down the stream. He has been unwilling to reside in the status quo. He continually seeks the next opportunity downstream, never focused behind him. As his sixth grade teacher shared one day, "The past is uninhabitable." Education allows him to look to the future and see that it is bright.

Chapter 46 – Real Estate

From years of playing football, Dennis learned valuable lessons of calculated risk resulting in appropriate reward. As he purchased control of Merchants Credit Bureau, he was taking a significant calculated risk that he could resolve the trust account issues, restore the trust of clients, placate the banking department, and pay back the money that he had borrowed from Waukesha State Bank to buy the business. He had extended himself beyond what is considered appropriate credit limits, as had the bank, by borrowing the money.

He got things straightened out with the business, was making payments to the bank, and felt that with the prospects for growth with the business and the money he was making, it was time to purchase a home for their family. Home ownership was, and is, an opportunity for capital accumulation that is quite unique in the U.S. as it extends to a much greater part of the general population than in many other countries. Dennis was ready to take advantage of that opportunity.

Dennis had become acquainted with Bob Manz, the son of one of his biology professors at Carroll, Ralph Manz. As they became good friends, Dennis realized that Bob was a genius, and, in spite of some funny quirks, he was very good at thinking through the logic of various issues. When Dennis was ready to purchase their home on Windsor Drive in Waukesha, Bob was instrumental in helping him gain the financing through Wauwatosa Savings and Loan and complete the home purchase.

In about 1963, shortly after the home purchase, Bob suggested that if Dennis was to buy rental properties at the then-current financing rates of 4 or 5%, he could ride the inflation trail from his cost of 4% until someone was ready to buy those properties when the cost to replace them would be 11 or 12%. The value of the buildings in such a scenario would continue to grow for the owner by doing nothing more than just riding the inflation. The conversation stuck with Dennis and he spent some time considering the implications.

Shortly after that conversation, Bob shared with Dennis that four four-family apartment properties on Greenfield Avenue in Waukesha were available for purchase. They could be purchased with very little money down, approximately $5,000 total for all four buildings, with the balance on a note at 4%. Dennis couldn't resist the opportunity, especially as he was convinced that Bob was correct in his thinking. Bob was just sharing the opportunity and wasn't looking to participate, so Dennis bought the buildings.

Ownership of apartment buildings brings a certain level of time demand as landlords qualify and place renters, collect rent, maintain the property, and deal with any problems that arise. The buildings were in great shape, with good tenants, and strong cash flow. The time demands were not overwhelming.

When interest rates started to climb, the value of the properties escalated, just as Bob had predicted. However, to capture the value growth one had to sell the property. When a buyer came forward and offered Dennis an amount for the properties that allowed him to net a

$60,000 gain on the sale, he couldn't resist. Rather than reinvest the $60,000 back into more real estate, he invested the proceeds in individual education trusts for his four children. He had outlined specific financial goals and the education trusts took priority over other investing at the time, but that financial kill in his first real estate deal whet his appetite for more real estate investing, even though it would be a few years before he would make that happen.

As the family grew, it made sense to look for space to stretch out a bit. When property became available in the Kettle Moraine Forest, Dennis purchased the 15 acre property and built a large home. After adding a pond in front of the house, it was a woodland paradise. When Dennis and Katie divorced, she remained in the house for a period of time and then the house was sold as part of the divorce settlement.

As Payco continued to grow, they moved the business several times. Eventually, Dennis realized that there would be a need for a facility where they could house the support infrastructure that would be required for a multi-location business. Dennis purchased a piece of property on Executive Drive in Brookfield and planned for the development of a 60,000 square foot facility. One of the keys of calculated risk is to know when to share some of that risk. In this case, Dennis determined to include his key Payco team in the ownership of a new building which, when completed, was fully leased by Payco. This building became more than a personal investment in real estate. It also gave Dennis an opportunity to hold his team together. The deal structure gave Dennis 50% of the ownership of the building and the other six of them split the remaining 50%. The building cost approximately $2.3 million to build and it later sold for $5.6 million. Not only did Dennis benefit from the transaction, his team walked away with significant gains as well.

When other opportunities presented themselves subsequent to the Payco building transaction, Dennis started to participate in limited partnerships, primarily on large rental projects. Over a period of time Dennis built up his portfolio to the point of having almost 1,000 apartment units. The projects varied in size up to approximately 220 units. Since they were major projects, for most of these apartment projects Dennis partnered with Tom Thompson, a real estate guru from Pewaukee, Wisconsin who put the deals together. With Tom's death in 2013, management of those projects moved to the company Tom founded, Thompson Real Estate.

Dennis has pursued a mix of new projects that develop a property, along with buying existing apartment complexes. He also invests in warehouses; including many in Florida, one that he bought and sold that was located on Capitol Drive in Brookfield, and another on the north side of Milwaukee just off Highway 145 and Appleton Avenue, a huge warehouse that is currently fully rented.

Real estate investment involves a level of speculation but is aided by the ability to look at a piece of property and to consider what might happen around the property. Dennis bought some raw land in St. Francis on the south side of Milwaukee next to the former Harnischfeger's headquarters. This 11 acre piece borders Lake Michigan and sits between two major building projects. Although his original thought was to develop the property, for now he is just sitting on the land. At some point, when one or the other of those two neighboring projects wants to expand, there will be a market for his piece of property. When they are ready, he will be ready.

Although he does invest in Milwaukee properties, such as one off of Janesville Road, Dennis' investment appetite is far-reaching. He has invested in properties in Middleton, Wisconsin, Bullhead City, Arizona, property in the Cayman Islands that houses cable and cell towers which generates income, a bunch of units in Vero Beach, Florida, additional units in Hobe Sound, Florida, spec units in Daytona Beach, Florida, and others in Destin, Florida. His resorts in Canada comprise a significant real estate investment.

Dennis has learned a couple of very important lessons from his real estate activity. As he reflects, "Sometimes it appears that when you have the momentum you might become convinced that you have the Midas touch. Sometimes the explanation can only be that. But, there are some low spots too!" Dennis had purchased a piece of property in Florida that was located next to a trailer park after negotiating a deal with the owner of that trailer park to partner with him and build a hotel. However, that could only happen after he got rid of the trailers. The other individual seemed to lose interest in either the transaction, or in working with Dennis, and made no move to get rid of the trailers. Recognizing that no one wants to stay in a hotel situated next to a trailer park, Dennis had $900,000 invested in a piece of property he couldn't develop. Noting that sometimes you have to take your licks, Dennis locked in a $400,000 loss when he sold the property for

$500,000. As he shared, "That is part of the getting ahead story – you have to be prepared to take some of those hits and some losses."

Chapter 47 – A Close Call

A serious early mistake came close to being financially disastrous for Dennis. After Payco had gone public a significant portion of his personal holdings was in Payco stock. Dennis had gotten involved with a friend who was putting together a condominium project in Boca Raton, Florida for which Dennis used his personal financial statement to leverage his own position in the transaction. He had initially limited his personal liability in the deal. However, as the project reached a critical point, at the 11th hour the person who had put the project together hit a serious financial snag. All of his guarantors jumped ship, leaving him seriously exposed financially and threatening the viability of the entire project. This individual came to Dennis, primarily because they were friends, and asked that Dennis stand in as a guarantor on the project. Recognizing that his own stake was at significant risk, and because of the friendship, Dennis agreed to act as a guarantor on the project.

He made a serious mistake when he agreed, not necessarily that the decision was wrong, but the big mistake was moving forward without legal advice. This was a complicated transaction and he had just created a significant personal financial exposure without legal assistance. Recognized as one of the worst mistakes that he has made in real estate investing, Dennis has made sure to never replicate the error. However, there were costly implications in this situation.

To make a long story short, soon after making the guarantee the market crashed and the friend defaulted on the project. Dennis was a guarantor and the lender, GECC (GE Credit Corp), who was upside down about $5 million on the project, was looking to Dennis for recovery to make them whole. Dennis had committed his cash and personal assets to Katie in the divorce, leaving him with little other than his Payco stock. As a result, Dennis was in a tough situation with minimal liquid assets but lots of Payco stock. Fortunately for him, the market had taken a dive and the Payco stock, while still a good value, didn't appear to be worth very much.

Dennis had to fly down to Miami to meet with the GECC people, their attorneys, and their accountants on the defaulted project. Determined that he wasn't going to face them alone, he made arrangements for his attorney, in spite of excluding him on the front end, to accompany him to Florida for the meetings. At the last minute, the attorney became deathly ill and couldn't make the trip. Although Dennis was also sick with the flu, he flew to Miami alone and soon found himself in a big conference room with four guys from GECC. They hammered at him telling him not only what they were going to do but also what they could do. He was sicker than a dog, but that didn't stop these four guys from pounding. All Dennis could think about was how dumb he had been for having put himself in such a situation. Of course, he had to take the blame because he was the one that had made the decision. He was caught in the garbage.

Terrified that they were going to demand all of his Payco holdings, Dennis was thrilled when he was presented with a deal that didn't include any of it. The GECC guys just didn't see any value in the stock. They could have wiped him out, but after going through his financial statement, apparently without doing much homework on the value of the stock, they omitted the stock as a recovery option. Dennis was prepared for the worst as they laid out the deal, expecting they would take everything he had. He listened intently as they said, "You are going to buy 10 of these condos, personally setting up outside financing for them, and you are going to pay us $50,000 as a slap on the wrist for us to let you off the hook." What a relief! Having 10 condos in a down market was onerous, but the fact that they left the Payco stock alone was fortuitous.

Dennis raised the $50,000, having to borrow much of it because he didn't have any ready cash, which he paid to GECC. He received the deeds for 10 units. Since he really couldn't go to commercial lenders for housing mortgages, he went to several of his friends and asked if they wanted to buy a unit in Florida at a reduced sales price. He made nothing on the transactions but was okay with that as he was only looking to cover his interest costs.   Over the following two-year period he sold all but one unit, which he decided to keep for a time, eventually selling that one as well. He realized that he came amazingly close to losing everything that he had worked for up until 1972. It could have been so much worse! It was a close call and he had learned his lesson.

As an established real estate investor, Dennis still sees great opportunity investing in real estate.   He would apply the lessons learned, including utilizing legal assistance, and maintains that the same logic still applies as it did when he purchased the first four buildings. Inflation will carry you beyond the cost of purchase to a point where replacement cost will exceed your original cost. Gain is in that spread and is almost imminent. However, you still have to purchase correctly because even if you have the best management group and they run the property extremely well, if you buy it wrong, you will never recover. The key is to be careful, look for projects that have upside potential in the rental market, and overlay the current economic situation to project where rental housing prices will go. For most individuals, Dennis would also suggest that real estate investment needs to come later in the scheme of things as you are building your wealth. Since you are taking on risk, use free cash so you don't endanger other aspects of your financial life.

The lessons are worth reiterating: 1) Never personally guarantee a project if you don't have control over the cost. 2) Don't frivolously sign your name on something because you're a good guy and want to help people. Leo Durocher used to say, "Nice guys finish last." 3) Involve someone who can give you appropriate guidance to find the right investment opportunity. 4) Use an attorney to review your commitments.

Chapter 48 – Banking & Other Investments

A natural extension of the collection business for Dennis was the banking business. Since they were doing some collection work for financial institutions, there seemed to be a connection. Most importantly, it piqued Dennis' interest. Sometimes when someone goes looking for an opportunity, they have to create that opportunity for themselves. In his case, Dennis invested in and helped set up a bank that would become the Greater Milwaukee Bank. His investment, at 15 – 20% of the total, was substantial enough that, as the largest shareholder, he was elected as the chairman of the bank. His bank involvement required him to pore over financial statements, sit on committees, consider lending and other policies, and to run the board meetings. As he found himself falling asleep at his own meetings, it wasn't hard to contrast a very boring banking enterprise with the vibrant collection business. Since Payco was where he was making the preponderance of his money that was also where he focused his primary energies. Greater Milwaukee Bank would grow enough under his leadership that M&I Bank would eventually purchase it, a sale that would net a small gain on his investment.

What started out as a learning experience to be involved in one bank wasn't enough, and Dennis would invest in two other banks. Dennis partnered with two other individuals, people with whom he played tennis and otherwise socialized, to take an ownership position in Continental Bank located on 8th and Wisconsin in Milwaukee. The three of them had determined to purchase a combined position that would give them control of the bank. In what he terms as one of the greatest disappointments of his life, the other two individuals moved forward without him, and they took control of the bank. He was stunned. How could his friends go behind his back? A born optimist, this disappointment rocked him. Now the lesson was not only that banking was boring but also reinforced in him the need to be very careful about whom he trusted. He found the situation distasteful and he wanted out. He didn't want anything more to do with these two men. When the opportunity came to sell the bank to Wells Fargo, Dennis gladly exited the bank business.

Finding it hard to end the experiment on a down note, and determined to control his own destiny during the next opportunity, Dennis invested in, and helped found, the Bank of Elm Grove. He would serve as chairman of this small bank until it was also purchased by M&I, returning a few dollars of profit on the sale. He had significant ownership and leadership positions in three different banks and had made a little money on the sale of each, yet he determined that it was time to focus all of his efforts back into Payco. He had learned some lessons from banking, probably some that he wished he hadn't experienced, but lessons, nonetheless. Probably the most important one was the need to be in control of his situation so that other people couldn't control his destiny. He didn't want anyone making decisions that would affect him.

He would later purchase a part of a start-up bank in Wisconsin Rapids at the invitation of his personal physician who also sat on the bank's board of directors. The members of the group that had put the bank together were truly neophytes in the banking industry, and, by this time, Dennis was a seasoned veteran having been involved in the startup of two different banks. The doctor informed the other members of the original group that they should include Dennis because of his experience. In spite of his significant investment level, he chose not to join the board, acknowledging that he had sufficient demands at Payco to occupy his time and focus; plus, it was such a small bank. He didn't pay much attention to the bank until one day he asked Bev to get a stock price from the bank. He had purchased shares at $20 and they offered him $65 per share for his stake. It didn't take long to make the decision to sell his position and take the long-term capital gain.

Dennis' banking experience is unusual for someone who had not made banking their career, and he had insights into the operation of a bank that few others had. His next major banking experience came when his personal portfolio and banking needs had outgrown the ability of the smaller banks in the area. They simply could not meet his needs. He had consolidated his bank accounts at First Wisconsin Bank, later known as Firstar, but he lost his banking contacts there due to organizational changes that came about as part of their many acquisitions.

In about 2008, when Wells Fargo sought to make a presence in the Milwaukee market, he switched all of his accounts to Wells, the new guys in town. A friend had contacted Dennis and suggested that Wells was looking for accounts like his, and that they were eager to show that they could work with him and service his needs. He established a

$3 million line of credit with the bank even though he had the cash and generally didn't need a line of credit. However, there were times when a real estate deal came along and he needed to move quickly. Sometimes the size of a project required a loan, and, rather than wait for the decision of a loan committee, he wanted to be able to write the check from the credit line immediately.

The banking team reviewed his financial statements, and, after determining the basis upon which they were willing to extend a line, they granted him the $3 million credit line. Unlike his experience with Waukesha State Bank, this would be a completely secured and collateralized loan. One of the stipulations was that they would not take any of his Collection House stock as collateral, noting that it was an Australian company and their bank policy didn't allow them to accept foreign stocks as collateral. Even though the stock was worth in excess of $5 million at the time, and the stock was traded on the Australian stock exchange, they demanded a position in apartment projects and other common stocks, but excluded Collection House. The thing that made him most unhappy was the fact that it was a bank policy issue, not a regulatory issue.

Dennis reluctantly agreed to the terms that were offered. When the stock market subsequently took a bit of a tumble, reducing the value of his collateral, all three of the bank representatives with whom he worked marched into his office one day dressed in black suits and looking like undertakers. It was an appropriate comparison. He was one of Wells Fargo's top five clients in Milwaukee, based on size of accounts, with accounts for each of his properties, for Canada, and for all of the things that he was doing, each of which was funneling back through Wells. There were significant transaction fees and his was a good account. But, now they demanded $50,000 in additional collateral on the $3 million line. He was furious!

Recognizing that this was once again a policy matter with directives from San Francisco thru Minneapolis to Milwaukee, Dennis asked, "You have the nerve to walk in here and ask me for another $50,000 of collateral on a $3 million line for which I've never missed an interest payment?" They could only reply that they had their marching orders. When he further queried whether or not, when the market went back up, they were going to free up some of his collateral that he had pledged to them, they stated that they could not do that. Giving them one more opportunity, he recapped the situation saying, "Let me understand this. You have millions of dollars of collateral on a line but your policy says it is $50,000 short and you now demand more collateral. If the market goes back up, you're not going to free up the collateral. Do I understand this correctly?" When they replied in the affirmative, he stated, "Neither you, nor the big shots in San Francisco or Minneapolis, know how to spell flexible. I don't need you. I am leaving."

Dennis contacted his friend Dave Baumgarten who had previously been with Associated Bank and had recently taken the role as President of Bank Mutual in Milwaukee. Dennis asked Dave how he would like to have a nice account at Bank Mutual, especially since he had just been appointed president of the bank. As they sat at the Kilbourn Towers, where they both lived, discussing the situation,

Dennis indicated that if Bank Mutual would take the Collection House stock as collateral, along with a little something else to give them some comfort, then he was ready to do business. Dave made the decision right there and said that they would work with that approach.

Dennis moved all of his accounts to Bank Mutual and has been with them now for several years. He pays down the line when he has ready cash, having learned during his stint in the banking business that you don't ever want to have what they call an "evergreen loan", one for which the principal is never paid off. Dennis pledged his Collection House stock as collateral, along with his Kilbourn Towers home in Milwaukee that overlooks Lake Michigan.

After getting the accounts set up at Bank Mutual, Dennis saw that their stock was trading at $3 a share and he purchased 20,000 shares. On July 19, 2013 Bank Mutual was trading for $6.54 per share. Ownership of stock in the bank had nothing to do with putting together the line of credit and account structure with Bank Mutual, but Dennis realized that this was a bank with a great president who would soon be the next CEO. The bank had gotten caught in the earlier real estate debacle and was still in the transition from being a Savings and Loan. They had a lot of REO (real estate owned) properties, something you don't want on your bank's balance sheet, but they were making progress on getting their financial house in order. Dennis is very happy as a Bank Mutual customer. But the most important thing is that, much like when he owned part of the banks, he was pleased to be back in control of his destiny. He couldn't control his situation with Wells Fargo because they were way too big and control was too far away. He was a big fish in a little banking pond in Milwaukee but realized that his accounts obviously didn't amount to much with Wells, or they wouldn't have chased him out of the bank.

A natural extension of Dennis' portfolio suggested that he invest in various common stocks. His investments in individual companies and in real estate are generally longer-term in nature. Stock investing has different tax implications so that is managed a little differently. An investment manager works with about $10 million of stocks and bonds outside of the Collection House stock. They work together to establish Dennis' risk profile, which is fairly conservative, and then invest accordingly. He gets quarterly reports and meets with them semiannually to review the investments which are focused primarily in oil, financials, and medical stocks. The common denominator lesson is to watch the spreads but avoid trying to time the market. He will share, "Trying to time the market is the best way to kill an investment." As with his real estate investments, Dennis tries to work in five-year segments and is a firm believer that if you are in the right quality stocks, you will double your investment every 5 to 7 years. That strategy has proven true in historical charts and information of the stock market. The key is to avoid getting antsy and moving at the wrong time.

The combination of assets, $105 million in total, is a far cry from seeking a dime from a shoeshine customer in the tavern. The pursuit has been relentless, with lots of excitement, fulfillment, and success, tinged with some disappointment and frustration. The assets capture, perhaps, the essence of a quest for financial relevance and independence.   Unlike his father who really couldn't afford to buy drinks for the house, Dennis has the wherewithal to do so.

Chapter 49 – Mingling with Celebrities

It has been suggested that variety is the spice of life. For Dennis, the individuals that he has met in his travels and activities have certainly added some of that spice to his life. Chance meetings with celebrities have yielded some fun memories and stories. When compared to the general population well-known figures make up a fairly small percentage, but Dennis has encountered his share.

Early in his business career, Dennis was in Houston preparing for a sales call with Exxon Oil. He had stayed overnight in the downtown area and had gone downstairs to have breakfast before his meetings. Having chosen to sit at the counter in the restaurant, he had already ordered his food when his attention was drawn to a big, muscular young man who had come into the restaurant. As this individual took a seat at the counter next to him, Dennis realized that he was sitting next to Cassius Clay, later to be known as Muhammad Ali. By this time, Clay had already become a boxing champion and his face was familiar. Dennis greeted him and they carried on a conversation while they ate elbow to elbow.

As they went their separate ways that day, Dennis had no idea what was in store for Clay who was headed to the Selective Service office to appear before his draft board. There he stated that, as a conscientious objector, he was unwilling to fulfill his duty in the armed services. His decision created a firestorm and Clay was eventually stripped of his heavyweight championship (which was later restored). He converted to Islam, and changed his name to Muhammad Ali.

Dennis recognized the value of golf during his business career, and, since he was a very good athlete, he enjoyed the exercise and developed into a pretty good golfer. He would often entertain clients or potential clients during a round of golf, drinks, and dinner. Success in business provided resources to buy a home in Florida and also allowed him more time to golf. After purchasing a home in Boca Raton in the mid '80s, he joined a local golf club and played as often as his schedule would permit.

Shortly after he joined the club, he signed up to play in a pro-am outing. Gary Player, a professional golfer, was the touring pro for the club. The two of them drew a pairing to play together in the event. As they played, they talked about their common interest in golf and in thoroughbred race-horses. They were soon very good friends.

Over the years that friendship would blossom. They would play golf together when the opportunity arose and would become partners in race-horses and horse breeding, addressed in a later chapter. Player was a successful professional golfer and would ultimately win 24 PGA Tour events, including what is called a Career Slam by winning all four major championships. He won the Masters three times, the U.S. Open once, the Open Championship three times, and the PGA Championship twice. As talented as he was, he went to great lengths to nurture this friendship and still calls Dennis regularly, often to invite him to play golf.

Because of his association with Gary, Dennis has also had opportunity to meet Arnold Palmer, Sam Snead, and Jack Nicklaus. Since Player is a good friend of Jack Nicklaus, and Dennis is a good friend of Gary Player, Dennis was invited to Jack's birthday party. There are not many individuals outside of the golf world that would be invited into that circle.

In spite of his attraction to golf, Dennis was not interested in buying a house on a golf course. Already a home owner in Boca Raton, Florida, he had visited a friend at Marina Bay in Fort Lauderdale who lived on a houseboat. This was not an ordinary houseboat; it was home built on the platform of a barge similar to what is used to transport goods on the Mississippi River. After seeing this home, a house on the golf course seemed really mundane.

Dennis soon sought out the acquaintance of someone who had access to the barges and found one that he could buy. Using the barge as the platform, he contracted the construction of a three-story home on top of the barge. Of course, with a moving foundation it is not an easy thing to construct such a building. Dennis had his personal quarters built on the main level, added two one-bedroom apartments for guests on the second level, and added a platform on the top floor for sunbathing and a place to barbecue. The boat is moored to the marina docks and is hooked up to city water and sewer. It is not a boat that you take out for a cruise as it has no means of propulsion, and its movement is limited to motion from the waves, generally when someone else comes into the harbor in a smaller boat.

His next-door neighbor at the Marina was Alfred Bloomingdale, of the Bloomingdale Store family. Al had started a credit card company which he soon merged with another fledgling company, Diners' Club. He would become the driving force behind the growth of that business. Dennis and Al would develop a casual acquaintance and would see one another periodically.

After completing the houseboat and moving in, Dennis tied his 49' sailboat to the houseboat to have it available when he felt a need to go boating. It was a unique home, one that he very much enjoyed. It also provided a wonderful retreat for entertaining clients.

Unbeknownst to Dennis, in late 1983, Paul Newman and Joanne Woodward were in Fort Lauderdale working on a movie called *Harry & Son*. Newman had gotten word of the Marina Bay community where Dennis lived on his houseboat. One evening, as Dennis was hosting several individuals from Citibank with whom Payco was doing business, there was a knock at the door. When Dennis responded, he was a bit surprised to find himself face to face with Paul Newman. Newman commented that he had been admiring Dennis' sailboat and wondered if he might take a look at it. Of course, when the women in the room realized that Paul Newman was there, they went from very talkative to very quiet. They couldn't believe that it was really Paul Newman walking through the door.

Dennis walked Paul through the house and showed him the door leading to the sailboat. After looking the boat over, Paul came back into the house and Dennis invited him to have a drink with the group.

"Sure, I'll have a Bud." As they stood at the bar talking, Paul commented that Dennis had an interesting houseboat and asked if they might rent the boat while they were filming the movie. Dennis had a home in Boca Raton at the time so was agreeable to renting the houseboat.

While Paul and Joanne were staying on the boat, Dennis decided to throw a party for them and invited the rest of the cast of the movie, including Bobby Benson and Morgan Freeman, to join them. Over the course of their various interactions, Dennis had a chance to get to know them pretty well, eventually leading to an invitation for Dennis to play a walk-on part in the movie. When people ask Dennis how he got to meet Paul Newman, Dennis will state, "It was Paul getting to meet me. He knocked on my door."

Dennis' interaction with Paul Newman subsequently led him to an opportunity to meet Tom Selleck and Don Ameche when they were in Fort Lauderdale filming the movie *Folks*. The director, Ted Kotcheff, stayed with Dennis while they were shooting the movie and gave Dennis a minor part in the movie.

When Hurricane Andrew came ashore in Florida in August of 1992, the home broke loose from the dock, as did several similar homes. After bumping together, they eventually sank. Although the home was insured, for Dennis the saddest part was the loss of the memorabilia that was on the boat when it went down that was never recovered, including pictures and other things that he had collected. He hated to lose the pictures of him with Paul, Joanne, and the others who had visited the home. Ironically, the one item that was recovered was a suit of armor that Dennis had purchased that somehow floated to the top of the water. That armor now stands in the doorway of Dennis' home in Jupiter, Florida.

Dennis had discovered a love for skiing when, as a family, they would venture to the slopes in Wisconsin or Colorado. Family vacations would often center on skiing in Colorado, with early trips to Aspen. That would lead to extensive skiing for Dennis at nearly every major ski run in Europe, including Val d'Isere's, Grindelwald, Davos, and Innsbruck - probably eight or 10 different resorts. He also enjoyed the après skiing, the after skiing associations, with the Europeans. Though there is no one well-known from those associations, they were important in helping him gain a great appreciation for the European approach to enjoyment, especially in their warmth towards one another.

With the amount of time that Dennis spent skiing in Colorado, especially as he tried to include the children, he purchased a home in Vail, Colorado. Because of the excellent golf in Vail, Dennis also spent some of his summer hours at his home there, as well as on the golf course. When former President Gerald Ford held a charity golf tournament in Vail, Dennis was invited to participate since it was at the course where he was a member. He recognized that it was for a good cause but also saw that it was a fairly exclusive group of attendees. This gave him an opportunity to meet President Ford, Bob Hope, as well as others who were also playing in the tournament. A special treat was when Dennis was seated with Tommie and Dickie Smothers, comedians and pioneers of television variety shows.

On the morning of December 26, 2004, a devastating earthquake measuring 9.3 on the Richter Scale struck off the coast of Sumatra. The movement of the ocean floor caused by the earthquake resulted in a tsunami wave that is estimated to have reached 80 feet tall, causing massive destruction from Thailand to the Horn of Africa, and ultimately was responsible for almost 300,000 deaths. Relief organizations quickly moved into action and sought funds wherever they could. President George W. Bush dispatched a delegation to the area to offer support, committing $350 million of relief funds from the United States. He also invited two former presidents, his father, George H.W. Bush, and Bill Clinton, to assist in fund raising efforts.[xix]

One of the events the two former presidents sponsored was a charity golf outing held at Medalist Golf Club in Hobe Sound, Florida. Greg Norman was the touring pro at the course and was also invited to participate as a host. Fundraisers have a fairly short list of who they can call on for significant contribution dollars, and Dennis was on that list. Familiar with the devastation, and unable to shake the images of destruction and loss of life, Dennis was quick to respond to the invitation to donate $25,000 to the tsunami relief fund.

The hosts made the outing memorable. Where else might you hobnob with two former presidents? Bill Clinton was particularly friendly and engaging. As Dennis was in the locker room, Bill threw an arm over

Dennis' shoulder, asked about his game, and was very willing to engage in small talk. The charisma had not abandoned him. While President Bush was less engaging, he was nonetheless a gracious host. Greg Norman is from Queensland, Australia - the home office location for Collection House. Dennis had met Greg at the 2000 Olympics in Australia and it was good to visit with him again at the charity outing.

On the day of the golf outing it rained like crazy in Florida, a fitting environment for a tsunami relief effort. By the time the golfers returned to the clubhouse they were soaking wet. As pictures were being taken with the former presidents, the golfers were encouraged to hurry to have their turn. Dennis hadn't had time to change his clothes and was still in his stocking feet. He would ask, "How often are you with two former presidents of the United States, much less, in your stocking feet?"

In each of the situations, Dennis was very comfortable in his interactions with these individuals. He, and they, recognized that he had significant influence in his role as CEO of a major public company. He was not intimidated at all by any of them. In fact, he just took the opportunity to enjoy the association and get to know them.

Chapter 50 –Horses, Golf, and Friendship

With a successful business, discretionary money, and some time, Dennis developed an interest in thoroughbred horses. With a continued focus on becoming a significantly successful businessman, as he looked at the horses as a business proposition, he determined that he would learn enough to make this a successful part of his business portfolio. He soon realized, however, that it was much more difficult to make this a successful business than he might have originally thought.

A significant element was bit more ethereal in nature. Dennis describes it as, "Later in life, when you don't participate in sports, you become a frustrated athlete, so I got into horseracing with thoroughbreds. Horseracing becomes a vicarious experience for a frustrated athlete. You see, the horse isn't running the race. You are running the race, except he's doing the physical work. As he's coming down the stretch and it looks like he's going to win, that's you winning! You are literally pulling that horse with your own charisma, or whatever, to the finish line. If you ask those that are serious in the business of horseracing they will all tell you about the same thing. It is not a real good business. You will not make a lot of money on it, but it is extremely interesting."

Many horse owners have horses that show promise but for whatever reason don't accomplish much on the track. Those horses come and go, and while very good animals, will take a place in less prominent racing circuits or in the breeding business. Most animals generate no story and are not talked about.

On the other hand, when an owner has a great horse, one that wins some races, there is a story to tell about that particular horse. Dennis had one such horse called *Spirit of Fighter.* This horse won almost $1 million for Dennis, had more first place finishes than any other filly mare in the country at the time, and in a total of 72 starts she had a record of 33 wins, 6 places, and 10 shows.[xx]

After meeting Gary Player at the golf outing in Florida, their common interests in golf and thoroughbred horses strengthened their friendship. That friendship eventually led to investing together in some horses.

Gary resides in South Africa on a ranch with about 200 thoroughbred horses and has developed a business of breeding and selling quality horses. After Dennis was invited to visit, he flew to South Africa and stayed at the Player ranch. The two men would also spend time together at the horse sales in Kentucky and would eventually partner in owning several race-horses together.

Over the years the two men have owned many horses together, first in the United States, but in more recent years all of the horses they own together are in South Africa. Gary is more interested in the breeding than the racing aspect of the business. The horses are an investment and they do okay; in fact, Dennis is in the black financially on the breeding. The racing horses are a different story. Although in addition to the horse that made almost $1 million he had another that had almost $400,000 in winnings, but these two horses are the exception to the rule. Most race-horses are money pits.

As an avid fitness nut, Gary suggested that Dennis should take off some weight and get back closer to his college athlete shape. They are the same age. Since Gary has maintained his athletic build, standing about 5'7" and weighing about 152 pounds, with enviable six-pack abs, he needles Dennis to get back in shape. Dennis has made strides and maintains his health but doesn't ever expect to replicate Gary's 1,000 pushups per day or his significant weight lifting. Dennis supports Gary's efforts to encourage young people to remain fit and healthy, and to avoid obesity. Although a very friendly individual, Gary still limits those who enter the inner sanctum of his friendship. Dennis is one such friend.

They still talk regularly, golf together as often as they can, and continue to work as partners in the horse breeding and racing business. Dennis still wonders sometimes and will share, "Can you imagine Gary Player calling you and asking if you'll play golf with him? And can you imagine turning him down?" They are good enough friends that each understands that the other has commitments, and then they work to get together at another time.

One time the two men had gone to Gulfstream Park in Hallandale Beach, Florida, to watch one of their horses run. They had parked the car and were walking in to see the race. As a professional golfer, Gary's was a familiar face because of the amount of television exposure. Many people would stop him for an autograph, something he was always willing to give. He would stand and listen as people would engage him with some tidbit of knowledge about his game, perhaps even describing a shot from a tournament. He was extremely patient with them. Dennis was soon pulling on his arm since their horse was to run in just a few minutes. But Gary would talk to anyone who wanted to have a conversation. When asked why he would do that he responded, "Someday I might not be able to play golf and when that occurs, I want to have some friends."

Dennis and Gary had an experience with a horse that they owned together that generated a telling story about horse ownership. As Dennis shares, "There are several steps you have to take to get into the Kentucky Derby. You have to pay a lot of fees from the time the horse is born all the way up until the time when the horse is three years old. Four thousand thoroughbreds are foaled every year and their owners all think that this will be the horse with which they are going to go to the Kentucky Derby. But only twenty horses run the Derby out of those four thousand. Everybody that wants to participate pays the fees associated. Not only do you pay fees, the horse is required to participate in, and win, certain qualifying races. Only by doing so might the horse be selected as one of 50 horses to be considered.

Dennis recalls, "We had a horse called GP's Black Knight (GP stands for Gary Player and Black Knight is his clothing line). The horse went out and won, fairly convincingly, the first two races in which it ran. We had paid $60,000 for the horse; $30,000 apiece. We got a call from one of the top trainers in New York, in fact, probably one of the top five trainers in the world; a guy by the name of Nick Zito. He said that he wanted to buy Black Knight and offered $240,000 for the horse. I was so excited because we had only paid $60,000. I called Gary in South Africa and told him that Zito wanted to give us $240,000 for the Black Knight. Since the horse was only two years old and had only won 2 races, this was an opportunity for great profit.

"When Gary responded that I needed to ask for $500,000, I told him that he was crazy. Zito won't pay that kind of money. But Gary insisted that I ask for $500,000.

"I got back on the line and told Zito that Player wanted $500,000 for the Knight. Zito responded no way on $500,000 but said he would give us $400,000 and not a penny more. I said, 'Sold!' without even calling Player back. So we took a horse for which we had paid $60,000 and sold it for $400,000, a $170,000 profit for each of us.

"The rest of the story was that the horse didn't pan out: he soured. Sometimes a horse will sour if you push them too hard, and although there is nothing physically wrong with the animal, it just loses its desire to run hard. I claimed the horse back for $5000. You can use a soured horse to run him against other horses that are not very competitive and eventually someone will want the horse. This was the case and someone claimed it from me for $10,000. The Knight later placed in a couple of races and won one race after that against nobody. The value of the horse went from $60,000 to $400,000 to $5,000 to $10,000.

"This strengthened a very important lesson which is that you don't fall in love with horses. They are not pets. They really are dumb animals with a very small brain. You have to treat it as a business. Since 1982 I have probably purchased $2 million worth of horses. I have owned over 300 and I can only talk about two or three specific horses. It is a very select few of the horses that gain notoriety."

Dennis knows the business very well and he knows horse flesh fairly well. He has partnered in the U.S. with an individual who is an expert in horses. More recently, Dennis and this partner bought a $50,000 horse that they have sent to Saratoga in New York to run. The horse is showing a lot of promise. Although Dennis will take opportunity to go and see the horse run, he leaves it to Danny, his trainer, to determine which horse to run when and where.

Although he does have partners in the horse business, Dennis likes to limit his partnerships. He currently partners with someone for his U.S. horse business and delights in his partnership with Gary Player. They each add something to the mix other than spending his money.

Chapter 51 –Other Ventures

Even though Collection House demanded a fair amount of his attention, Dennis still had time and money to invest in other things that showed promise.   Shortly after selling Payco, he invested approximately $2 million in real estate, mostly apartments. He also invested $1.5 million in a company called Call_Solutions, later known as NOVO 1. He soon found out that when word gets out that you have available cash, you will be inundated with invitations from others who have a use for that cash. He was willing to listen to the sales pitches, and periodically one would catch his attention.

One such opportunity was an oxygen business called SMS, Specialized Medical Services, headquartered in Milwaukee. A couple of guys who belong to North Hills Country Club, the club to which Dennis belongs, had started a company to sell oxygen to rest homes, assisted living facilities, and hospice organizations for individuals who needed oxygen assistance to breathe. They approached Dennis, outlining the need for additional capital to grow the business. After he looked at the financials and did his due diligence, he invested $750,000 into SMS for a 20% ownership stake. Over the following three or four years there wasn't much return to the shareholders which caused him to refer to his investment as *patience money*. But the company continued to grow. A key component of the business, one that drew Dennis' attention when they were seeking his investment, was their software. Their IT system helped them accelerate payment from the government, a key to the business since a significant portion of their income came from Medicare and Medicaid payments. Instead of the normal 60 to 90 days for payment, the software helped put them at the head of the list for payments, substantially shrinking the days outstanding on receivables.

The company grew as they added more and more clients. Even though they had a bunch of debt when Dennis got involved, through the growth of the business and the patience of the investors who took no compensation during that time, they worked hard to pay down the debt of the business.

With a 20% ownership stake, Dennis was very active in the business. He sat on the board and helped guide them with their plans. His presence at the meetings was sometimes intimidating, but that was his intent. He knew that they needed his help to stay focused on the business and make decisions that would result in the big payout at the end. He wasn't interested in having any of them demand immediate gratification. The managing partners had to stay focused and hard charging. For example, when they wanted to get new company cars to replace a couple that were a few years old, Dennis was quick to note that they had company cars and suggested that the same ones would do fine for a period of time. Then he would remind them of where they had set the targets for the business, showed them that he knew what the performance was against those targets, and held them accountable for meeting those targets. He was adamant about helping them stay focused and to see that the little things really did combine to make a big difference.

During Dennis' fifth or sixth year of association with the company, the principals were approached by a similar business out of Indianapolis that wanted to merge the two companies. Of the outside investors, three were old farts, as Dennis refers to them, who were fine with an exit strategy. Excellent offers were made to the two managing partners from Milwaukee to run the combined companies. The other company had a VC that was funding them who came up with the money to buy out the three outside investors. Dennis parlayed $750,000 of patience money into $3.1 million, with another $200,000 coming as soon as a claw back provision expires; a rather nice, long-term capital gain.[xxi]

After Dennis exited the oxygen business, an opportunity came to him in the security business that caught his attention. This business works with larger businesses who want to control door openings within their facilities from a central point. With intellectual property as the primary asset of the business, their efforts were focused in selling complete hardware and software systems.

A unique feature of the business is its scalable capacity using the same technology. The system provides cost-effective solutions for applications ranging from 10 doors up to 2,000 doors while providing the ability to control all activity from a central point. The prison in Leavenworth, Kansas is running their software to control the opening of the doors in the prison. A hospital in New Jersey uses their system to control the doors on rooms where they store medications and drugs, even using the system to lock someone inside one of the rooms if they somehow gain unauthorized access. The Army Corps of Engineers is building a huge complex in Florida and the business is bidding to control every opening in that facility.

The system requires someone to monitor cameras, or be alerted through a buzzer, and then they use the system to open the door. It also provides notice if someone is trying to gain entry into an area to which they shouldn't have access. As new buildings are being built, security has become a big thing.

As of 2013, Dennis has been involved in this security business for four years. In that time they have made progress and are starting to get things turned around and performing better. However, after realizing that two of the four original partners, including the CEO, were not performing at the level they needed to, Dennis was called on to play the part of the ax man and relieve them of their duties. With about 23% of the ownership, Dennis had much at stake. The bylaws of the business gave the board oversight and power to make such changes, and Dennis was the board's representative in addressing the issue. Severance packages were provided, the individuals departed, and then they focused on getting expenses under control.

As with any investment in a privately held business, the financial performance is critical for the success of the investment. Dennis sees the likely exit path, recognizes what they need to do to position the company, and remains focused on guiding them to that success. He is determined to take the business in a different direction than the original owners who brought the technology from Israel to the U.S. but then tried to do too many things and outpaced their capital. As the largest shareholder, he is very active in the planning and execution of the business plans, defining his role as helping them stay focused on the business goals.

Additional real estate transactions were sprinkled in among the business holdings. These seemed to add the spice and hold his interest. But he is willing, as with many business opportunities, to say no. He invests in those with which he is comfortable and confident. Other than for the rental unit projects, he doesn't carry mortgages on his properties. However, when dealing with $10-$15 million apartment projects, ones in which he owns 25 or 50% of the project, those require commercial borrowing. Although his appetite for additional deals has waned somewhat, he retains strong interest in those that he owns and currently has over $30 million invested in real estate.

Dennis recognizes that his involvement in these businesses has helped him to remain mentally active and engaged. Although Bev deals with much of the detail and tracking, he is still the driver, helping his partners stay focused on the investment goals, whether in real estate or another business. As long as his brain stays active he will stay active in the business world. There is no intent to turn from producer to consumer, even though he is often encouraged to be a more extravagant consumer. Not only does he see that his activity keeps him alert, he sees that he has the ability to make a difference for a business; he still adds value to a project.

While he continues to entertain invitations to participate in opportunities, as he laughingly shares, "I don't even buy green bananas anymore." That being said, with Bev's attention to detail and his nose for the right deal, assuming that he lives until he is 85 there is no reason that he won't grow his $100 million in assets to $150 million in the next 8 years. In the meantime, he will live well on the dividends paid by Collection House and the oil company preferred stocks.

Dennis pays careful attention to the financial forecasts and changes in the trends of the markets. He refuses to succumb to the temptation to try to time the market. Instead, when he sees changes coming in the economy, he uses that information, along with his understanding of the international markets, to guide his investing. A perfect example was his analysis of the Detroit car business as it tanked several years ago. It was impossible to compete with a competitor (Japan) that was building cars at $37 per hour when your (U.S. automaker) cost was $78; long term viability was doomed.

Chapter 52 – Fishing Resorts

Dennis became an excellent fisherman through hours of observation while he manned the oars of the fishing boat for his dad, from his interactions with his good friend, John Taylor, who taught him how to fly fish, and from his experiences with salt-water fishing. He knows what he is doing with a fishing rod in his hands and still finds pleasure in landing a nice fish.

With a background in real estate coupled with a love of fishing, it was natural that Dennis would be drawn to a venture that would include both. In about 2005 Dennis partnered with several individuals to purchase a five-star lodge and fishing facility located on beautiful Knee Lake which is situated 400 miles north of Winnipeg, Manitoba, Canada, called North Star Resort. This property had a great history of drawing fisherman eager to catch a trophy fish. The facility boasted gourmet meals, its own landing strip, 13 cabins, a main lodge, boats, motors, and docks, and drew up to one thousand fishermen per year in its short 13-week season. But it also represented a heavy investment in facility and equipment.

Twisting a John Wayne quote to fit his own purposes, Dennis will chuckle, "The only good partner is a dead partner." He soon realized that with a downturn in the economy, his partners didn't have much stomach for the costs of operating a luxury fishing resort, and they bailed out, leaving him to sink or swim. After operating the facility for two years at a $200,000 annual loss, he took the resort into receivership. Dennis was able to buy the resort from the receiver, a testament to the difficulties of owning and running a fishing resort.

As he looked to get the resort on stable financial footing, and with the realities of the economy, he saw the need to change the pricing structure to make the destination more affordable. He decided to cut back on some of the amenities such that it was not as exclusive a resort, thinking that he could draw additional individuals with a lower price structure. He maintained some of the most popular features, such as the ability to hire a guide, at extra expense, for the first day to learn where to find the fish. The individual fisherman was then generally comfortable with the idea of taking out his own boat without a guide. Further changes were introduced in 2013 to make the facility more of an outpost establishment where guests will do their own cooking, while still providing an excellent fishing adventure for a very reasonable price.

Several miners who were rescued after a cave-in from a mine in West Virginia appeared with Oprah Winfrey on her television show. When she asked them what they would like to do to celebrate life, they indicated that they would like to go fishing, sharing that they'd heard about Knee Lake. Arrangements were made for them to go on a fishing trip at the North Star Resort, after which Oprah talked about the wonderful trip that Dennis had donated. Oprah didn't pay a penny yet she received the recognition for the fishing trip. The saving grace was that it did generate some positive publicity for the resort.

Located about forty miles away from the North Star Resort is Dennis' Bear Lake Outpost, an offshoot of the Resort. The guests are flown by float plane and landed with their pre-selected food, something they will prepare themselves. A cabin is provided with kitchen and living quarters. Boats and motors are ready for their use. With fairly Spartan facilities, fishing is the entertainment, so a guest should be committed before they land. The only communication is via radio and no one will stop by until the plane lands to fly the guest out at the end of their stay. But this provides an excellent value for a great fishing experience. The facility currently has three cabins, with the possibility of adding more. However, the challenges of having sufficient boats and motors for many more individuals becomes such that five cabins seems to be the appropriate limit. One of the salient features is that no one else is on the lake other than those who stay at the Outpost.

His experience with selling spots at North Star and Bear Lake Outpost helped Dennis to realize that there were multiple segments of the fishing market. There were those who were looking for the luxurious accommodations to go with fantastic fishing, those who were looking for nice accommodations and fantastic fishing, and those who were willing to do much of the work themselves, coupled with fantastic fishing. They already had facilities focused on the middle and lower end of the market, both with excellent fishing lakes, but they lacked a high-end resort where guests were again looking for the luxury of a five-star resort.

Dennis had hired Dave Brahm to assist him in marketing the resorts and to attend the fishing shows. As Dave would visit with those at the show, he realized that they were attracting many blue-collar, older, overweight men. These individuals were interested in the outpost facilities as they were quite cost conscious, and it was from these individuals that they drew most of their clients for North Star and Bear Lake.   But he also found a group of people who had responsibility for planning executive retreats and incentive trips for key employees.   There was a demand for a high-end resort.

The question became, does it make sense to open another resort?

Chapter 53 – North Haven Resort

With the demand increasing for a high-end resort, Dennis determined to build one. After acquiring fishing rights from the Canadian Government, he began construction of a luxury resort on the shores of Utik Lake, located about fifty miles from his facility on Knee Lake. He named it North Haven and determined that it would be the shining star of the resorts. Because of its remote location, the only way to get materials to the site was either by air or by truck traveling the network of winter ice roads after the lakes froze. In fact, the resort was highlighted in a 2013 Discovery Channel episode of the popular show, *Ice Road Truckers*. That inconvenience came with a hefty price tag, costing $2 million just to build the facility. The construction cost was in addition to the land acquisition costs, the licensing by the Canadian Government, outfitting the rooms, providing boats and motors, hiring staff, and all of the other expenses that come with a facility of this nature - costs that were much higher because it was located in the middle of nowhere.

Since they were building a facility that was unlike any other, much thought went into development of their approach to their customer's fishing experience. The result of that planning was what is called the four F's, as noted below. (Dennis' commentary is in parentheses). The four F's of the North Haven resort, upon which they built their business, include **F**ish (the Almighty gave us those), **F**ood (they bring in a chef and provide gourmet meals at dinner), **F**acility (which is brand-new, approximately 4 years old, with Hilton type beds, fireplaces, Sirius radio, and everything except TV, which is in the main lodge), and **F**riendly. Dennis and his team keep a close eye on each of those elements to make sure that this is what is delivered to every guest. When they have large groups at the resort, either Dennis, Bev, or Robbie (who takes care of Dennis' properties in Florida) will also be there to make sure that everything runs well and according to the four F's. Repeat business is the resort's anchor to success, and they are pleased when a group will sign up for time the following year, especially if they commit to bring a bigger group. Groups of 12 or 20 guests are common, and they have hosted groups of as many as 34 people.

The cost of a 2013 North Haven trip was $4800 per person for a four-day stay which includes everything except the cost of booze (guests can bring their own), the cost of the fishing license, and the gratuity. Even with a significant pricing structure, the North Haven resort is a one-of-a-kind and is drawing a good clientele. The common response is disbelief that there is such a facility in the middle of nowhere.

All guests are guaranteed to gain 5 pounds while staying at North Haven. A large breakfast is served each morning at 7a.m. so that the fishermen can be out on the lake fishing by about 8 a.m. The early fishing activity is focused on walleye. The morning catch is prepared and cooked, accompanied by appropriate side dishes, for a shore lunch which is served about noon. A gourmet dinner is served at seven o'clock in the evening.

The key draw is the experience for a fisherman, many of whom only fish once a year, who may catch as many as 100 fish during their stay. It is not uncommon for at least one of those to be a trophy size fish. The first class treatment is enjoyed by all and is a draw for many to return.

Because of the remote location, guests fly into Winnipeg and stay the night in a hotel. Early morning transportation is provided back to the Winnipeg airport for a chartered flight north to Thompson, overflying the resort. In Thompson, the guests are then transferred to the resort's floatplane and fly the 40 minutes back south to the resort.

It is hard to imagine an upgrade to the experience, but a current construction project will do just that. Dennis is building an airstrip for North Haven that will be ready for the season that begins in June of 2014. The new airstrip will cost approximately $1.4 million because it required chopping down trees, removing the tree roots, blasting the rock, crushing the rock, and then laying and grading the gravel strip. All of the equipment had to be hauled in over the ice roads. Since they will land airplanes of up to 34 passenger capacity on the strip, it has to be a solid base. Mother Nature conspires against such a project, dropping heavy summer rains which require the strip be pitched so that the water will drain off, and it has to be built to withstand the freeze-thaw cycles caused by the fluctuation in temperature. Since it is not uncommon to experience temperatures of 60 below zero, pavement was out of the question as it would not hold up under the extreme conditions.

The new airstrip at North Haven will eliminate the flight into Thompson, allowing guests to fly directly from Winnipeg to the resort, significantly reducing the time they will spend flying instead of fishing. Once they land, they will jump on a pontoon boat which will ferry them to the resort, about a 300 yard trip. The change will also allow the guests to leave Winnipeg a little later in the morning and lessen the chance of mechanical and other delays that sometimes creep in.

The current operation requires the ownership of two float planes, a Beaver and an Otter, with operating costs in excess of $300,000 per year. Dennis should be able to sell both planes for about the amount of the construction costs of the airstrip. Maintenance costs for an airstrip will be much less than the maintenance costs for those float planes. Planes will be chartered out of Winnipeg depending on the size of the group coming in, so the operating costs can be adjusted appropriately.

In spite of the great fishing on Utik Lake, as well as on Knee, or Bear, there are still those guests who are curious about the fishing on another lake. The resorts offer fly-outs that allow fishermen access to a different lake to fish during their stay. Once the Otter and Beaver are sold, the resort will then refer these individuals to a charter company and the guest will pay the charter company directly for the extra trip. It allows the resort to offer the accommodation without bearing the associated costs.

With the exception of the walleye that are kept for the shore lunch, all of the fish caught at the resort are released. Each of the guides is trained to show a fisherman how to hold a fish for a photo and then to quickly, and correctly, return the fish to the water. When someone catches a trophy fish, or maybe just a bigger fish than they have ever previously caught, they get excited. But the long-term viability of the resort is dependent on the fishery; if the fish population is killed, the business will be destroyed.

Since a fish that has been caught has just spent many minutes fighting the fisherman, by the time it gets to the boat it is exhausted. For picture taking, guests are cautioned to never grasp a fish by its gills; rather, they cradle the fish just below the head, under the gills with the other hand placed under the fish towards the tail. All of this should be done in less than a minute because the fish is not only worn out, it is gasping for air. After a quick picture, once the fish is back in the water, the fisherman grasps the fish by the tail and gently moves it forward and back in the water so the water goes through their gills. It usually takes a couple of minutes to revive the fish and eventually the fisherman can feel the trauma lessening as the fish gains strength. But it is critical to make sure that the fish is healthy. Soon it will gain strength and swim away, and sometimes will splash water with its tail as it departs, as if to say goodbye.

The catch and release program has been a big help to the fishery on each of the lakes. However, it did take a couple of years to get people out of the mindset that they needed to take fish home. Similar to Dennis' experience, many of the guests' earlier fishing experience was to provide food for their families. But this is a different scenario and a couple of arguments help sell the idea. The first is that it would be good to have the guests' children or grandchildren come back and catch that fish when the fish is a little bigger. Second of all, if a guest really wants to take home some fish, there is a fish house in Winnipeg from which to order some. Most have readily conceded that it is a good idea to return the fish to the water.

Manitoba has introduced a program intended to entice sportsmen to catch and release trophy fish by developing their Master Angler recognition. Guests that catch northern pike 40+ inches long can register the catch with a picture and an accurate measurement of the fish, and receive a certificate. Many find it much easier to mount a picture and certificate on the wall and have the additional satisfaction of knowing that the same fish is still in the water to be caught by someone else.

The spawn takes place in late May or early June. Early guests might see these big female northern pike as they swim up into the shallow water where they dig out a depression with their tails and lay their eggs. They don't go too far away from those eggs as they guard the nest. It is especially important to protect these females.

Since the guests are there to have a great fishing experience, the goal is to help them catch big fish. But they also have to understand that the way they treat the fish, especially the females when they are full of eggs, will determine if the fish are there in the future for them or following generations. The resorts have exclusive licenses for the lakes; no one else can fish there except for the native population. A trophy northern pike of 45 inches will be 30+ years old.   Photos of the fish and fisherman have, for the most part, replaced the mounting of trophy fish.

The quality of the fishing is such that a fisherman, even a poor one, will often catch as many as 50 fish per day. In some cases, several of those will be trophy size fish of 40 inches or better. To hook a fish that size, which weighs more than 20 pounds, the fisherman has a fight on their hands, and it is especially exciting if they are using a light action fly rod. On a trip with a group this summer, Robbie Durston caught three trophy-size fish of 41, 45, and 46 inches on the same day, each on a fly rod.

The fishing is so good, in fact, that after several days of such productive fishing, some fishermen have grown tired of catching so many fish. They have been observed watching a 30-inch northern following their lure towards the boat. Rather than hook the fish, the fisherman has jerked the lure out of the water. The lure then goes back in the water to try to attract a bigger fish.

As noted, the only fish that are caught and kept are walleye for the shore lunch - and only enough for the fisherman, his partner, and the guide. Generally they keep five fish which produce ten filets. Although that might sound like a lot of fish, after spending the morning on the boat in the fresh air and working hard to land fish, people are hungry. There are few foods that will rival fresh walleye straight from the lake and cooked right on the shore. The guides serve as the chefs and compete with one another to see who can come up with the best dish. Standard fare would certainly include battered fish, but other favorites have been developed which include honey garlic, chipotle, and honey mustard. All of the fish is cooked over an open fire. With 10 different spots on Utik Lake where they can do the shore lunch, the guests see a variety of scenery. Each location is stocked with a fire grate, firewood, and a picnic table. Sometimes several groups of fishermen gather in one spot for the shore lunch and other times it is just a few people. No matter how many are at a given site, this is a great time to talk about the morning's fishing and swap stories of the one that got away. After a couple of lunches, and dinners together in the evening, the individuals have gotten to know one another fairly well.

The stunning North Haven property continues to grow in popularity. The first year it was open it drew about 80 guests, a year in which they spent a lot of time ironing out the wrinkles and making sure they were set to handle bigger groups. The second year they drew about 170, and the third they drew 280 guests. 2013 is the fourth year in operation and it has been a very good year, expected to draw almost 500 guests for the 13 week season. The resort attracts a lot of interesting people, including, as a recent guest, the owner of the Chicago Cubs, Tom Ricketts. The positive word of mouth advertising that they have received from guests has shown great rewards as those guests rave about their experience. With Winnipeg only an hour-long flight north of Minneapolis and the new airstrip allowing a quick trip into North Haven, it will be fairly reasonable to get there even though the resort is remote.

One variable over which they have no control is the weather. If the ice is late coming off of the lake, guests can't fish. If early storms come, the late weeks in the season are in jeopardy. Yet, as they focus on the target guests, they see that they are drawing those individuals. After all, this is intended to provide a good old boy's retreat where they can belly up to the bar and have a couple of drinks, tell a few fish stories (lies), enjoy excellent food, and delight in superb fishing.

By the time the airstrip is done at North Haven, Dennis' total investment in the resort will be about $12 million. Although he takes great pride in the facility and personally enjoys being there, he anticipates a time when he will sell. It will take the right person, one who has a lot of money, loves fishing and the outdoors, and wants to run a resort.   The resort will likely have its first profitable year in 2013, looking strictly at operating costs, and although that is not a fully loaded number, it is still tracking in the right direction.

In the meantime, Dennis will enjoy the resort properties, meet new and interesting people, exchange ideas with some bright folks, and catch a trophy fish or two. The investment has yielded dividends beyond those anticipated.

Chapter 54 – Giving Back

In Richard Bach's book, *Illusions – The Adventures of a Reluctant Messiah*, he describes creatures that cling tenaciously to the twigs and rocks at the bottom of a stream, unwilling to let go for fear of the unknown downstream. Inevitably, the trip would involve some bumps and bruises, but there is no way to experience what is downstream unless you let go.

Very early in his life, Dennis determined that he was unwilling to cling to past prejudices, limitations that others tried to impose on him, or situational difficulties. He determined to let go of the rocks and twigs and experience the downstream adventure. That willingness to experience life spills over into his view of helping others. Even though frugal in his personal spending habits, he is generous with others, especially those in need of a hand-up.

Since athletics played a tremendous role in his personal development and, frankly, made his education possible, when Dennis was asked to give back to the athletic department, he was happy to comply. His football coach during his senior season, Mickey McCormick,[xxii] had suffered a stroke and died. When Lisle Blackbourn, formerly a coach for the Green Bay Packers, took over the Carroll football program, Dennis couldn't turn down the invitation to be a "volunteer" scout for the team. Although he was incredibly busy with his business and a young family, here was an opportunity to give back to the school and the athletic program in a way that few other individuals could do. His direct expenses were covered by the program but his time, a most valuable commodity, was given freely and willingly. In a specific case of the giver being a receiver, Dennis was also the recipient of excellent coaching from Blackbourn, not only in the art of football, but also in the art of life.

Since he still lived in the area and had been connected with the football program after graduation, Dennis seemed to be a natural selection when Carroll College asked him to serve as the head of the Alumni Association. He had given a lot of time to the school as a football scout. All of the demands on his time were still there, and increasing. But he was unwilling to turn them down. Dennis was living proof of the idiom, "If you want to get something done, give it to a busy man." This was not a paid position. When they asked, he did his best to step up and do the job.

Over the next couple of years, Dennis worked hard to encourage greater participation in the alumni association and, by extension, greater involvement in the school. The alumni group was small and the number of those who were willing to open their wallets was even smaller. Even though there was (and is) only an enrollment of about 2,200 students, it was critical to the mission of the school to keep them involved. Dennis struggled to show the example. When a golf outing was scheduled to raise funds, even though people signed up to participate, the fees they paid barely covered the cost of the golf, dinner, and other expenses. It was particularly distressing to know the background of some in the room who had the ability to give significant dollars but would not. Unfortunately, he still sees some of this same attitude today, and it still frustrates him. His sole remedy is to try to set the example. When auction items are available, his bids are generous.

In his role with the alumni association, Dennis spent a couple of years rubbing elbows with members of the Carroll College administration. They saw his abilities and drive and were impressed. His alumni involvement would subsequently lead to a more extensive association with Carroll.

Dennis and his family were members of the Presbyterian Church in Waukesha. When the church decided to create a mission church to better serve individuals on the south side of Waukesha, Dennis and several others were called on to assist in founding that church. Southminster Presbyterian, located on Richard Street just off of Grand and Sunset, started with a dozen parishioners and subsequently grew to 200. Dennis contributed extensively for the initial expenses, assisted in the planning and approach, and even served as a member of their lay clergy, assisting with collections and other activities. Changes in the family situation, including the move to Wales, changed the involvement with the church, but Dennis has continued to contribute regularly to their programs.

Dennis would see this activity come full circle as, after his marriage to Angela, she and her daughters, Stacy and Alice, were baptized at Southminster Presbyterian. Angela had grown up in Ukraine, part of the former Soviet Union, and had never been baptized because they didn't encourage religion in the country.

In the mid '80s, an invitation was extended to Dennis to become a trustee of Carroll College. This was not a position that he had applied for; indeed, it is not a position for which one can apply. His name was suggested, reviewed by a selection committee, and then approved by the president of the college. Not only were they looking for leadership skills, it was quite obvious that they were trying to gather individuals who had personal access to money they might contribute, or access to other money that might be contributed. Dennis fit both criteria and was invited to serve as a trustee, and accepted; he was one of 30 trustees.

This was a learning experience as he observed and thought about how he might make a difference in his role. The board sets policy and hires presidents, but it is the president and his staff, especially the CFO who controls the expenses, that run the school. Realizing that they were probably most interested in his money, he made the commitment to be generous with the school but was clear that they should not expect him to attend a lot of the meetings. It simply wasn't going to happen.

For some time, the college had relied heavily on Presbyterian ministers as their CEOs since the school was Presbyterian sponsored. Although well-versed and trained, training for the clergy doesn't necessarily translate into being a good businessman. By the end of Dr. West's service, in June of 1992, the college was operating in the red. Dennis was asked to serve on the search committee to find a new CEO. He had listened and observed over the prior several years and now was quite adamant that they not hire a minister. Some members of the search committee were a little taken aback when he strongly suggested that they needed a street fighter, one who knew how to read a balance sheet. However, they would later come to agree with him.

That approach led to the hire of Frank Falcone. He was truly a street fighter. He went to work cutting costs, cutting faculty, getting rid of courses that should not have been offered (such as a German class with only two students), and other such things that were wasteful. There was a rebalancing of the classes that were offered with the students available and a return to a core, liberal arts type of school. Frank got it turned around and Dennis was a significant supporter.

Chapter 55 –Punches Sports Complex

Cost cutting, although necessary, was not the solution to all of the financial challenges of the school. It was up to Frank Falcone, the street fighter, to ask for the big dollars to meet the needs of the university. Since the school needed money for some major projects, he reached out to his short list of potential donors. As one of those potential donors, Dennis was invited to contribute $1 million to the school's *Building Champions Campaign*, money that was to be put into an income producing trust. The timing was correct, Dennis was up to the invitation, and his million dollar contribution was monumental. Falcone was also able to raise funds from other individuals and organizations and was successful in returning the school to a positive financial position.

Similar to the situation with investing in fledgling companies, Dennis was aware that once he contributed money he could expect to be inundated with other requests, even from those to whom he had already given money. But he wasn't going to let that stop him from giving back to his alma mater. Other than for football, the Carroll athletic teams, as a matter of course, "borrowed" fields from the local high schools or the local community to host their competitions. It was somewhat embarrassing to the student athletes and, frankly, made it very difficult to recruit athletes to the school. The school realized there was a need for extensive funding and was determined to correct the situation.

Once again, they caught Dennis at a time when he had some money available and was in a situation that would be tax effective for him. Unlike the first campaign where they sought money from many individuals, this time Dennis was asked to personally fund a major project. For this effort he was asked to contribute a million dollars which constituted the total anticipated funding for the project. The money would allow the school to acquire land, demolish existing buildings on the property, and construct a first-class athletic facility to include a state of the art track surface, a soccer field, and a ball diamond. What became known as the Dennis G. Punches Sports Complex was an incredible upgrade for the university. Sports teams in the Midwest seek opportunity to use the track because of the quality of the surface and the beautiful facility. Cost considerations ultimately expanded that total commitment for Dennis to $1.5 million. In a gesture to thank him for his generosity in providing such a significant improvement to the school, Dennis and his family were invited to be the guests of honor at a homecoming football game.

Dennis' grandson, Jonathan, was a member of the Carroll soccer team and played for four years on high school fields. There is a particular satisfaction knowing that will not happen in the future for other athletes. The soccer teams now play on the sports complex field, never again to have to borrow an athletic venue. A side benefit is that this beautiful facility replaced rundown buildings, helping to revitalize that part of the city. It was one of the initial projects in an area that now boasts of new student housing along with a retail complex focused on serving the student population. There was direct and indirect benefit from the generous gift.

Dennis has always recognized that one of his most valuable resources is his time. He doesn't take any commitment lightly, and even though he indicated he would not attend many of the meetings of the Carroll Board of Trustees, he served a complete 10-year term, retired from the board for a period of time, and then was reappointed. He has almost completed his second 10-year term. During his tenure on the board, Dennis has served with five different presidents of the college.

In the early years of his participation, Dennis acknowledges that he had the poorest attendance record of the trustees, yet they continued to invite him to sit on the board. It didn't make sense to him to fly home from somewhere else in the country for a three hour meeting where they discussed student housing or a similar topic as, even though important to the students and the school, it wasn't important enough to him to take the time to study so that he could give valuable input. Yet, they recognized that he added value, both from his perspective of the school as a graduate, but especially as a businessman. And they certainly liked that he was a successful businessman that was willing to add some dollars to their operations. His attendance has been better in the recent past, something they attribute to him being semi-retired, a status that he strongly denies. He has just been willing to give more of his time – still a precious commodity.

Dennis will acknowledge that he doesn't talk a lot in the meetings, but when he does have something to say he is not at all bashful about stating how he feels because he generally has a strong opinion about the issue. For example, when the college faculty made a move to unionize, there were members of the board who sympathized with the faculty, suggesting that the school recognize their collective bargaining unit. Dennis felt very strongly that this would be to the detriment of the school, and especially to the students. In fact, he stated, in no uncertain terms, that if the faculty did unionize he would no longer sit on the board nor would he have any of his children or grandchildren attend the school. Noted for their quality of education, he saw this as a significant threat to that quality. He was pretty noisy about his position.

After sharing the example of Hillsdale College in Michigan, an extremely conservative college funded primarily by contributions from alumni, he shared how successful they were in providing a quality education and suggested that they needed to model that school rather than a liberal, union driven school. He wasn't about to have the administration roll over and play dead on the issue.

Following his vocal leadership, the school set a budget and fought the unionization efforts. The school was able to thwart the faculty's first effort because of the school's affiliation with the Presbyterian Church as the school faced the potential of sanctions by the church. By the time the second effort came around, the faculty really wasn't behind the efforts as those who had been most vocal were no longer employed by the school. This was a situation that Dennis felt required that he take a stand.

Dennis recognizes the need to pay his fair tax burden but is also careful to avail himself of the tax advantages available under the law. He created a charitable trust through which he contributes, thus making his contributions much more effective for him and, as a result, allows him to donate more to the organization.

One of his greatest frustrations continues to be that the significant giving is limited to a handful of individuals. He sees that it is time for the other graduates to step up and share the burden, and the satisfaction, of perpetuating the quality education available at Carroll.

As a result of his extensive involvement with the school, several of Dennis' grandchildren have attended Carroll College. On one occasion, Dennis was invited, as a trustee, to present a grandson's diploma to him on graduation day. A function normally performed by the president, Doug Hastad invited Dennis to present his diploma to Jonathan, a total surprise to his grandson. Of course the president shook his hand as well, but to see the look in Jonathan's eyes was something that Dennis will never forget.

Dennis' stepdaughter, Alice, plans to start her Carroll education in the fall of 2014. Her wardrobe already has many Carroll shirts and sweatshirts. But to her, an excellent student, the big draw is the quality of education. It has come full circle as Dennis has taken the value of his education, parlayed that into an ability to assist the school and others, and now his family is benefiting from the difference that he has made in the quality of the school through his leadership and his contributions.

Chapter 56 – Watching out for Individuals

When Dennis and the other small group of individuals took on the challenge of starting Southminster Presbyterian Church in Waukesha, they were fairly visible in their efforts. Certainly, the gift of the sports complex has high visibility on the campus of Carroll College, now Carroll University. However, since the majority of Dennis' giving takes the approach of making a difference in the lives of individuals, it is anything but highly visible.

Through church associations, business contacts, friends of the family, or when individuals see a need, Dennis is one to whom the person in need might be guided. His goal is to help individuals, families, and people for whom he thinks he can make a difference, rather than seeking a cause. If a family is headed in the wrong direction, he might step in and help.

Dennis was recently made aware of a large family that was having difficulty meeting their personal obligations and was in jeopardy of losing their housing. He stepped in and paid the back rent, the current rent, and provided money for food and transportation. He saw it as an opportunity to give a *hand up*, not a hand out. He made a difference because he kept the family together, got them out of a current mess, and provided some breathing room to get them back on their feet. As if this wasn't enough, he added a personal touch when he took a couple of the older children out on Lake Michigan on a fishing trip, something that they otherwise would likely never have a chance to do.

The fish that were caught went home with the boys, providing a few meals as well. Often, it hasn't taken a lot of money to address a problem, but the message that someone cares has been appreciated and, at times, is overwhelming to the recipients. A common question is, "Why is he doing this for me?"

When he is made aware of a situation or a need, Dennis will look at the information and situation to see if he thinks he can make a difference. If he feels that he can, he will focus on those areas while doing all he can to ensure that the help doesn't go to feed a drug or alcohol problem. While he is careful not to take away the personal responsibility of individuals to provide for themselves, if the initial help doesn't resolve the problem, he has shown a willingness to step in again.

Many times the help was just what the individual or family needed to get them beyond a rough spot. Those have been very satisfying for Dennis, knowing that he made a difference. On the other hand, there have been situations where he has extended assistance, sometimes over an extended period, only to see the opportunity squandered and the individual no further ahead for the assistance. In spite of those periodic disappointments, he has determined that he will not let those experiences keep him from making the effort in the future. Few, other than the ones who receive the help, will ever know it happened.

Other assistance that he provides is of a longer duration, not only the time during which he gives help but also the lasting nature of the help. A firm believer in the value of education, Dennis has assisted a number of individuals to complete their college education. They are then able to go on, find a good job, and provide for themselves and their families. Other assistance has come to individuals who were starting a new business where a small infusion of capital was sufficient to make the difference between great success and failure.

Dennis' son, Skip, has chosen a career in the ministry and works as a chaplain. He is a gifted linguist and a very unselfish person. After a short stint in the collection business, Skip realized that he was not cut out to be a collector. That quickly ended the dream for Dennis that Skip might someday take over the business. Dennis had the wisdom to realize that his children each needed to follow their own path, and though there was some disappointment that Skip headed a different direction, Dennis was there to support and encourage.

After college, Skip worked for a Bible Institute for a period of time while he raised money for an extended mission to Africa. While living in the Republic of Cameroon, he was instrumental in recording a language, a combination of French and the native dialect that had not been written previously, and then translated the New Testament into that language. He had found his purpose, which was to help people. Dennis was visibly proud of his son when he visited him in Cameroon.

As a result of Skip's focus on others, Dennis supports many of the activities with which Skip is involved. It gives them a chance to talk about a need and to assess whether or not the project will really do any good. After they have a chance to analyze it, Dennis determines whether or not he wants to participate; most of the time he does, especially as Skip has come to understand the nature of what Dennis might support. As a result, Dennis uses his philanthropic capacity to work through his son, using his son's judgment, to support worthy causes. The agreement is, "Dennis makes the money, and Skip gives it away." It has allowed them each to make a difference and has strengthened their relationship.

Dennis has made a difference for the church, for Carroll, for the football team at Carroll, and for countless individuals and families. It is hard to hide a church or a sports complex. Those are visible reminders of his efforts. Less noticeable are the others that he has quietly helped. He is okay with that.

Chapter 57 – Giving Advice

Though he might have felt some regrets about not developing the next generation of leaders at Payco, Dennis has more recently had opportunities to share some of his business learning with the younger generation. The following ideas were shared with the son of a friend, an aspiring entrepreneur. While not the "formula for success," Dennis views these as keys to business success.

He shared the following ideas:

1. You have to develop an intense focus on what you wish to accomplish. Sometimes that focus can cost you personally and professionally, as it did with Dennis' first marriage.

2. If you are serious about success, you have to set goals and include the qualitative and the quantitative. What do you wish to accomplish and by when?

3. Read some books that will guide your decision making, including *Think and Grow Rich* and *Illusions.*

4. Don't expect your vocation to be your avocation. "I didn't wake up one morning and decide to be a bill collector," Dennis shared. Once you pick your vocation, strive to be the best at what you do. Never settle for mediocrity.

5. Don't get caught in the calf path. When cows are let out of the barn, they will generally follow one another on the

same path back out into the field. They eventually create a trench where they walk over and over again. The trench can get pretty deep and as a result, they don't vary much from that path. The longer you stay in it, the more difficult it is to get out. And the view never changes. So don't get caught in the calf path. Avoid it at all cost.

6. Work smart! Yes, hard work is important but one can work hard on a treadmill, getting tired and sweaty in the process, and never go anywhere. Make sure your hard work is of value.

7. Few people will make excessive amounts of money working for someone else. Choose to be responsible for your destiny.

8. Be generous once you find your vision and then put the vision in play. Dennis gave away 49% of Payco in the beginning as he rewarded those who shared the vision.

9. Assess your risk tolerance and once you know what you are willing to risk, go all out to achieve. (Dennis took significant risk, especially with a young family, but as he will recall, he had nothing to lose other than to start over. He had a teaching certificate and had the class-work completed that would have allowed him the ability to apply for medical school.) As you look at your risk levels, you also need to decide if you can be patient for the big payout at the end, or if you are solely interested in the immediate gratification.

10. Be careful with your time. Allot it appropriately to those who will help you achieve your goals but if you let them distract you, and get you focused on their issues, that time will not come back. Decide if you are the dominant or the recessive player.

11. Don't get caught in the garbage of life. As Coach Blackbourn taught, "Stay focused on your job and where you are supposed to be. Don't get knocked on your ass because you weren't paying attention."

Certainly, some of that conversation sounded like it came out of a textbook, but the items came from Dennis' personal experience. He was willing to share to make a difference for someone.

Chapter 58 – Looking Back

At 77 years of age it is difficult to avoid waxing a little philosophical. Although he has long viewed time as his most important asset, Dennis realizes that now it is even more precious than in the past. Periodically, he finds himself thinking about what his contributions have been to mankind and what will be the impact when he slips off of the dish.

Dennis recalls clearly the day that his 6th grade teacher wrote the following on the chalkboard: "The past is uninhabitable!" As he recalls, most of the other kids had no idea what she was saying, but he got the message that he couldn't live in the past. His look back at his life is by no means an effort to live in the past; rather, it is a reflection of what he has accomplished, and what is yet to be done.

It is a challenging exercise to determine how to measure one's life. When looking at the elements of his life, for Dennis each of these has had a specific role.

1. Recognizing that he wanted to be the best at whatever he did, he set goals, addressing the quantitative and the qualitative. Not only did he know *what* he wanted to accomplish, he was clear on *when* he wanted to accomplish it.

2. Dennis developed a laser-like focus early in his life. Always busy, he understood that activity alone wasn't going to help him accomplish his goals. The focus on his objective could not waver.

3. Accumulating assets was important, and doing good things with the assets was paramount.

4. Time was his most valuable asset. He didn't tolerate anyone wasting his time. Work, family time, and relaxation were all acceptable and appropriate uses of the time.

As a science major with the anticipation of working as a high school science teacher, Dennis acknowledges that he has drawn many of his personal theories from his education. One that has received his particular attention is the idea that the success that an individual might achieve is 70% a result of their genetic makeup and 30% a result of their environment. Though his own early environment was humble and sometimes difficult, he attributes his station in life heavily to his gene pool. He will acknowledge that his children have benefited from the combined gene pool of the Punches and the Truesdales, but he also worked hard to create an environment of learning and achievement for his children. He has sought to understand his genetic makeup and correlate that with his environment.

Dennis can see that his father was limited by his own environment, including the fact that he only had an eighth grade education. Herb and his five siblings were distant with one another, lacking closeness or familiarity. Dennis recalls that it was like being among strangers when he was with his father's family. Yet, on the other hand, Dennis' mother was much softer in temperament and affection. She was a gentle soul and Dennis still has fond memories of how she would care for him when he was sick. What was Dennis to have gained through genetics? He is a product of both parents; stoic and straightforward, yet with a bent to kindness and nurturing.

Dennis developed a skill early in his life, one that was not genetic driven, but rather was a product of his environment. He was able to picture himself in another person's shoes to try and sense how they felt about a situation. He realized the need to control his own emotions while he looked at the situation from their perspective, and then he would react. There was no thought that everyone should be like him; it was just him trying to understand the other. With the confidence he developed as he practiced that skill, he realized that it helped him avoid that constant battle of wills with other individuals. He knew where he was headed and was able to say, "I'm okay."

Even though his family was split apart when his parents divorced, the siblings remained very close. Dennis has often been the instigator in creating situations to gather the family, even though now he and his brother Bill are the only ones still living. Herb, Shirley, Pat and Bob have slipped off the dish.

Dennis is very proud of his youngest brother, Bill, who worked with Dennis at Payco for almost 25 years. Dennis encouraged Bill to complete his education while working which resulted in some class time at Milwaukee Area Technical College, but the most important thing that Dennis felt he could give his brother was an opportunity. Bill has a very likeable personality, which fit well in the business. He would eventually move all over the country for Payco before finally settling in Florida as a regional manager.

Before Payco was sold, Bill had recognized that there was an opportunity in a segment of the healthcare industry for a collection business but had not had sufficient time to develop the opportunity. When the business was sold, Dennis provided some seed money for Bill to pursue that market. Bill built a very successful business, paid the money back, and would ultimately sell the business for $5 million. Dennis derives great satisfaction from his brother's success.

Dennis felt that he accomplished far more in teaching his children by example than he ever could by preaching at them, and he tried hard, while his children were growing up, to allow them opportunities to grow. He was one who could allow his children a chance to run up against a stumbling block and, rather than saving them from it, would help them see the value of figuring out how to surmount the challenge. He taught them the value of time, the importance of goal setting, and helped them see the importance of focus. His travel schedule, coupled with having them live apart with their mother, meant that his interaction was primarily on weekends, holidays, and vacations. This meant that they often enjoyed dinner together, attended athletic events, frequently at Carroll College, skied, and vacationed, often in Europe. Those activities generally had an educational element with them, especially when they were younger, as he imparted his philosophy on life and the importance of understanding what was going on around them. One particularly memorable trip was a stay in a castle in Austria for Dennis, Debbie, and Laurie. He encouraged them to let go of the rocks and experience the journey down the stream. He was swimming right there along with them.

Having established the education trust funds with the proceeds from the sale of the apartment buildings in Waukesha, supplemented by additional contributions, education was paramount. Although none of his children would choose to attend Carroll, they each chose a school where they could gain an excellent education. Debbie attended Wheaton College in Illinois and subsequently earned a Master's degree from the University of Minnesota. Laurie and Skip attended Westmont College in California, and Emma attended college in North Carolina. Debbie now works with individuals with addictions. Laurie is the extreme optimist and is a fitness buff; she looks the part of someone half her age. Skip is well on his way to completing the hours necessary for becoming an end-of-life chaplain. Emma has established her career in North Carolina. Dennis is extremely proud of his children and remains grateful to Katie for bearing them.

Dennis takes great delight in the fact that his children like to spend time together. Since Debbie lives in Wisconsin, Skip and Laurie in California, and Emma in North Carolina, it takes some doing to get together, but they go out of their way to be together. In fact, if anything they probably spend more money than Dennis thinks they ought to watching out for one another. But he says that with pride. With eleven grandchildren and a great granddaughter, it is a large and active group when they are together. He eagerly anticipates having the landing strip completed at North Haven in 2014 and has planned a family reunion in Canada at the resort. He shared, anticipating the reunion, "It is nice to have a place that can handle that size group and give them a place to enjoy being together for four or five days."

Dennis has lost the sight in his left eye, which is his dominant shooting eye. Rather than give up shooting, Dennis found an individual who builds offset stocks, and had him build one for him. Now when he pulls the gun into his left shoulder the barrel lines up over his right eye. If he hadn't found that option he would have had to give up bird hunting. The gun modification allows him opportunity to continue to hunt, and he especially enjoys the chance to go with Skip and with grandsons.

As a successful businessman who was also a young father, Dennis realized that if he waited until he died (slipped off the dish) before he passed some of his wealth on to the next generation, his children would be too old to really enjoy it. He implemented a plan to help them improve their quality of life while they were still young. Since he had the ability to act as a safety net, he was able to discourage their purchase of life insurance, saving significant dollars. Acknowledging that he had the ability to alleviate some financial pressure, he helped with things like their education, funding the education of their children (his grandchildren), or buying a home. He didn't take over their personal responsibility; he just gave them some assistance.

Chapter 59 – Look Forward & Wrap Up

Recognizing that communication was an important part of estate planning, in a family meeting Dennis spent time with his children in a financial planning discussion helping them to set their personal expectations and for him to communicate his own to them. He wanted them to understand, "Even after Uncle Sam takes a big bite out of the pie, there will still be some nice size pieces left for my family."

Part of that planning has come in the form of education trusts which Dennis has established for each of his grandchildren. Not only have the trusts alleviated a significant financial burden from the families, they have also allowed him to perpetuate the idea that the Punches family is educated. He is adamant that the family legacy is education. He structured trusts such that at age 30 his grandchildren will receive the money that is remaining in their individual trust, and his expectation is that his grandchildren will use that remaining money to fund educations for their own children; thus extending that legacy. As he states, with only a slight laugh, "I will turn over in my grave if you don't pass that money on to continue the legacy of education. I will be there to haunt you. Even if you don't believe in ghosts, you are going to see one." It is too early to see what they will do for the next generation, as the sole great- granddaughter is but seven years old. But all eleven of Dennis' grandchildren have now graduated from college, and it was grandpa's opportunity to give them a running start.

After Dennis' oldest grandson had finished his undergraduate degree, he entered a physical therapy program in California. Ryan is a very frugal individual and, even after the expenses of an undergraduate degree, had a substantial amount remaining in his educational trust. Dennis was incredibly pleased when Ryan approached him and said, "Grandpa, I know I can have the money when I'm 30, but would you continue to invest for me? I want my children to be able to have what I have." That was exactly the perpetuation that Dennis was looking for in the scheme of things.

As he might say, in his best Fibber McGee imitation, "Overall, I believe my family is going to think well of me; I hope, I hope, I hope."

An unexpected twist to his life occurred in 2008 when Dennis and Bill walked into a Milwaukee restaurant and Dennis saw Angela Vilenski for the first time. He found himself immediately attracted to her and his recollection of the conversation with Bill was, "That one is mine." After introducing himself and asking her for a date, Dennis and Angela dated for the next four years, traveling, boating, and doing many things together.

Angela, her first husband, and oldest daughter, Stacy, had immigrated to the United States from Kiev in the Ukraine with another daughter, Alice, born after they arrived in Milwaukee. They had run a very successful beauty salon in Milwaukee. Although that marriage later ended in divorce, Angela had become a naturalized citizen and continued to provide for her family. She is incredibly grateful for the opportunities that the U.S. has afforded her.

As the relationship got serious, Dennis took some time for introspection. He realized that not only was he turning 74 years old, he had been single for a long time and had become rather set in his ways. It was to be a significant change from having only himself for whom to be responsible; he now not only had to think of including someone else in his decision making, there was also a teenage daughter that came with the package. Although that didn't particularly bother him, it was another consideration. He was far enough along in his estate planning that he already had a good idea of the destiny of his assets, but he could see the path to include Angela in that planning.

There were also considerations for Angela, including a teenage daughter to care for plus her employment required her attention. She was 35 years younger than he was, but she found that they were compatible and that she really enjoyed being with him.

With the necessary considerations dealt with, Dennis and Angela married on December 3, 2011. They now enjoy splitting their time between homes in Milwaukee and Jupiter, Florida, and periodically at the home in the Bahamas.

An important consideration after the marriage was where to reside. Dennis had moved to Florida almost 20 years earlier and enjoyed getting out of the cold. Wisconsin ties were still strong so he retained residences in the Milwaukee area. With a high school student, and an excellent one at that, there was a decision to be made. Alice was a straight A student through her first two years at Whitefish Bay High School, with many advanced placement classes. But Dennis didn't want to spend the winters in Milwaukee. He wanted to enjoy the weather, his boat, golf, travel, and the things that were important to him, and to Angela. He was willing to fund a private education for Alice to make that happen.

Much to Alice's chagrin, the decision was made for her to attend school in Florida, where she was enrolled at Jupiter Christian High School. This was a serious stumbling block for her, but it was more than just an issue of attending a Christian school and having to leave her friends; she was also very concerned about the quality of education. Jupiter provides an excellent education with many advanced placement classes. During her first year at the school, she had her opportunity to let go of the rocks and twigs and make the journey down the stream. Alice made new friends, has excelled in the environment, and is preparing for entry to college at Carroll University back in Waukesha.

Since Angela's extended family is still in the Ukraine, Dennis spends time with her traveling to that part of the world. Since he doesn't speak the language, he assumes the role of "conversational dropout, trying to laugh when others laugh." Angela works hard to interpret for him and keep him involved in the conversations, but his mind does wander to other things as it is hard to stay engaged when you don't understand.

Dennis still likes to surround himself with interesting people and has a fairly broad diversity of friends. Angela has enjoyed, for the most part, getting to know Dennis' friends, recognizing that it has been a learning experience for her.

A very important element in Dennis' life continues to be his friendships, but he will state, "As you go through life you have really very few friends, as you think about it. One can often count them on one hand, and if it not, on two." Dennis cherishes his continued close ties with Gary Player. At the same time he recounts that many of his friends are departing, slipping off the dish, as it were. It was very difficult for Dennis when his good friend John Taylor died after a tree that John was chopping down fell on him. Dennis honors this good friend, sharing, "John, I appreciate all that you have added to my life. You are a good friend."

As he takes a look back and considers his legacy, Dennis would share with his children and grandchildren that as he set out on what he thought to be his quest, he realized that he had an opportunity to alter the direction of the family. He didn't really expect to change it, but to at least alter the course. He saw education as the key. It was always there in his mind, looking to see how he could positively impact multiple generations. Everything that has been accomplished has been part of that quest. He has been able to do many things for his family. They came first and they will always come first. Along with that is his expectation that succeeding generations will follow that example. He states, "If you can teach your children that, I think they will go a long, long way, and do a lot of good things in life."

He continues, "The rest of the legacy, if there is one, since I am now on what you would call the downhill slide, although I don't feel like I'm sliding because I am very active, would include my activities in Australia and the rest of the world. I am going to keep it up. I am well, fit, and healthy. I haven't forgotten too many things and that's why I'm doing this now, by the way, before that sets in. It has been a great, great experience. I wish you all the best. Carry on!"

End Notes

[i] http://www.u-s-history.com/pages/h1586.html

[ii]

Signers of the Declaration of Independence – Joseph Hewes signature is just below that of John Adams – lower middle of page

[iii] http://www.revolutionary-war-and-beyond.com/joseph-hewes.html

[iv] Humboldt Park is not an area of Chicago where you would choose to go into today as it has changed dramatically, especially as things began to polarize between the ethnic groups.

[v] 1955 Carroll College Football Results
Coach McCormick / 5-2-1

@ Millikin	W 20-7
@ Hope (MI)	L 19-13
Illinois Wesleyan	W 20-17
@ Beloit	L 9-6
@ North Central	W 20-7
Wabash	T 7-7
Milwaukee State	W 25-7
St. Norbert	W 27-20

[vi] 1956 Carroll Football Results
Coach McCormick / 5-3-0

St. Norbert	L 26-20
Millikin	L 14-6
@ Illinois Wesleyan	W 20-7
@ Elmhurst	W 34-0
North Central	W 26-14
@ Augustana	W 19-12
Wheaton	L 21-14
@ Lake Forest	W 14-13

1957 Carroll Football Results
Coach McCormick / 2-6-0

@ St. Norbert	L 38-13
@ Millikin	L 15-6
Illinois Wesleyan	W 14-0
Elmhurst	W 71-0
@ North Central	L 6-0
Augustana	L 34-20
@ Wheaton	L 19-0
Lake Forest	L 6-0

[vii] At a brewery if the bottling machine didn't fill a bottle completely it was called a short-fill, and was rejected. It could not be sold to the public. A friend of Dennis, someone who played football with him, worked for Gettelman brewery who would sell the short-fill's to their workers for one dollar per case of 24 bottles. These short-fill cases would show up at various functions at the college.

[viii] from Fiddler on the Roof
[ix] http://www.fiftiesweb.com/cars/chevrolet-55-59.htm - '59 Chevy Impala cost $2,715
[x] John Davies sat for a period of time on the Carroll University Board of Trustees with Dennis
[xi] 1958 Carroll Football Record
Coach Blackbourn / 6-2-0

Whitewater State	W 26-13
@ Elmhurst	W 47-0
@ Illinois Wesleyan	W 26-13
Millikin	W 32-12
@ Lake Forest	W 12-7
Wheaton	L 16-12
@ Augustana	W 34-18
North Central	L 18-6

[xii] Long-time radio personality from the 1930s and 1940s

[xiii] Over the counter securities trade directly between two parties, rather than the established stock exchanges, which trades require the intervention of a broker. These are often low-value shares that have little market activity. The Pink Sheets is a private company that provides quotes for such over the counter securities, although they do not execute the trades.

[xiv] **Merger of Payco American Corp. and OSI will create leading outsourcing company.**

NEW YORK--(BUSINESS WIRE)--Aug. 14, 1996--Payco American Corp. (NASDAQ:PAYC) and OSI Holdings Corp., a McCown De Leeuw & Co. portfolio company, announced today that they have entered into a definitive merger agreement in which Payco American Corp. will become a wholly-owned subsidiary of OSI Holdings Corp., thereby creating the largest accounts receivable management company in the United States.

The transaction (including assumed indebtedness) values Milwaukee-based Payco at approximately $150 million. Under terms of the agreement, the shareholders of Payco will receive $14.00 in cash for each share of Payco common stock. As part of the merger, certain members of management, whose holdings comprise approximately 20% of Payco's outstanding common stock, have entered into agreements with OSI Holdings Corp. to vote their shares in favor of the merger. The merger is subject to various conditions, including approval by holders of a majority of Payco's outstanding shares, and is terminable under certain circumstances. The merger is expected to close in October.

Payco American Corp. is a leading provider of a full range of accounts receivable management services, including customer service outsourcing. Payco provides nationwide account coverage through its network of 37 offices across the United States and Puerto Rico and employs more than 3,300 people. Payco also is a majority owner of joint ventures in Mexico City, Mexico and Tokyo, Japan that provide receivable management services.

"The Payco management team and employees are extremely excited about joining OSI. Payco has been a leader in the accounts receivable management industry for the past 25 years and with this partnership we can accelerate the implementation of our growth plan. Payco and OSI share a common vision of becoming outsourcing partners with our customers," Dennis G. Punches, Payco's chairman and founder, said.

OSI Holdings Corp., based in Atlanta, was formed in September 1995 by McCown De Leeuw & Co. to build the largest single-source provider of a full range of accounts receivable management services to credit issuers. OSI's strategy is to acquire leaders in various accounts receivable management businesses, including contingent fee collection services, debt portfolio purchasing, billing, teleservicing and complete functional outsourcing. OSI currently has three separate operating companies, Account Portfolios Inc., A.M. Miller & Associates and Continental Credit Services.

"The employees of Payco have built the company into an industry leader through years of diligent effort and outstanding service to clients. We are very enthusiastic about welcoming them into the OSI family," Jeffrey Stiefler, chairman of OSI Holdings Corp. and former president of American Express, said. "This merger will give OSI a broader range of capabilities across more industry groups than any of our competitors. We will then be perfectly positioned to serve every aspect of our clients' receivable management business needs, including complete functional outsourcing."

McCown De Leeuw & Co., a private investment firm that manages approximately $500 million in capital, specializes in buying and building middle market companies in partnership with management. Since its formation in 1984, the firm has invested in 28 companies that collectively generate more than $3.5 billion in annual sales. McCown De Leeuw & Co. works with management to build its companies through both internal growth and strategic acquisitions. McCown De Leeuw & Co. has offices in New York City and Menlo Park, Calif.

[xv] An old English term - the dish is the earth. You don't die, you slip off the dish.

[xvi] **If**

If you can keep your head when all about you
Are losing theirs and blaming it on you,
If you can trust yourself when all men doubt you
But make allowance for their doubting too,
If you can wait and not be tired by waiting,
Or being lied about, don't deal in lies,
Or being hated, don't give way to hating,
And yet don't look too good, nor talk too wise:
If you can dream-and not make dreams your master,
If you can think-and not make thoughts your aim;
If you can meet with Triumph and Disaster
And treat those two impostors just the same;
If you can bear to hear the truth you've spoken
Twisted by knaves to make a trap for fools,
Or watch the things you gave your life to, broken,
And stoop and build 'em up with worn-out tools:
If you can make one heap of all your winnings
And risk it all on one turn of pitch-and-toss,
And lose, and start again at your beginnings
And never breath a word about your loss;
If you can force your heart and nerve and sinew
To serve your turn long after they are gone,
And so hold on when there is nothing in you
Except the Will which says to them: 'Hold on! '
If you can talk with crowds and keep your virtue,
Or walk with kings-nor lose the common touch,
If neither foes nor loving friends can hurt you;
If all men count with you, but none too much,
If you can fill the unforgiving minute
With sixty seconds' worth of distance run,
Yours is the Earth and everything that's in it,
And-which is more-you'll be a Man, my son!

by Rudyard Kipling

[xvii] Shakespeare – from *Hamlet*

[xviii] **Stopping by Woods on a Snowy Evening**

Whose woods these are I think I know.
His house is in the village, though;
He will not see me stopping here
To watch his woods fill up with snow.

My little horse must think it queer
To stop without a farmhouse near
Between the woods and frozen lake
The darkest evening of the year.

He gives his harness bells a shake
To ask if there is some mistake.
The only other sound's the sweep
Of easy wind and downy flake.

The woods are lovely, dark, and deep,
But I have promises to keep,
And miles to go before I sleep,
And miles to go before I sleep.

[xix] **President Asks Bush and Clinton to Help Raise Funds for Tsunami Relief**
The Roosevelt Room

10:15 A.M. EST – January 3, 2005

THE PRESIDENT: I'm honored to be standing here with two former Presidents, President Bush 41, President Clinton 42. We have come together to express our country's sympathy for the victims of a great tragedy. We're here to ask our fellow citizens to join in a broad humanitarian relief effort.

Eight days ago, the most powerful earthquake in 40 years shook the island of Sumatra. The earthquake caused violent tsunamis in the Indian Ocean, which left an arc of destruction from Thailand to the Horn of Africa. The devastation in the region defies comprehension. More than 150,000 lives are estimated to be lost, including 90,000 in Indonesia, alone. As many as 5 million people are thought to be homeless, or without food or shelter; thousands more are missing, and millions are vulnerable to disease.

...To draw even greater amounts of private donations, I have asked two of America's most distinguished private citizens to head a nationwide charitable fundraising effort. Both men, both Presidents, know the great decency of our people. They bring tremendous leadership experience to this role, and they bring good hearts. I am grateful to the former Presidents, Clinton and Bush, for taking on this important responsibility and for serving our country once again.

In the coming days, President Clinton and Bush will ask Americans to donate directly to reliable charities already providing help to tsunami victims. Many of these organizations have dispatched experts to the disaster area, and they have an in-depth understanding of the resources required to meet the needs on the ground. In this situation, cash donations are most useful, and I've asked the former Presidents to solicit contributions both large and small.

http://georgewbush-whitehouse.archives.gov/news/releases/2005/01/20050103-12.html

[xx] http://www.pedigreequery.com/

SPIRIT OF FIGHTER ① (USA) dkb/br. M, 1983 DP = 8-5-2-4-1 (20) DI = 2.33   CD = 0.75 - 72 Starts, 33 Wins, 6 Places, 10 Shows **Career Earnings:** $847,454.

Owner: D. Punches
Breeder: E.R. De Vries
State Bred: FL
Winnings: 72 Starts: 33 - 6 - 10, $847,454.

won Miss Dade H.,etc.

(CLOSE)

GALLANT KNAVE (USA) b. 1970	GALLANT MAN (GB) b. 1954 [BI]	MIGOLI (GB) gr. 1944	BOIS ROUSSEL (FR)	b
			MAH IRAN (GB)	4
		MAJIDEH (GB)* ch. 1939	MAHMOUD (FR)	2
			QURRAT-AL-AIN (GB)	b
	PLOTTER (USA) br. 1953	DOUBLE JAY (USA) blk/br. 1944 [B]	BALLADIER (USA)	b
			BROOMSHOT (USA)	b
		CONNIVER (USA)* br. 1944	DISCOVERY (USA)	c
			THE SCHEMER (USA)	c
SOME ONE FINER (USA) ch. 1979	LORD REBEAU (USA) dkb/br. 1971	MARIBEAU (USA) b. 1962	RIBOT (GB)	b
			COSMAH (USA)	b
		CRESWOOD DOTTIE (USA) ch. 1957	CALL OVER (USA)	d
			VIRGINIA BEACH (USA)	d
	SOME ONE FINE (USA) ch. 1969	SUNSTRUCK (USA) b. 1960	TIM TAM (USA)	b
			SIENNA (GB)	b
		WHO DUDETTE (USA) ch. 1959	FIRST NIGHTER (USA)	c
			DUDES BABY (GB)	b

xxi

http://www.riversidecompany.com/News_and_Media/Press_Releases/SMS_News_Release.aspx - sale of SMS

xxii

(http://athletics.carrollu.edu/documents/2012/11/12/Football_Individual_Records_Coaching_Records.pdf)